Contents

Your Living Trust & Estate Plan

How to Maximize Your Family's Assets and Protect Your Loved Ones

THIRD EDITION

Harvey J. Platt

Attorney-at-Law

ALLWORTH PRESS
NEW YORK

11 10 09 08   10 9 8 7

Published by Allworth Press
An imprint of Allworth Communications
10 East 23rd Street, New York, NY 10010

Cover design by Douglas Design Associates, New York, NY

Page composition/typography by Sharp Des!gns, Inc., Lansing, MI
SR Desktop Services, Ridge, NY

Library of Congress Cataloging-in-Publication Data
Platt, Harvey J.
Your living trust and estate plan : how to maximize your family's assets
and protect your loved ones / Harvey J. Platt.—3rd ed.
p.   cm.
Includes index.
ISBN-10: 1-58115-217-5
ISBN-13: 978-1-58115-217-3
1. Estate planning—United States—Popular works.   2. Living trusts—
United States—Popular works.   I. Title.
KF755.Z9   P55   2002
346.7305'2—dc21   2001007469

Your Living Trust
& Estate Plan

Preface

$\mathscr{S}$ince the first edition of this book was written, there has been some dramatic legislation in the state and federal laws involving gifts and estates. The changes, among other things, have created further reductions and tax credits and have caused widespread interest.

The second edition was updated in 1999 and included an overview of the federal and gift estate tax provisions in the Taxpayer Relief Act of 1997, detailed explanations of federal and state regulations that revised various types of trusts, plus new material to help readers understand the ramifications of other legal changes that had taken place up until that date.

This third edition contains new material, including a detailed explanation of the important provisions of the Estate, Gift, and Generation-Skipping Transfer Tax Act that George W. Bush signed into law on June 7, 2001 (see chapter 9). Chapter 22 sets forth the highlights of the Proposed New Regulations for Required Minimum Distributions established by the Internal Revenue Service on January 11, 2000.

In addition, revisions and updated material and information are included in revised Chapters 8, 10, 11, 12, 19, 22, 23, 25, 26, 27, 28, and 29. Chapter 28, The Cutting Edge: Value Reduction Strategy in Discount Planning, is a new chapter, created for those who are potentially faced with substantial estate tax. That chapter carefully outlines many of the significant wealth-transfer devises that are employed today in sophisticated estate planning.

This edition of *Your Living Trust and Estate Plan* is even more comprehensive than the previous revision. It should more than meet your needs in helping you formulate and create your estate plan.

Acknowledgments

My thanks to Nicole Potter, a superb editor and writer, who has helped in putting this book together. Lastly, I am forever indebted to my clients for their support and inspiration.

What This Book Means and Why You Should Read It

*E*state planning is a complex, ongoing process. One must put together and assemble various available devices, techniques, and strategies to accomplish two main objectives: an effective, orderly continuity of your affairs after your death, and the maximum sheltering of your property against transfer taxes.

Good estate planning is complicated. Every person, as well as every family, has his own special needs. Estate planning, generally speaking, is divided into two separate and distinct phases. The first phase takes place during your lifetime, when you do the actual planning and creation. During this period, you will set up the wealth protection and transfer cost reduction devices that are available and applicable to your circumstances. This phase includes the ongoing need to make revisions as dictated by life's changes.

The second phase occurs after your death. During this very important period, action needs to be taken in the following areas: (1) postmortem tax planning elections that can reduce taxation; (2) the administration and settlement of your affairs; and (3) the eventual transfer of your assets to your beneficiaries.

In many states, the legal procedure implemented to effectuate the settlement of an estate is the probate process. This proceeding is administered by the courts, which both validates the will of the estate owner and supervises the transactions that take place during the administration of the estate. Whenever possible, the probate process should be avoided. The probating of a will gives rise to unnecessary and often excessive expenses and delays that are both frustrating and time consuming. Fortunately, in the vast majority of situations, probate is not inevitable, and alternatives can be adopted.

In selecting the format for passing your property to your heirs, you basically have two choices: the use of a trust or the use of a will. The theme of this book focuses on the benefits of selecting a living trust to achieve this goal. The concept of the living trust is to provide you and your heirs with continuity in the ownership and management of your property, along with the traditional estate tax deferrals and avoidances. If it is important to you that your property is transferred to your heirs without the interruption and involvement of third parties and the unnecessary costs incident thereto, the living trust is for you.

Thanks to recent media attention and publicity, people have become much more aware of the existence of the living trust and its benefits. There is, however, a dearth of professionals possessing the expertise to both advise and prepare one. The living trust itself must be extensive! If it is not, it cannot cover all the contingencies that could arise during your lifetime and those of your survivors. Even though most of these contingencies will never occur, they need to be addressed for the trust agreement to be effective.

In order for you to fully understand and appreciate what a living trust is and what it can do for you, you *must* have an awareness of the basics of the estate planning process and an overall understanding of its fundamental elements. This book will take you step by step, using clear and concise language, through the gamut of options available and help you find the solutions to the puzzles that are inherent in the estate planning process. You will be presented with every important detail of creating what should be the basic document of every estate plan, the living trust. The reasons why you should avoid probate and the important instances in which you should avoid the joint ownership of property are discussed as well.

This book is designed for individuals with estates of all sizes. When estates are large, there are various methods available to save, reduce, avoid, and defer estate and income taxes. These are usually found in the form of different types of trusts. This book explains, in simple and plain language, how these strategies can be implemented. The benefits of the many available estate planning methods are described; their downsides are explained as well.

The use of the living trust, no matter the amount or kind of property involved, eliminates the need and expense of probate and does not require the blessings of the courts for the transfer of your property. There is no downside to it. Everyone should have a living trust no matter the size of his or her estate.

This book is not a do-it-yourself kit. It is not intended to be a substitute for competent advisors. However, after reading it, you should be able to understand the options that are open to you and intelligently work with your professional advisor in the creation of your specific plan.

Included also are important subjects that are not traditionally covered in books of this kind. These include retirement benefits, Medicaid, asset protection, planning for children with special needs, and estate planning for persons who are at the risk of AIDS.

This book is the product of more than thirty-five years of experience in this field. After you have read it and familiarized yourself with its contents, I honestly believe it will give you the impetus to think about your own circumstances and proceed with the formulation of your own plan. Of course, you should seek the advice of an expert familiar with estate planning.

I know of no greater emotional and material benefit than having your heirs avoid the annoyance, nuisance, and unnecessary costs of probate. Creating a plan that gives your heirs maximum wealth protection, avoidance of unnecessary capital gains taxation, and the sheltering of assets from estate taxes to the highest amount possible is probably the greatest material gift any person can bestow. The living trust can do all of this for you and your family.

❖

CHAPTER 1

The Development of an Estate Plan

*T*his chapter provides an overview of the entire process of the planning of an estate. In other words, what are the things that must be considered and prioritized, e.g., where and what are my assets; what form should my estate plan take (living trust or will); who will inherit my estate; how much will he or she receive and in what manner (outright or in trust); who should assist in the development of my plan; what steps should I consider to reduce the eventual taxes both during my lifetime and upon my death; who shall be the managers of my estate; who will take care of my minor children; have I forgotten anything or overlooked anyone; have I balanced the inheritances depending on the needs of my survivors; have I created potential litigation among my survivors; and have I coordinated all strategies and devices?

The answers to these questions will form the foundation for the plan itself.

What Is an Estate?

An estate includes all property owned by you less all of your liabilities. To plan an estate, its values and components must be first determined. Therefore, a critical and important step in the process of estate planning is the creation of a written inventory. Not only is the identity of assets important, but where they are located can be just as significant. Assets that are held in a safe deposit box or property not readily identifiable, such as foreign bank accounts or real property, may never be found.

The inventory should contain the following information: (1) the description and location of the property; (2) the ownership (individual, tenancy-in-common, joint or shared) and the percentage owned; (3) the cost and fair market value of each of the assets; (4) liabilities and debts; (5) beneficiary designations (who is to receive retirement benefits, life insurance proceeds, annuities, and similar benefits); (6) whether any assets are subject to any agreements (corporate or partnership interests); and (7) whether it is community or separate property.

A complete inventory of your property will not only avoid the headaches that can be created in locating the property after your death, but also minimize the costs that are incident to such a process. At the end of this book there is a suggested inventory form to aid in the preparation of this information.

The Probate Estate

This is the portion of the estate that must go through the probate process before it can be transferred. Property left by a will is normally subject to this procedure. All property that is inherited at death by various probate avoidance methods such as the living trust, joint tenancy, insurance, and beneficiary designations, is not included in the probate estate. Property that is held in the living trust is not subject to probate because it is not owned by you. The optimum estate plan should be totally free of probate assets.

The Taxable Estate

This is the property that's subject to federal and state estate tax, if any, when you die. It is the gross value of all property owned by you less all administration and funeral expenses, claims against the estate, debts, marital and charitable deductions, and casualty and theft losses.

The Beneficiaries

The selection of the beneficiaries is a basic element of the estate plan. The choice of who will inherit what depends upon many factors, i.e., personal, need, tax considerations, age, and competence. Questions have to be posed and resolved: Can my survivors manage their affairs? What will be required for their support and maintenance? What is best for their comfort and welfare?

Special Assets

Certain assets may require special consideration, such as an asset that will have to be sold after your death, like a business interest. Thought has to be given as to its valuation and the method of its liquidation. If similar types of interests are to be retained by your survivors, you should determine who will manage such interests and the liquidity needs of assets of this nature.

Participants in the Process

Those participants who are necessary to create and implement your plan and assume the final responsibility for the achievement of the desired results must be included in the planning process. The attorney is usually responsible for the overall creation of the plan. An accountant may be called upon to provide financial information required to properly identify and define your assets and liabilities. Other individuals, such as life insurance agents, financial consultants, and financial planners may help to provide a view as to other aspects of the financial plan such as benefit recommendations, tax information, budgets, and investment management.

Liquidity Needs

The liquidity needs of an estate must be considered and defined. This would include deciding whether the size of the estate should be increased. Steps can be put into place, for both short- and long-term planning, to achieve these results, such as: (1) an increase in life insurance coverage; (2) gifts of income-producing property to lower-tax-bracket family members; (3) an increase in employee benefit programs; (4) changes in existing portfolio investments; and (5) consideration of the asset appreciation potential of tax shelter annuities.

Reduction of Estate Costs

In addition, you must consider in this process the various ways to reduce costs that will arise at death. These will include: (1) making lifetime gifts and sales; (2) maximizing the use of the estate deductions, tax deferrals, avoidances, and credits that are available; (3) the use of life insurance trusts; (4) providing instructions for the management and assistance in the distribution of certain assets that require special expertise; (5) creating a structure for the valuation of assets that do not have a readily ascertainable fair market value, such as shares of stock of closely held corporations, real estate, or certain tangible personal property; (6) contemplation of making the estate eligible for the use of Section 6166 of the Code (deferred payment of estate taxes) and Section 303 of the Code (redemption of shares of stock to the extent of funeral and administration expenses); (7) avoiding probate through the use of trusts and survivor property arrangements; (8) setting up private annuity arrangements which can avoid probate, gift, and estate taxes; and (9) consideration of the state of your domicile when you die. Each state maintains its own laws controlling property located in it, in addition to potentially imposing gift and estate taxes.

Fiduciaries

The selection of fiduciaries (executors or personal representatives, trustees, or guardians) is probably one of the most difficult tasks in formulating an estate plan. Consideration in this regard must be given, where applicable, to corporate representatives such as banks and trust companies, in the appropriate situations.

Coordination of All Plans

The increased use of probate avoidance devices makes estate planning even more complicated. As such, consideration must be given to the coordination of the disposition of probate and nonprobate assets. You should consider nonprobate assets as property that you have transferred during your lifetime except that you have retained the total right during your lifetime to alter the distribution upon your death. This would include life insurance, Totten trusts, joint bank accounts, and plans with beneficiary designations. Your living trust, will, and any other documents providing death payment instructions must be reviewed to be sure there are no ambiguities among all of these devices.

Personal Concerns

In the planning process, an order of priorities must be observed. For example, if your assets are insufficient to provide financial security for your surviving spouse and children, your spouse is usually given the larger share of your estate and your children are provided solely for their educational needs. This is a personal decision that you must make. Consideration must be given to the short- and long-term needs of the beneficiaries—their competency, ability to be self-supporting, and ability to manage money and property. Their ages and health must be weighed in this process as well. You may wish to favor a handicapped beneficiary. On the other hand, irresponsible beneficiaries may be given a larger share than their siblings, on the theory that their needs or their families' needs may be greater than those of beneficiaries who are committed to a work ethic.

The Human Element

The success of any estate plan depends on the human element. An estate plan that is balanced should not cause litigation or dissension among family members or hatred of you. Money, it has been said, "is the root of all evil." Weaknesses such as greed, dishonesty, and divisiveness, often surface when money is involved. Measures should be taken to deflect conflicts of this kind, such as: (1) the equalization of bequests to children both in amounts and in the manner of the distribution (outright or in trust); (2) careful selection of the guardian for a minor child, since the guardian must supervise the management of the minor's property; and (3) the proper balance if you have had multiple marriages and you have multiple sets of children. Other considerations include children who have special needs that require planning by special experts in order to coordinate the programs available to them. Unmarried couples who have no statutory rights to inherit the other's property must create special methods for transferring their property to the survivor in order, in many cases, to avoid litigation with a hostile family. Finally, it is worth noting that, just as we have the right to leave our property to whomever we want (subject to statutory restrictions), we have the right to disinherit anyone (subject to the same restrictions).

Preventing a Challenge to the Estate

An excellent method of preventing a challenge to your estate is an "in terrorem" provision in your living trust or will that provides for the revocation or forfeiture of a legacy if a beneficiary contests the validity of the document or its distribution of property.

Funeral and Burial Plans

Your estate plan should consider funeral and burial plans as well, which may include cremation arrangements and the donation of body parts to organ banks for medical transplants and/or research.

The use of a will or a living trust as a device for an anatomical gift is usually not a good idea. The effectiveness of any organ for transplant depends upon immediate removal. Usually this can be best planned by creating an instrument in the form of a card (which should be witnessed by at least two witnesses) or other documents to provide for the anatomical gift, which can be carried by you.

❖

CHAPTER 2

Selecting Who Receives the Benefits of Your Estate

*T*his chapter describes the process of designating those who will receive your property: who they are, how much you should leave them, and in what form (outright or in trust). You will also find out whether you can disinherit anyone (which in many cases depends upon the laws of the state where you live); what happens if you fail to provide for alternatives in case a beneficiary should predecease you, and what can be done with pets.

A beneficiary is the recipient of all or a portion of your estate. Beneficiaries can be members of your immediate family, charities, trusts, relatives, friends, and other organizations.

The selection process requires consideration of: (1) the laws of the state which controls the distributions; (2) the estate tax consequences; and (3) the needs of the particular individuals involved. Your beneficiaries can receive their inheritances either outright or in trust. If a beneficiary is a child, his or her share will be held by a custodian until he or she attains majority (usually eighteen years of age). Bequests can be made in a dollar amount or of a percent of the estate.

Alternates

Alternate beneficiaries should be selected in the event the primary beneficiaries predecease the estate owner. If a primary beneficiary dies before the estate owner, the inheritance might lapse. Bequests that lapse will either pass through a residuary disposition or by intestacy, if none exists. A residuary disposition can be effectuated by including a provision in your living trust or will that sets forth who is to receive all of your remaining property not specifically given to the named beneficiaries.

Certain inheritances, however, are prevented from lapsing by state law, as the result of the blood relationship of the parties. In New York State, for example, a bequest to a child who predeceases a parent will not lapse, but will pass down to the children of the predeceased child.

Intestacy

Passing assets by intestacy means that, if one dies owning assets in his or her name and has not created a distribution instrument (living trust or will), the property will pass to the closest blood heirs of that person under the laws of the state where he or she maintained permanent residence (domicile) at the time of death. In such event, it is the state which provides the terms of the stream of distribution. This would not apply, however, if the asset itself has a distribution beneficiary, such as the designation of a beneficiary of an insurance policy, a retirement plan, or a jointly held asset.

Surviving Spouse

In most states a surviving spouse is protected by law and must receive part of the estate. Therefore, appropriate provisions must be made for the spouse in order for that person to receive no less than his or her legal share. An example of the protection afforded spouses by law is illustrated in community property states. In this case, a surviving spouse has no legal claim to the other spouse's property. This is because community property states automatically divide property between the spouses as they acquire it during their marriage. Each spouse has the right to dispose of his or her one-half of the community property as he or she sees fit. Unmarried couples living together, however, have no such rights of inheritance unless a binding agreement, giving the other person specific rights of inheritance, has been entered into during their lifetimes.

Minors

When minors are named as beneficiaries they can receive their share outright or it can be placed in a trust. Most states prevent a minor (someone under eighteen years of age) from owning property outright. A guardian of the property can be designated to be responsible for managing the bequest until the minor attains majority. The guardian's management is subject to whatever restrictions are placed on the gift. (For a more detailed description of minors as beneficiaries, see chapter 18.)

Common Disaster

The laws of most states provide that, in the event of a common disaster, each of the people involved is presumed to have survived the other. That means if you and your spouse die in a common accident and it cannot be ascertained who died first, each of you will be deemed to have survived the other and your estates will be distributed accordingly. This means that each of your respective estates would pass as if the other person had died first. States that follow the Uniform Probate Code require a beneficiary to survive the estate owner by 120 hours. A clause can be inserted in a living trust or will that not only creates a different presumption, but provides that a beneficiary must survive by a certain amount of time to be considered to have survived the other person. However, for a spouse, the estate tax laws limit the period to six months for the unlimited marital deduction to be available.

Pets

Pets are an estate planning challenge. In most jurisdictions, pets are considered just another piece of property. However, for many, a pet is extremely important and considered a person and not just property.

Certain states, like California, allow people to leave part of their estate to an animal in 'honorary trust' (which is not a legal trust).

Seven states already had legislation similar to that passed in New York in 1996, which allows a pet owner to create a trust, either inter vivos (during lifetime) or testamentary (by living trust or will) to provide for the care of a pet. Before this law was passed, a trust could not be established for a pet nor could a pet be the beneficiary of a trust or receive an outright gift.

The use of the principal and income of the trust may be enforced by a person designated for that purpose, or if no one is appointed, the court may appoint an enforcer. The trust must terminate upon the death of all the animals covered by the trust or the expiration of twenty-one years, whichever comes first. The court has the right to reduce a fund that appears to be too large for the care of a pet. Any overage would be paid to the estate owner's estate.

New York is the seventh state to enact pet-trust provisions.

The Residuary Beneficiary

Your living trust or will should name a residuary beneficiary or beneficiaries and alternates as well. These are the persons or organizations that will receive the balance of your property not specifically given and will also work to pass those gifts which may have lapsed.

9

Personal Expressions

In recent years, explanations or personal commentaries have been omitted in many living trusts and wills. There are instances, however, when reasons for particular gifts or disinheritances are meaningful and may even discourage legal challenges.

For example, a parent may leave unequal shares to two children and give a reason, i.e., one child is wealthy and the other is not. Given such an explanation, the advantaged child might not seek to challenge the legacy; or if one child may be disadvantaged, physically or mentally, and therefore will have special needs, an expression of this fact may have the same dissuasive effect.

Disinheritance

The laws of most states do not protect children from disinheritance. The best formula for disinheriting a child is to leave the child a token amount that effectively serves as a disinheritance. This can include a provision of explanation. Alternatively, you can expressly disinherit a child by a specific clause, which could also include a statement as to why.

Forgiving Debts

Any debt, whether written or oral, can be forgiven. This works to release the person who is responsible for the debt and has no income tax impact.

Unmarried Partners

Unmarried couples or partners living together have no rights of inheritance. They are free to deal with their property as they see fit. If they have entered into an agreement that provides for specific rights of inheritance, an agreement of this nature will usually be enforceable.

Abatement

If your estate does not have sufficient assets to satisfy all of your bequests and debts, then your bequests will be proportionately reduced. Specific bequests, which are those that give a beneficiary a specific article, (for example, a car or certain shares of stock), are usually the last items that are reduced, with residuary and cash bequests being reduced first.

In creating a selection of beneficiaries, you should set down all of the potential persons, their order of priority, any special needs they might have, and what your legal obligations are, if any, to any of them. Once this and your assets, liabilities, and the tax consequences are determined, you can then determine who is to get what and how.

CHAPTER 3

Wills

When you think of estate planning, your thoughts usually focus on a will. The most common questions asked are: What is a will? Must you have a will? What happens if you die without one? This chapter answers these questions and describes this form of passing your property. At the end of this chapter is a list of the important elements that must be provided in a will.

Since people differ, their wills differ. There is no single prototype of a will. However, the basic goals are all the same. This chapter tells you when a will is necessary, who can execute a will, when a will is a legal document, the different kinds of wills, what are the common and uncommon elements of a will, and what can be incorporated into a will by reference. Understanding the role of a will in the overall estate planning process is very important. A will is nothing more than a simple statement of what you want to happen with your property after you die.

It has been estimated that one out of every three wills is contested. This is an unbelievably high statistic. Because of the history of fraud and undue influence, the laws of our states are very strict insofar as wills are concerned.

What Is a Will?

A will is usually the first thing you contemplate when planning your estate. It is the written document that provides for the distribution of your property when you die. Every will must go through probate. Because of this, in most instances, a will is not the best way to pass your property to your survivors. Other devices, such as a living trust, are generally preferable. However, a will is still a useful document that should be created as a stopgap to any other probate avoidance devices used and for certain other purposes. There are certain limitations on what you can do under a will, however, and they must always be considered.

These are:

- What are the rights of my surviving spouse? (Most states afford the spouse a right to inherit.)
- What are the rights of my children? (Most states do not require you to leave anything to your children.)
- If I create a trust, how long can it last and can the income from it be accumulated? (All states limit how long a noncharitable trust can last and some limit how long income can be accumulated and not distributed.)
- Can I give an unlimited amount to a charity? (Many states limit the amount that can be given to charity if there are surviving family members.)

When Is a Will Necessary?

A will is necessary to designate guardians for the person and property of minor children (under eighteen years of age). In the vast majority of jurisdictions in our country, a living trust cannot designate a guardian to both care for the child and manage the child's property. It must be done in a will.

A will is also necessary to transfer property to your living trust that was not transferred before your death. This is known as a pour-over will. A will is also necessary in most jurisdictions to disinherit someone.

In order for a will to be a legal document, most states require the following:

- You must be a legal adult (at least eighteen years old)
- You must have *testamentary capacity*
- The will must comply with the technical will-drafting requirements of the state
- The will should be typewritten or printed
- The will must have at least one provision setting forth the plan of distribution of your property
- You must appoint at least one executor or personal representative
- You must date the will
- You must sign the will in the presence of witnesses (usually not less than two)

Since laws vary from state to state, it is always advisable to verify the legal status of your will if you move.

Testamentary Capacity

In order to create a legally valid will, the law requires that you possess "testamentary capacity," meaning: (1) you must know the nature and extent of your property; (2) you must know who the people are who would inherit your estate, if there was no will; and (3) you must understand the distribution plan you have created under your will. Once you have created a legally valid will you are called the "testator" (male) or "testatrix" (female), of that will.

Witnesses

A will must be signed and witnessed in accordance with the technical requirements of each state. Most states have similar rules for the execution of wills. A will need not be notarized, recorded, or filed in the court.

Witnesses are usually persons who do not inherit under the will. These people witness your signature and then sign the will themselves as witnesses. You must tell the witnesses that the instrument they are witnessing is your will, but the witnesses do not have to read it or be told what it contains.

Like the testator, the witnesses must be competent. This generally means that, at the time the will is executed, the witnesses must be mature enough and of sufficient mental capacity to understand and appreciate the nature of the act they are witnessing and be able to testify in court, should it be necessary.

Formalities of Execution

The appropriate formality of execution is to have the testator and the witnesses in the same room. All should sign the document, using the same pen, with the testator signing or initialing each page. After a will has been executed it should never be taken apart once it has been stapled together.

Self-Proving Wills

The great majority of states have adopted a self-proving will procedure. After executing the will, the testator and the witnesses, in the presence of a notary public, should sign an affidavit stating that all of the requisites for due execution have been complied with. If this is done, certain formalities later on required by the courts in the proving of the will can be dispensed with.

Safeguarding a Will

Once a will has been executed, it is important to safeguard it. It is best if the will is safeguarded by the lawyer who prepared it. A will placed in a safe deposit box may not be conveniently available to the heirs, since safe deposit boxes may under local law be sealed for a period of time after the death of the box holder. Most states that had statutes restricting the probate of lost wills have repealed them. If a will is lost or destroyed without the consent of the testator, in many states this does not prevent its probate, provided its contents are proved.

Statutory Wills

In response to a public demand for a legally valid will that can be written on an easily available printed form, several states have authorized simple "statutory wills." Presently, California, Maine, Michigan, and Wisconsin have approved statutory wills. In a statutory will, spaces are provided where the testator simply writes in the names of the beneficiaries. However, these instruments have been highly criticized in the legal profession because they can create a great deal of problems. Individuals should not try to write their own wills, as they may do more harm than good. Trying to cut corners in the making of a will could create great problems for the testator's estate.

Holographic Wills

A holographic will is one written entirely in the testator's hand and signed by the testator. Generally, in states that recognize holographic wills, attesting witnesses are not required. The rationale is that it is difficult to forge a person's handwriting. However, because of the possibility of forgery, these documents are viewed very strictly by the courts.

About half of the states permit holographic wills. In those states, a holographic will supersedes a prior formally executed will. Under the Uniform Probate Code, a holographic will is valid, whether or not it has been witnessed, if the signature and the material provisions are in the handwriting of the testator. If any printed-material provisions are eliminated, the handwritten portion must show the testator's intentions, and the key distribution provisions must be in the testator's handwriting. The State Attorney's office of each state should be checked to verify if holographic wills are valid in that state.

Divorce

The effect of a divorce upon the validity of certain provisions of a will varies from state to state. In New York State, for example, if a marriage is ended by divorce, then all provisions to a spouse in a will are void. In some states, the law treats the former spouse as if he or she predeceased the decedent, so as to protect the children in the estate plan. In other states, the transfer to the former spouse is simply "null and void." However, in a life insurance policy, the former spouse named as the beneficiary will be held as the beneficiary by contract law, if there was no legal change made by the policyholder during his or her lifetime.

Marriage

What happens if you execute a will and subsequently marry? A large majority of our states have laws that award the spouse an intestate share, unless it appears from the will that the omission was intentional. If the spouse is provided for in the will or by certain will substitutes, which meet the statutory requirement as to amount, then he or she will not be awarded an intestate share. An example of this is a trust annuity created during the life of the testator which will pay income for the life of the surviving spouse.

A Residuary Clause

A will should include a residuary clause. This clause in a will is usually the most important. It provides for a distribution of the remainder of the estate after all of the other specific and cash bequests have been made. The residuary bequest can be made to a single beneficiary, either outright or in trust, to two or more beneficiaries in stated proportions, or to a class of beneficiaries such as "children." The residuary clause can function as a blanket contingency clause should any bequest or contingent bequest made under the will fail. A bequest that fails, for whatever reason, would turn over to and be added into the residue of the estate. As previously mentioned, this residue also includes any assets not specifically accounted for in the will. Therefore, it is important that you select a residuary beneficiary or beneficiaries.

It is always a good idea to incorporate a residuary clause into the will even if you have selected contingent beneficiaries for all bequests. There is always the possibility that a contingent beneficiary might die before you. Furthermore, even if all beneficiaries do survive the testator, there may still be estate assets remaining that were not disposed of, and therefore, could be subject to intestacy, which means that since you have died without a will, your property would be distributed to your nearest blood heirs in accordance with the order of distribution as set forth under the laws of your state. Your property *escheats* (that is, goes to the state government) after passing through intestacy, if no blood heirs can be found. A residuary clause is a good way to avoid the undesirable prospect of estate assets falling into the coffers of the state government.

Oral Wills

Oral wills (also called "nuncupative" wills) are only valid in a minority of states and, even where valid, are acceptable only if made under special circumstances, such as the will-maker's perception of imminent death. Some states impose far more restrictive limits. In some states an oral will can be made only by someone serving in the armed forces, just before death being certain, and only for a limited amount of personal property.

Video or Film Wills

At present, no video or film wills are recognized by state law. Indiana is the only state with legislation specifically addressing the use of videotape in the probate process.

The Indiana statute permits the use of a videotape as proof of the testator's intentions, mental state and capacity, the authenticity of the will, and any other matter the court determines relevant to the probate of the will. No other states have passed laws dealing with this subject.

A videotape of the will-execution ceremony can have potential advantages. Unlike witnesses, whose memories may fade as time passes, a videotape is highly accurate. It allows the court to better evaluate the testator's condition by preserving evidence, such as demeanor, voice tone and inflection, facial expressions, and gestures. A videotape may also have psychological benefits for both the testator and the survivors. The testator may feel more confident that his intended plan will take effect, and the survivors may be comforted by viewing the testator delivering a final message.

Although videotaping a will execution ceremony may have significant benefits, there are potential problems. In some cases, steps can be taken to reduce or eliminate these problems; in others, it might be better to forego taping the ceremony.

If the testator's physical appearance or demeanor is poor, it may be advisable not to videotape the ceremony. Although a situation may otherwise seem appropriate for videotaping, a video should not be used if the testator's outward appearance, age, disability, or other habits may prejudice a judge or jury, or lead them to conclude that the testator was incompetent or unduly influenced.

Another potential problem is the possibility that someone might alter the videotape. The alteration could be accidental, although careful storage procedures should reduce the risk. A videotape could also be intentionally altered; however, it is more difficult to alter a videotape than a written document.

Joint Wills

A joint will is a will made by two people, usually a married couple. When the first spouse dies the will leaves everything to the survivor and designates how the estate will pass on when he or she dies. A joint will is, in effect, a contract and does not allow changes to the final disposition of the estate. There is no guarantee, however, that the final beneficiaries will receive anything, since there is nothing to prevent the survivor from consuming all the property. If you wish to control the ultimate distribution of your estate after your spouse dies, you are better off selecting a legal device known as a QTIP trust (see chapter 9). This type of trust will also insure the benefit of the estate tax marital deduction, which might not be available in the estate of the first spouse who dies under a joint will.

Challenges to a Will

Challenges to a will are common. A will can be contested on grounds of mental incompetency (lack of testamentary capacity) or by proving that the will was procured by fraud, duress, or undue influence. For this to be successful, it must be shown that a third party was able to manipulate the testator in creating a document which was not his or her will, but that of another person.

After-Born Children

If children are born after you make a will, it is wise to revise it to reflect your new situation. Most states, however, have specific statutes providing for "after-born children," treating them as if they were alive at the time of the making of the original will.

Incorporation by Reference

In a majority of states, memos or other writings can become part of a will by incorporation by reference thereto, provided that the writing is identifiable with reasonable certainty and that the writing is in existence at the time the will is created. However, this view is not universally accepted.

Under the majority view, a person may provide in his or her will that tangible personal property is to be divided among individuals who are named in a memo located in a safe deposit box. In addition, the Uniform Probate Code and the State of Florida permit incorporation by reference provided that the list is signed and describes with "reasonable certainty" the items and the beneficiaries. The list may be prepared either before or after the execution of the will and may be changed after its initial preparation. It is not necessary to physically attach the list to the will.

In a minority of states, including New York, however, such memos or lists are not secure estate planning devices. These jurisdictions feel that incorporation by reference should not be permitted out of concern that such an unattested document could invite fraud. In a classic New York case in which incorporation by reference was denied, the decedent's will directed that a parcel of real estate be divided into four parcels among each of decedent's four sons. The will included a legal description of the property. A diagram of the property was physically attached to the will following the signatures of the decedent and the witnesses; one paragraph of the will referred to the diagram and stated "I do hereby incorporate the same herein." Even so, the Surrogate's Court held that the diagram violated the New York rule against incorporation by reference and thus had no legal significance.

Even in states where incorporation by reference is not allowed, there are exceptions to the rule. A New York Court has held that a reference in the testator's will that half of his residuary estate was to be distributed to individuals named in his wife's will was valid. The testator and his wife both died when the *Lusitania* was torpedoed at the beginning of World War I. Of course it can be argued that this is not a true exception to the incorporation by reference doctrine because the wife's will had been executed in accordance with statutory requirements.

The New York Estates, Powers, and Trust Law allows a person to distribute all or part of his estate to an inter vivos trust (a "pour-over") if the trust was executed before or concurrently with his or her will and was executed in the manner required by state law for recording the conveyance of real property.

Another exception to the doctrine of incorporation by reference in states such as New York is the doctrine of "facts of independent significance." If a testator leaves a cash bequest to each person "who is an employee of mine at the time of my death," or leaves "all my tangible property located in my apartment at the time of my death" to a beneficiary, the bequest, although the exact details of it are not set forth in the will, is not necessarily invalid. As long as the facts can be readily ascertained, for example, what tangible property is actually located in the apartment at such time, the bequest can be valid under the doctrine of independent significance. A New York Surrogate Court has applied this doctrine to hold that a testator's direction to pay the claims of those persons taking care of him during his last illness created valid claims by those persons.

Lastly, on the subject of incorporation by reference, an interesting variation to that means of including other memos or writings in a will is where a will refers to a list of personal property that is itself attached to the will as the last page. In another New York case, the three-page will was signed on the third page. The will referred to an attached list of personal property and the list was attached as page four. The court found that the attached schedule was "constructively inserted" at the point referred to in the will.

Even though a will that refers to an outside list may not be valid to dispose of such property, the will may, nevertheless, be admitted to probate and the other portions of the will given effect.

Codicils

A codicil is a supplement to an existing will. It has to be executed with the same formality as the will. Because both the will and any codicil to it have to be offered for probate, it is often better to create a new will. There are certain circumstances though when the use of a codicil is preferable to a new will. For example, when a testator whose competency may be questioned wishes to change his or her will. In such a case the use of a codicil would be a better choice than creating a new will, because if a new will was signed and denied probate, former wills would have to be located which might have been destroyed or lost. If a codicil were used, then even if it were not admitted to probate, at least the prior will could be.

Forms of Wills and Provisions

There is no set standard form for a will. However, the underlying purpose of the will is basic: to transfer property from the estate owner to the beneficiaries.

The following is a list of the elements, both common and less common, that should be included in a will:

a. The identity of the person who created the will by name and family relationships.

b. The declaration by the testator of his or her residence. A statement to this effect, even though not legally binding, is at least some indication of the testator's thinking.

c. The revocation of all prior wills and codicils.

d. Burial, funeral directives, donation of body parts, and perpetual care directions. As a result of the delay between death and probate, anatomical gifts should be covered by arrangements made during your lifetime.

e. Payment of debts and administration expenses.

f. Distribution of tangible personal property.

g. Distribution of real estate to include specific gifts ("devises") and "legal life estates." A legal life estate is the same as a bequest in trust, wherein a person is given the life use of certain real property and no trustee is required. A legal life estate will qualify for the estate tax marital deduction as QTIP property.

h. Legacies which fall into the following four categories:
- Specific bequests
- General cash bequests
- Cash bequests payable out of certain property
- Residuary bequests

If, at the time of death, the testator no longer owns an asset specifically given, that particular legacy will not be effective. As such, alternate provisions for such an event should be provided, such as a cash bequest.

i. Trusts can be created out of the property of the testator for spouses, children, or others; however, consideration has to be given to the extent to which trust principal may be withdrawn by or on behalf of trust beneficiaries.

j. Legacies that terminate. If a beneficiary dies prior to the testator, the legacy lapses and as a general rule would pass down to the residuary beneficiary. Anti-lapse statutes in most states prevent the lapsing of a bequest to a child who predeceases his or her parent by in turn passing down the legacy to the children of such predeceased child. Will provisions can direct what happens if a beneficiary should die before the testator by making alternate directives.

k. Where appropriate, disinheritance may be provided for.

l. Allocation of the payment of death taxes.

m. Appointment of fiduciaries: executors, personal representatives, trustees, custodians of gifts to minors, and guardians of the person and property.

n. Survivorship. In certain situations it is important to set forth in what order individuals have died in order for their respective estates to be distributed to designated beneficiaries in the event of a common disaster.

o. Investment and other powers of the fiduciary should be expressed, including those concerning a business owned by the testator. The will should expressly set forth whether the business is to continue or be sold or liquidated.

p. If the testator holds any powers to withdraw the principal of a trust or to direct its eventual distribution or its termination, the exercise or nonexercise of these rights should be considered. As a general rule, the testator is deemed to have exercised them under a residuary clause contained in a will.

q. Precatory provisions. These are expressions of wishes that are not binding, as they are intended as something the testator would like to see happen but does not direct them to take place.

r. Explanations that offer personal touches to a will have generally been abandoned today. This may be because lawyers do not want to be burdened with this type of preparation. A statement by the testator can, however, make a gift more meaningful and perhaps even discourage contests. For example, the wish of Benjamin Franklin in his will dated July 17, 1788, provides an insight as to his taste regarding jewelry:

> "The king of France's picture, set with 408 diamonds, I give to my daughter Sarah, requesting that she not form any of those diamonds into ornaments . . . and thereby introduce or countenance the expensive, vain and useless fashion of wearing jewels in this country."

The will of Doris Duke, who left no part of her estate ($1.2 billion) to the companion she adopted at age thirty-five, sets forth her state of mind regarding this person:

> "I am convinced that I should not have adopted Chawdi Heffner—I have come to the realization that her primary motive was financial gain. I believe that, like me, my father would not have wanted her to have benefitted under the trusts which he created, and similarly, I do not wish her to benefit from my estate."

(Miss Heffner later commenced litigation challenging the will.)

s. Gifts may be made to a class of persons such as children, issue, grandchildren, nieces, and nephews.

t. Charitable bequests, which can be outright or in trust.

u. Certain limitations, such as the following, have to be considered as well:
  • Rights of a surviving spouse
  • Rights, if any, of children
  • The rule against perpetuities limiting the time property can be held in trust

v. As discussed in chapter 9, disclaimers are very significant postmortem planning tools. The use of a disclaimer permits the shifting of property from the intended person to other individuals without the imposition of gift or estate taxes to anyone. As such, a provision providing for such an event should be included if it is a part of the overall plan.

Trusts

In addition to a will, a living trust should be created. The size of the estate will determine the type of living trust that should be employed and the kind of sub-trusts that will come into existence after your death. Most of the states in this country require a formal probate proceeding if the estate owners' assets exceed ten thousand dollars.

A "testamentary trust" is created under a will and takes effect only after death, which means after the assets have been subject to the probate process.

If you die owning property in your name, your will has to be probated. What the probate process is about and its impact is set forth in detail in the next chapter of this book.

❖

CHAPTER 4

Understanding the Probate Process

*M*ost people really do not understand what probate is. The probate process can be torturous and agonizing. It can be costly, frustrating, and time consuming. With proper estate planning, it can be avoided. The value of an estate will usually determine whether a formal probate proceeding is required. In most states, if the value of the assets in your name is less than ten thousand dollars, an informal proceeding—usually by affidavit—is permitted to pass title to property. In this chapter you will learn all about the legal procedures involved in the administration of an estate by the courts. It explains who participates in it, how compensation is fixed for the managers of an estate, where probate originated, and whether it's necessary.

What Is It?

Probate is one of the ways to pass absolute title to your property to your survivors. It is the legal process by which a court validates your will and supervises the administration of the estate thereafter. For some, the word "probate" has taken on a sinister meaning. This is because it is complex, tediously slow, costly (legal fees in many instances are determined by the size of the estate), and, in most instances, totally unnecessary. The complexity of the process includes: the filing of the necessary court documents to institute the proceedings; notification to creditors and disposition of any claims; the gathering and valuation of the assets of the estate; the filing of the tax and accounting proceedings; and the eventual transfer of the assets to the heirs and closing of the estate. If, however, you create a living trust, your estate can be settled in a matter of hours as opposed to a matter of years. Avoiding the probate

23

process is, in most instances, the most significant reason to establish a living trust.

If your will is not a valid legal document or if you die without a will, your property will pass to your closest blood relatives, who will be determined by the law of your home state. This is called dying "intestate," which means in Latin, "without a will." In either of these events your estate is subject to the courts.

The Fiduciary

In your will you designate an executor or personal representative. This person (the "fiduciary") is in charge of administering the affairs of the estate and of carrying out the terms of your will. The fiduciary marshals and takes possession of your assets, manages and invests them, settles the debts, completes unfinished business, settles the estate tax proceedings, and eventually transfers the assets to your beneficiaries in accordance with the terms of your will. It is therefore important that you select a fiduciary who is responsible and competent. The executor usually hires an attorney who is experienced in probate matters. The executor and attorney are usually compensated based upon the existing formats in the state where the services are performed. The commissions paid to executors or personal representatives are usually based upon a percentage of the value of the estate as determined by a set sliding scale rate under the law of the state; for example, 5 percent of the first $100,000 of the estate, 4 percent of the next $200,000, and 3 percent of the next $700,000. Attorneys can be compensated either by a percent of the gross value of the probate estate or on a fee fixed by the court. In addition, the estate is required to pay the court costs, which include filing fees and similar expenses. Many lawyers charge estates at an hourly rate for their services in matters of this kind. In some states the courts will set the fees solely on a "reasonable" basis. In addition, there are court-processing fees and other transaction costs that an estate incurs during the probate administration period. The varying range of probate costs will depend on the size and complexity of the estate as well as the state in which it is administered. These fees can range from 4.5 percent of the gross estate on large estates to 9 percent or more on small estates.

When Is Probate Necessary?

There are a few instances when probate is mandatory:
- To designate guardians (persons and property for minor children) that can only be designated in a will.
- To distribute property not transferred during one's lifetime to probate avoidance devices. This is usually accomplished by a simple

pour-over will, which provides that any property not transferred during one's lifetime be transferred to a trust or other device to be held and distributed in accordance with its terms.

- If the decedent was involved in litigation.
- If the decedent was heavily in debt, the probate process is a good forum to settle those matters and cut off creditors' claims.

Probate's Origin

The history of probate is rooted in England, and our current formal proceedings were started after the American Revolution.

In England today, however, they have simplified their system to provide that the executor named in the will is only required to file an accounting of the assets and liabilities of the estate with the tax department which values the property and assesses the estate tax. The actual validating of the will, called a "Grant of Probate," is routinely performed on a very prompt basis. The executor administers the estate without the intervention of the courts, and only if a contest arises or any other kind of dispute evolves does the court get involved.

In most civil law countries the probate system is even less complicated. In these jurisdictions, when you sign your will, it is notarized by a notary who has semi-judicial authority. After your death, the executor can perform all administration functions without the intervention of the court. Disputes are taken care of in the same manner as any other legal dispute.

Length of Probate

Because of the court's requirements and office delays, the usual probate proceeding can last for years. This can result in an erosion of assets through the imposition of fees or a deterioration in property values through improper management and investment. By comparison, except for the filing and completion of tax proceedings, property placed in a living trust can be transferred shortly after the death of the estate owner.

Probate Avoidances

In response to the system of probate, and in order to avoid it, many methods have been developed. This means you can employ alternate techniques to pass property to your heirs when you die, without incurring the costs associated with probate. The major avoidance vehicles are: the living trust, joint-tenancy ownership, life insurance, irrevocable trusts, and bank accounts. All of these methods are discussed at length in this book. The living trust is the most important means of avoiding probate and is really coming into its own. It is legal in every state, and attorneys have finally acknowledged its benefit and the fact that it has no downside. Even certified public accountants, who do not usually focus on estate planning for their clients, are confirming the advisability of using a living trust.

New Disclosure Requirements for Attorneys

In 1995, New York State enacted a statute (covering all wills and codicils executed after January 1, 1996) providing that attorneys who are named as executors in wills that they, or anyone affiliated with them, have prepared must disclose to the testator, prior to execution of the will, that: (1) subject to limited statutory exceptions, any person, including an attorney, is eligible to serve as an executor; (2) absent an agreement to the contrary, such person, including an attorney, will receive a statutory commission for serving as executor; and (3) if an attorney serves as executor, such attorney is entitled to both executor's statutory commissions and reasonable compensation for legal services. Attorneys must also obtain a written acknowledgment of disclosure from the testator. Model disclosure forms that satisfy the disclosure requirements of the statute are provided in the statute.

Drafting a will naming oneself as an executor poses a unique conflict to the attorney/draftsperson. On the one hand, with few exceptions, the testator or testatrix has the right to name whomever he or she pleases to serve as executor. On the other hand, there is a confidential relationship between the attorney and his or her client. Under the Code of Professional Responsibility the attorney/draftsperson is directed to avoid even the appearance of abuse of that relationship. Thus, he or she must avoid "consciously influencing a client to name the lawyer as executor."

The new statute is designed to address situations where the client may think or presume that naming his or her attorney as executor will reduce the commissions and/or legal fees charged to the estate.

The new law applies only to attorneys, not other professionals, and only if such attorney or an "affiliated" attorney drafts a will naming such attorney as an executor.

The failure to obtain a written acknowledgment of disclosure from the testator will result in the commissions of the attorney/executor being reduced by one-half. If the executor is serving as a coexecutor, the reduction is based upon the statutory commission due that executor.

It is important to note that the law does not apply to trustees of inter vivos (revocable or irrevocable) or testamentary trusts. The statute may serve to encourage increased use of revocable inter vivos trusts.

Acknowledgment of Disclosure Forms

The following are models of the testator's written acknowledgment of disclosure:

  A. When set forth in a writing executed *prior to or concurrently* with a will:

Prior to signing my will, I was informed that:

1. Subject to limited statutory exceptions, any person, including an attorney, is eligible to serve as my executor;
2. Absent an agreement to the contrary, any person, including an attorney, who serves as executor for me is entitled to receive statutory commissions for executorial services rendered to my estate;
3. If such attorney serves as my executor, and he or she or another attorney affiliated with such attorney renders legal services in connection with the executor's official duties, he or she is entitled to receive just and reasonable compensation for those legal services, in addition to the commissions to which an executor is entitled.

_____ _____
WITNESS   TESTATOR

_____ _____
DATED   DATED

  B. When set forth in a writing executed *subsequently* to the will:

I, _____ have designated my attorney _____, a(n) Executor/Alternate Executor/Coexecutor [delete what is inapplicable] in my will dated _____.

Prior to signing my will, I was informed that:

1. Subject to limited statutory exceptions, any person, including an attorney, is eligible to serve as my executor;
2. Absent an agreement to the contrary, any person, including an attorney, who serves as an executor for me is entitled to receive statutory commissions for executorial services rendered to my estate;
3. If such attorney serves as my executor, and he or she or another attorney affiliated with such attorney renders legal services in connection with the executor's official duties, he or she is entitled to receive just and reasonable compensation for those legal services, in addition to the commissions to which an executor is entitled.

_____ _____
WITNESS   TESTATOR

_____ _____
DATED   DATED

CHAPTER 5

Co-ownership of Property

This chapter gives you a broad overview of the various forms of co-ownership, what they mean, and how they work. Certain states have abolished joint tenancy in certain situations and these are described as well.

Ownership in a community property jurisdiction is described in detail and you will learn which states have it and what it's all about.

There are three basic types of co-ownership of property:

1. Joint ownership with a right of survivorship and tenancies by the entirety, which can only be created between individuals who are married
2. Tenancies-in-common, in which each co-owner owns an undivided fractional interest in the property, and which form of ownership subjects the property to probate
3. Community property, a special form of co-ownership between spouses that exists in nine states

Joint ownership of property should not be created or used as a substitute for a will or living trust. If the joint owners were to die simultaneously and there were no will or living trust in existence, the assets would pass to those perhaps not intended, which would be the nearest blood relatives of each joint owner (on a one-half-each basis).

Joint ownership of property, although it allows you to avoid probate, carries with it distinct downsides. These deal mainly in the loss of a "stepped-up value" of the property at the time of the death of the co-owner (not in community property states). The stepped-up value is the value property is increased to (fair market value) at the time of the owner's death, which is the income tax basis to the heirs. If the alternate valuation date is cited, the basis is the fair market value of the property on the alternate valuation date (six months after the date of death). This could reduce or eliminate capital gains taxes upon its eventual sale. The failure to obtain an increased value could result in adverse income tax consequences to the heirs of an estate.

Upon the death of the survivor of jointly owned property, his or her assets will be subject to probate, so that joint ownership does not fully eliminate the probate process. A joint owner could be subject to creditor's claims and the asset could be lost. A living trust offers the benefits of co-ownership without these risks. It provides for the survivorship aspect, avoidance of probate, and provides the survivors with assets needed immediately after the person's death.

Joint Tenancy

Joint tenancy is the simplest probate avoidance method. In this type of ownership each person's interest can be disposed of without the consent of the other owner. It also can provide for the "right of survivorship," allowing the survivor to inherit the deceased owner's share without probate. In approximately thirty states, a similar form of ownership called a "tenancy-by-the-entirety" is allowable. This method, which can only be used by a married couple, offers the right of survivorship (like a joint tenancy) except that in the tenancy-by-the-entirety, each joint tenant is deemed to own the entire interest. This prevents the sale or transfer of property without the consent of the other joint owner.

The disadvantages of these forms of ownership are: (1) if the value of the estate is larger than the amount of the current applicable unified credit for estate tax purposes ($650,000), the joint ownership will cost the heirs a certain amount of their inheritance because the unified credit may not be applicable in the estate of the first to die (for a detailed explanation see chapter 9); (2) in certain instances, the creation of a joint interest is subject to gift taxes; and (3) a partial loss of increased tax basis as a result of the inability to step-up the value to the value at the date of death.

Tenancy-in-Common

A tenancy-in-common is another form of joint tenancy that permits each owner to dispose of his or her share independently. When one owner dies, his or her share will usually pass on to his or her heirs rather than to the joint owner. The advantage of this form of joint ownership is that the asset can be transferred to a living trust and thus avoid probate and provide a survivorship feature.

Bank Accounts

You can use joint tenancy bank accounts to avoid probate and provide funds to heirs. Most forms of bank accounts can be owned in joint tenancy, including checking, savings, and certificates of deposit. To open such an account, everyone involved signs as joint tenants with right of survivorship. When one joint tenant dies, the survivor(s) can have access to the account, with no need to go through probate.

Under the Uniform Probate Code, during the owner's lifetime a joint account belongs proportionately to each contributor, thereby permitting each to revoke the joint ownership at any time. Under the laws of many states, including the State of New York, each joint owner has the right to an equal percentage of the joint account.

Under a joint tenancy arrangement the property automatically is inherited by the surviving owner(s). Other forms of shared ownership such as tenancy-in-common and community property (see below) do not create a survivorship right. In those cases, how each share owner's interest will be disposed of is determined by a will or living trust.

Multiple individuals can own the same property as joint tenants provided they each have an equal interest. If they own different interests in the property, the form of ownership is a tenancy-in-common which does not allow the right of survivorship.

While states have laws spelling out the legal consequences of joint accounts, most states leave it to the persons who create the account to define the rights of the joint holders of the account per an agreement signed when the account is opened. Joint bank accounts generally fall into one of the three following categories:

1. *Joint tenancy with immediate vesting:* Each joint owner, on the creation of the account, acquires an interest in one-half of the funds deposited, and neither can withdraw more than half without accounting to the other.
2. *Revocable account:* Each can withdraw the full amount on deposit without accounting to the other. Avoid using this type of account if there is any serious possibility that the would-be named joint tenant would "misappropriate" the funds.
3. *Convenience account:* One person deposits all the funds and has the sole right to the funds while both are alive. The other can make deposits and withdrawals only as "agent" for the owner.

All three types provide for survivorship. In the case of the convenience account, however, while it is clear that the individual supplying the funds receives the funds when he or she is the survivor, if the other person survives, whether he or she receives the funds depends on the deposit agreement and the local law.

In New York (effective January 10, 1991), the "convenience account," if funded with separate property, will remain the separate property of the depositor. No gift is inferred upon the opening of such an account and on the death of the depositor the other person does not have a right of survivorship.

You can create bank accounts that prevent a joint owner from withdrawing any funds before your death. During your lifetime, the beneficiary of such an account normally has no rights to the account and is entitled to such funds only after your death. If the beneficiary of such an account should predecease you, an account of this kind would pass under the residuary clause of your will. In the State of New York, these accounts are commonly called Totten trust accounts and this form of nonprobate passing is limited only to bank accounts.

Safe Deposit Box

A joint tenancy safe deposit box can be a sensible place to keep important personal documents. Either joint tenant can obtain access to the documents when they are required.

In many states with state death taxes, safe deposit boxes are sealed by the bank as soon as it is notified of the death of an owner. The contents cannot be released until the box is inventoried by a government official or a waiver is obtained, which is usually a relatively simple procedure.

State Laws on Joint Tenancy

The following states have limited or abolished joint tenancy as described:
- *Alaska:* No joint tenancy in real estate except for husband and wife
- *North Carolina:* No joint tenancy for any property except joint bank accounts
- *Pennsylvania:* No joint tenancy in real estate (has been questioned in court decisions)
- *South Carolina:* Real estate joint tenancy must include words with right of survivorship
- *Tennessee:* No joint tenancy for any property except in the case of husband and wife
- *Texas:* No joint tenancy in any property unless there is an agreement in writing between joint owners

Joint Tenancy in Community Property States

Nine states—Arizona, California, Idaho, Louisiana, Nevada, New Mexico, Texas, Washington, and Wisconsin—have a form of co-ownership of property known as community property.

The community property systems may vary from state to state, but there are certain common concepts. All property acquired by a husband and wife during their marriage, while they reside in a community property state, is community property. It belongs to each of the marriage partners, share and share alike, each owning one-half thereof. They share not only in the physical property acquired, but also in the income from the property and their salaries, wages, and other compensation for services.

At the same time, each person may still own separate property. They may also hold property between them in joint tenancy. A married couple can convert community property to separate property or vice versa. A change in the form of ownership can be decided by the couple. Any such changes should be formalized by an agreement in order to have a clear, written record of the parties' desires, should a future dispute arise as to ownership rights.

Spouses can agree prior to their marriage through a prenuptial agreement that they will not be bound by the community property laws of their state of residence.

In general, community property assets retain that character even after the parties have moved to a noncommunity property state, unless the parties themselves are able to adjust their rights between themselves. Thus, if you are living in a community property state, you and your spouse may have acquired a community property bank account. If you move into a noncommunity property state and take the proceeds of the account with you, the money still retains its community character. If you then invest it in real estate in your new home state, the real estate may still be viewed as community real estate.

If you are a couple who moves from a noncommunity property state to a community property state, the personal property you acquired in the former state, whether tangible or intangible (stocks and bonds and the like), retains its character as separate, joint, or whatever other form of ownership it originally had. Real estate will retain the form of ownership assigned to it. Real estate in a community property state acquired by either spouse while married may be treated as community property without regard to the domicile or residence of the spouses. It has been held that the law of the state where the real estate is situated determines whether the income therefrom is community property.

Basis of Decedent's and Survivor's Interest

The general rule is that the values for income tax purposes of property acquired from a decedent is the fair market value of the property on the date of his or her death or on the alternate valuation date if the executor so elects. Where property is held jointly by spouses in common law states, the surviving spouse receives a stepped-up basis of only one-half of the value of the property. The survivor's half carries over his or her original basis.

Uniform Marital Property Act

The Uniform Marital Property Act (UMPA), adopted in Wisconsin and under consideration in a number of other states, is a form of "community property" law similar to the existing community property laws. Its principal effect is to institute a legal presumption, which may be rebutted by evidence, that all property owned by a married couple is presumed to be so-called marital property that is equally divisible between the spouses. It will apply in cases of property divisions upon divorce and at death.

Most states have adopted "equitable distribution" statutes that govern the dispositions of property upon divorce. UMPA represents a modification of equitable distribution policy in that the parties are presumed to own all property acquired after the marriage equally.

Like community property laws, UMPA provides a full step-up in the tax basis of property received by a surviving spouse. This has the effect of reducing post-death property capital gains on any appreciated property sold after the death of a spouse.

Third Parties

If a spouse considers placing property into joint tenancy with someone other than his or her spouse, and if the property is the separate property of the spouse, that's permissible. However, if the property is community property, the surviving spouse would have a claim against the estate of the deceased spouse and the surviving joint tenant for his or her one-half interest in the property. The surviving spouse could successfully contend that the deceased spouse had the authority only to transfer his or her half of the community property into joint tenancy with someone else.

Simultaneous Death

If joint tenants die simultaneously, their interest in the property will pass according to their wills. Usually the residuary clause in the will passes this on to the residuary beneficiaries of the estate. This cannot be done with a living trust since it only works to dispose of property transferred to it. A pour-over backup will would transfer the jointly owned property to the trust which in turn would distribute it under the terms of the trust.

Tax Rules

The value of jointly owned property is included in your taxable estate. The amount is based on how much you contributed when the jointly owned property was created or bought. If you put up all the money to purchase a piece of joint property, the full market value of the property will be included in your taxable estate.

Federal Estate Taxes

The federal regulations presume that for estate tax purposes, except for married persons, the first joint tenant to die contributed all the property to joint tenancy. The estate can reduce this by proving the amount of the contribution of the surviving joint tenant to the property.

As to spouses, only half the value of the joint tenancy property is included in the federal taxable estate of the first spouse to die, no matter how much either spouse contributed to the property.

However, the 50 percent rule of inclusion does not apply to spousal joint interests created before 1977. The rule for all spousal joint tenancies created prior to 1977 is that, if the decedent spouse paid the entire consideration for the property, the entire property is included in the decedent spouse's estate and the surviving spouse receives a stepped-up basis for the entire property.

Since there is no estate tax covering property jointly owned by spouses, for income tax purposes, the form of ownership is relevant only to determine the basis of property to the survivor and the qualification of the estate for three special estate tax benefits: (1) special use valuation of farm and business realty under Code Sec. 2032A; (2) deferred payment of estate tax under Code Sec. 6166; and (3) death tax stock redemptions under Code Sec. 303. These special benefits are discussed in detail in chapter 9.

Generally, from a tax standpoint, it is not advisable for spouses to jointly own property. The advantage of avoiding probate can be vastly outweighed by the tax disadvantages. If ownership in property is retained solely by one spouse, the survivor will receive the property at a cost basis stepped-up to the fair market value at the date of the first spouse's death rather than having two different cost bases (half at the survivor's original basis and half at the deceased spouse's stepped-up basis). This could effectively eliminate a capital gains tax on the subsequent sale of the asset.

In addition, from an estate tax standpoint, the joint ownership of an asset eliminates its potential use to fund a credit shelter trust since it will not pass through a will or living trust.

Liability for Tax

There is a danger of estate tax liability on a joint owner of property, other than a spouse. Code Sec. 6324(a)(2) imposes estate tax liability on a transferee who receives or has on the date of the decedent's death property included in the decedent's gross estate (to the extent of the value of such property). If the decedent had only jointly owned assets or jointly owned and nonliquid assets, then the Internal Revenue Service might pursue the joint owner to obtain payment of the tax. In that event, the joint owner would have a right of reimbursement from the estate or contribution from other legatees. In *A. Fillman and First Interstate Bank* v. *USA*, DC Iowa, 90-2 USTC 60,064, the decedent had substantial real estate holdings. One parcel was owned jointly with a sister of the decedent. The balance of the realty was transferred to a trust and the estate did not have sufficient assets to pay the estate tax. The Internal Revenue Service levied against the sister's accounts rather than against the property included in the estate. The court held that under state law (Iowa) the Internal Revenue Service did not have to first proceed against the trust or jointly held property.

Joint Tenancy as a Taxable Gift

When a person purchases property in joint tenancy or holds property as a sole owner and creates a joint tenancy in the property, there probably will be a taxable gift unless each of the joint tenants makes the same amount of contribution. This impact is nothing more than the general rule that, where property is transferred for less than full and adequate consideration in money or money's worth, the amount by which the property exceeds the value of the consideration is a gift.

If the value of that gift exceeds $11,000, the donor must file a gift tax return and gift taxes are assessed, subject to the availability of the applicable lifetime exemption of the donor ($1,000,000 in 2002).

There are some limited exceptions to the rule that a gift is made whenever a sole owner places property in joint tenancy. If a joint bank account is created, with one person actually contributing all the funds, no taxable gift is created at that time. The same rule applies for buying United States savings bonds in joint tenancy. Only when the person who didn't contribute half the original deposit or cost takes possession of more than his original contribution (by withdrawing money from the bank account, or selling an interest in the bond) will there be a taxable gift.

No gift taxes are assessed against any gift made between husband and wife. Either spouse may transfer any separately owned property into joint tenancy with the other spouse without concern over gift taxes.

Taxation of Community Property

The creation of joint ownership can permit the splitting of income, with each joint owner paid up to his or her respective share. This may generate some savings. These benefits are not available with savings bonds and most bank savings accounts where one depositor creates the account. In addition, creation of an account with a child under fourteen years of age will not afford any savings since a child under fourteen is taxed at his or her parent's tax rate on unearned income in excess of $1,000.

For community property held in joint tenancy the tax basis rules are different for married couples. Both shares of community property held in joint tenancy are entitled to a stepped-up basis upon the death of a spouse, no matter what contributions were made to the initial purchase. Thus, if a husband and wife own community property real estate in joint tenancy worth $500,000 at the husband's death, the basis of both the husband's and wife's share of that real estate is stepped up to $500,000 (no matter who paid for what, originally).

To get the full stepped-up basis, however, you must prove that the joint tenancy property is community property. Otherwise, only the half belonging to the deceased spouse gets the stepped-up basis. Under the tax law there is a presumption that joint tenancy property is not community property. In certain situations, a couple may hold title to community property solely as a probate avoidance device. Records should be kept to properly identify the property and its origin. One way to do this is to place a notation on the property ownership document itself.

The use of the living trust as a probate avoidance device, rather than joint tenancy, permits a married couple to avoid probate and qualify both halves of the property for the beneficial increase in the value of the entire property to its date-of-death value. No matter what the form of ownership, if the property is community property, it will be entitled to a stepped-up basis.

Termination

In most states, as long as joint tenants are alive, any of them can terminate the joint tenancy, without consent of the other.

Creditors

Creditors of a joint tenant can legally pursue that joint tenant's interest, but not the other joint tenants' interests. If there is an attachment, a court may order the whole property sold to reach the debtor's share.

As a general rule, upon the death of a joint owner, the survivor will take the property outside of the deceased tenant's obligations.

Deathbed Creations

If an owner of property is terminal, creating a joint tenancy of his or her property is a last minute probate avoidance device, if no previous estate planning has been done. Since the surviving joint tenant did not contribute towards the property, he or she (other than a spouse) will get a full stepped-up basis to market value on the death of the individual creating the joint tenancy.

Personal Property

Joint tenancies for personal property can be created without documents of title for all tangible personal property. To create a joint tenancy for personal property that doesn't have a formal document of title, all you have to do is declare in an acknowledged written document that you and the co-owners own the property "in joint tenancy" or "as joint tenants."

In spite of the pitfalls and disadvantages of spouses owning property jointly, there may be limited situations where it may be desirable. In addition to avoidance of probate, a bank account jointly owned will provide easy access for both spouses during their lifetimes and after the death of one, for his or her survivor.

If a person owns a closely held business, placing other property in joint ownership with a spouse could qualify the business for certain estate tax benefits. If property other than the business property (which could be fully included in the person's gross estate) was placed in joint ownership, half of the value would be removed from the person's estate, which could aid in achieving the percentage. Because of the unlimited marital deduction, this type of transfer can be accomplished without any gift tax imposition. See chapter 26 for a detailed explanation of these benefits.

Lastly, in many jurisdictions, a spouse who may be vulnerable to claims of third-parties could protect a home or other real estate from such claims by owning such property with a spouse as tenants by the entirety.

❖

CHAPTER 6

Trusts

*T*his chapter discusses trusts, including their particular characteristics and components, such as the grantor, the beneficiary, the
trustee, the written provisions, and property. Each one has a significant
importance in the operation and workings of the device. Trusts are
either irrevocable or revocable. They are either inter vivos (created during lifetime) or testamentary (created upon death). Since trusts are
income-producing entities, they must respond to the Tax Code.

An important reason for creating a trust is to avoid putting substantial amounts of income-producing property in the hands of a child or an
adult who is not financially mature.

By having a basic understanding of a trust and what it can be used
for, you will have a better understanding of other chapters in this book,
including the living trust and the various roles that a trust plays in the
estate planning process.

The trust is an extremely flexible device that is free from the downsides of other estate planning devices.

What Is It?

A trust is a legal device that can satisfy a multitude of needs in personal
financial planning. The written trust permits you to transfer the enjoyment of property to others, while leaving legal ownership out of their
hands. Certain property interests created by trusts may be considered
gifts and may be subject to gift tax.

Trusts may be created to avoid, defer, or decrease federal income and
estate taxes; or to provide steady and controlled support for minors,
incompetents, and other dependents. Trusts may be used in the business

place. Employee benefit trusts and voting trusts are examples of this kind of use. To understand how a trust works you must first become familiar with the basic terms and the necessary requirements for establishing a trust.

The Grantor

The individual who creates the trust is known as the "grantor." The grantor decides what property will be transferred into the trust; the purpose of the trust; who the trustee will be; whom the beneficiaries will be; the terms of the trust; and how the trust funds may be utilized.

The Trustee

The "trustee" is the owner of legal title to the property in the trust. The trust exists exclusively for the benefit of the beneficiary, with the trustee being responsible for the management of the trust assets, keeping them separate and accounted for. The trustee is entitled to a fee or commission for these services but receives no benefit from the trust, unless he or she is also a beneficiary. A trust may have more than one trustee. The trustee is designated by the grantor. However, if the grantor fails to designate a successor trustee, the court will name a successor.

The selection of the trustee can be in many instances the most difficult part of creating a trust. The trustee is responsible for carrying out the intentions of the grantor as expressed in the trust instrument. Therefore, the trustee must not only be willing and able, but must be familiar with the beneficiary and his or her needs. The trustee must also be qualified to handle all management, financial, and accounting duties necessary to properly administer the property of the trust.

The Beneficiary

The "beneficiary" is the individual or group of individuals who receive(s) the primary benefits from the trust property. The primary beneficiary is usually entitled to any income the trust may earn. The "remainder beneficiaries" are those individuals or organizations who are entitled to the trust property (principal) after the entitlement of the primary beneficiary terminates in accordance with the terms of the trust agreement. If trust assets are mismanaged, the remainder beneficiary, can, in addition to the primary beneficiary, assert claims against the trustee.

Primary and remainder beneficiaries may have conflicting investment interests with regard to the use of the trust property. The primary beneficiary will normally seek to receive as high a return as possible in order to maximize the trust's current income. In order to gain these higher rates of return, the trust property will be subject to a greater risk of being lost. Primary beneficiaries will be more than willing to take such risks if they do not have an interest in the principal itself. The main goal of the remainder beneficiaries, on the other hand, will be to preserve and protect the principal for their eventual inheritance. Therefore, the remainder beneficiaries would want the trust property to be invested in lower-yielding, lower-risk investments. Trustees must balance the interests of both classes of beneficiaries in order to fulfill their fiduciary obligations. Trustees, therefore, have a high degree of legal responsibility to the beneficiaries of a trust. They have, in most instances, the obligations of obtaining a reasonable income for the primary beneficiaries and a reasonable appreciation of the value of the trust's assets for those who will eventually receive those benefits.

The most common standard by which the investment decisions made by a trustee are evaluated is the "prudent man rule." This rule requires that a trustee act in the same manner with trust property as a person of prudence, discretion, and intelligence acts in the management of his or her own assets. The origin of this standard was an 1830 court case, *Harvard College* v. *Armory*. A restatement of this rule has been adopted which recognizes investment practices in the modern era. In 1992, a version of the prudent investment rule was adopted by the State of Illinois.

Recently, New York State passed the Prudent Investor Act. The new prudent investor rule represents a substantial shift in the standards of trust administration, investment, and trustee conduct. This is a departure from the long-established prudent man rule.

The underlying concept of the new prudent investor rule is that no type of investment or strategy is imprudent or prudent per se. Therefore, trustees are given wider latitude in analyzing their choices. Their prudence (or imprudence) will be assessed based on a broader range of factors, such as the terms of the trust, the risk tolerance of the trust, the beneficiaries' needs, and the amount of property in the trust. Another fundamental change is that the determination of a trustee's prudence is made on the entire portfolio of the trust and the strategy and investment techniques employed, rather than on isolated individual investments. According to the prior New York rule, a trustee's decision regarding one poor investment could be deemed imprudent even though the rest of the portfolio was properly allocated and performing well.

The Corpus

The property that the grantor of the trust transfers to the trustee is known as the "corpus" or "principal." It may be transferred in different ways, depending on the nature of the property. If the property is "personal property" such as stock, then either actual delivery or a transfer document is required. If the trust property is "real property," such as land, then a written instrument transferring it to the trust will be needed.

The Beneficiary/Trustee

A beneficiary who is also serving as a trustee may be prohibited from engaging in certain actions. Under New York law, for example, if a beneficiary is serving as trustee of a discretionary trust, the beneficiary, as trustee, cannot participate in a decision to distribute income or principal to himself or herself.

Consequently, if a grantor wishes to appoint a beneficiary as trustee and the beneficiary as trustee is unable under applicable state law to exercise certain powers, the grantor should also appoint an independent cotrustee who can exercise those powers.

The value of all property over which a person possessed a general power of appointment is includable, at death, in the decedent's gross estate. The term "power of appointment" is applicable to a power given to the possessor by another (rather than to a power that has been created and retained by the same person).

In order to prevent the assets of a trust from being included in the gross taxable estate of a person who is both a beneficiary and trustee, or having the exercise or failure to exercise a power by such a person treated as a gift, none of the powers granted to the beneficiary as trustee may fall within the purview of a "general power of appointment" as defined under the Internal Revenue Code.

In other words, if a beneficiary is serving as trustee, and as trustee the beneficiary has the power to participate in decisions concerning the exercise of unrestricted discretion to distribute income or principal to himself or herself, the beneficiary will have a taxable general power of appointment and the assets of the trust will be included in his or her estate, even if such power is never exercised. Similarly, if the beneficiary/trustee has the unlimited discretion to permit the use of the trust assets by the beneficiary, the beneficiary would also have a general power of appointment.

However, if under the trust instrument the beneficiary /trustee has a fixed right to income from the trust or an interest in income or principal of the trust, limited by an ascertainable standard, the beneficiary/trustee will have the power to participate in decisions with respect to the distribution of income or principal to himself or herself without adverse tax effects.

A power is considered limited by an ascertainable standard to the extent that the holder's ability to exercise or not exercise the power is reasonably measurable in terms of the possessor's needs for health, education, or support. Examples of powers limited by an ascertainable standard are powers exercisable by the beneficiary/trustee for his or her "support," "support and reasonable comfort," "support in his or her custom manner of living," "education, including college and professional education," "health," and "medical, dental, hospital and nursing expenses, and expenses of invalidism." However, a power to use property for the comfort, welfare, or happiness of the powerholder is not limited by the requisite standard.

Common Trust Provisions

Typically, a trust provides standard provisions setting forth the following:
- A description of the property transferred to the trust
- The name of the trustee and the powers of the trustee
- The names of the primary and contingent (remainder) beneficiaries and the conditions under which they are to receive the income and principal (discretionary, accumulated, or distributed)
- The powers of the trustee to distribute a portion of the principal of the trust for the support and maintenance of a beneficiary
- A provision that prevents the beneficiary from transferring his or her interest in the trust and states that the interest of the beneficiary is not subject to claims of creditors of the beneficiary (spendthrift)
- A provision setting forth the state rule concerning when the trust must terminate
- A provision stating that the named trustee/successor trustee is not required to post a bond
- A provision providing for the naming of a successor trustee or the method for the successor to be designated and the payment of compensation to the trustee
- The term or duration of the trust

The spendthrift provision imposes a restraint upon the equitable interest of the beneficiary. A spendthrift is a person who is incapable of managing assets prudently; so essentially, this type of trust provision prevents a beneficiary from selling or losing his or her interest in the trust to others. It imposes a disabling restraint on the beneficiary and creditors: the beneficiary cannot voluntarily transfer his or her interest, and his or her creditors cannot reach his or her interest. In New York State, all trusts are considered spendthrift unless the grantor expressly makes the beneficiary's interest transferable. There are, however, certain statutory exceptions to this presumption. For example, the Uniform Probate Code works the opposite way: A trust is not considered spendthrift unless the creator expressly makes the beneficiaries' rights in the trust property nontransferable.

Special Trust Provisions

Because a trust is usually set up for an extensive period of time, flexibility must be incorporated into its provisions. The trustee has to have the ability to respond to changing times and circumstances. Typical provisions providing for this flexibility are the following:

- A provision permitting the trustee the right to distribute or apply the income and even the principal of the trust to other persons. These are usually persons on the same level (siblings) but may also be descendants of the beneficiary.
- The discretion of the trustee to use the principal of the trust for the beneficiary and the standards under which such permission is given.
- The power of the beneficiary to withdraw or invade the principal of the trust. Giving the beneficiary a limited power, such as the right to withdraw in any one year the greater of $5,000 or 5 percent of the value of the trust assets, will not leave the beneficiary completely at the mercy of a trustee's discretion when a need arises. Such a limited power will not place the beneficiary in a prejudicial estate tax position either.
- If a beneficiary is disabled and could qualify for government assistance, special provisions must be incorporated.
- A clause permitting a change of "situs" of the trust for administrative convenience or favorable tax laws. Normally, the location or situs of the trust is where the trustee is located. The trust is usually therefore subject to the rules and regulations of the situs jurisdiction.
- A clause permitting the primary trust beneficiary to designate who will enjoy the remainder rights to the trust property. This is known as a power of appointment and can be general, specific, or limited.
- A clause permitting limited amendments of the trust to protect it against adverse tax consequences if subsequent changes in the law render certain provisions of an irrevocable trust undesirable or not within the original intention of the grantor.
- A power reserved by the grantor in an irrevocable trust to replace a trustee with another trustee (who normally cannot be the grantor).

Irrevocable Trusts

One of the main purposes of creating an irrevocable trust is the reduction of estate taxes by removing the trust property from the owner's estate. Under a trust of this type, the grantor is not supposed to retain any right to amend, revoke, or alter the trust in any way. Additionally, the grantor cannot retain, directly or indirectly, any right to control the ownership or enjoyment of the property placed in the trust or the income generated by such property. As a result of these rules, the grantor in most instances should not act as a trustee.

Forms of Trusts

There are only two principal forms of trusts: the "inter vivos trust," which is created during lifetime; and the "testamentary trust," which is created under a will. An inter vivos trust may be revocable or irrevocable.

Inter Vivos Trust

An inter vivos trust is a trust agreement made while the grantor is still alive. A trust of this kind may be created in one of two ways. As grantor, you simply declare the holding of personal property for the benefit of another. This is known as a "declaration of trust" and the grantor becomes the trustee. Alternatively, as the grantor, you may transfer title in property to a trustee for the benefit of yourself or another person or group of persons.

The inter vivos trust may be revocable or irrevocable, depending upon state laws and the language of the trust instrument. Some states require that if a trust is to be revocable there must be specific language in the instrument stating so. It is extremely important to consult the applicable state laws before setting up any type of trust.

The inter vivos trust has tax advantages, as it can permit a shifting of income from one person to another. The amount of control the grantor retains over the trust can raise questions regarding intent, and thus the validity of the trust. The validity of a trust where the grantor maintains the right to revoke the trust during his or her lifetime is usually accepted. However, where the grantor is the trustee and the sole beneficiary of the trust and no valid trust intent can be found, some courts have invalidated the arrangement. Generally, as long as an interest is created for a beneficiary other than the grantor, the trust will be valid even if the grantor retains extensive powers.

Amendment of a Trust

Can you amend a trust? Most revocable trusts, if properly prepared, provide the authorization for the trust to be altered or amended, in whole or in part, during the grantor's lifetime. In most states, if the grantor is alive and competent and all of the interested parties to the trust are adults and consent to such a procedure, an irrevocable trust can be amended or revoked. If the grantor is not alive or his or her consent cannot be obtained, or if the consents of the other intended parties cannot be obtained, it would be practicably impossible to amend a trust. A testamentary trust is not amendable or revocable except by the courts under certain circumstances (i.e., tax reformation, mistakes in the drafting of the document, or under certain circumstances covering charitable gifts).

Recently, the state of New York enacted a section of the law enabling a trustee who has discretion to invade the principal of a trust to appoint that principal to the trustee of a different trust so long as the following conditions exist:

- There is no reduction in the income interest of the primary beneficiary
- There is no change in the beneficiaries of the trust
- The compensation of the trustee does not increase

If the trustee wishes to proceed without prior Court approval, the consent of all persons interested in the trust must be obtained, or the Court provides notice to such persons. As such, by utilizing this procedure, an indirect amendment may be attained even though the rest of the provisions of the different trust are not the same.

Income Taxation of Trusts

Trusts and estates are income-producing entities recognized by the Internal Revenue Code. At one time, trusts were used as splitting devices by those in higher tax brackets to shift income to a lower tax bracket. The typical plan was to distribute income-producing assets to a spouse or child in trust, and the spouse or child in a lower tax bracket would pay less in taxes. The savings could be quite significant if one spouse was in the 50 percent tax bracket and the other was in the 20 to 30 percent tax bracket. Much of the tax advantage of this type of planning was removed by the tax revisions enacted in 1986.

The new tax law (Revenue Reconciliation Act of 1993) sharply increases income taxes on trust funds commonly used by families to set aside money for minors and young adults. This change raises questions as to how existing trusts should be managed. Many people find that the

46

income retained by a trust will now be taxed at a higher rate than if held by the grantor or beneficiary. It simply won't be worthwhile to accumulate much income in a trust. The tax rate has nearly doubled for some trust income. Previously, the first $3,750 was taxed at 15 percent and the maximum tax rate was approximately 28 percent. Under the new law, which is retroactive to January 1, 1993, the tax rate jumps to 29 percent on trust income of more than $1,500 with brackets up to 39.6 percent.

Parents who put money in a trust fund when a child is born and who make regular contributions over the years in anticipation of college and graduate school costs might easily find their funds in the highest tax brackets.

As a result of revision of the tax laws, a trustee must now consider shifting trust capital to investments that are expected to grow in value rather than to produce current income, such as stocks instead of bonds. Capital gains on stocks currently is taxed at 28 percent, while trust income, like dividends/interest, can be taxed at rates as high as 39.6 percent. This approach can be tricky, because investing for growth may mean taking on greater risk—something a cautious trustee does not like to do.

A trustee can distribute a portion of the income of the trust to the beneficiary, instead of retaining it in the trust. Investment income for a child under the age of fourteen is taxed at the parents' rate after the first few hundred dollars. But when they turn fourteen, children are taxed at their own individual rate, which is likely to be much lower than the trust's rate or their parents' rate.

Because trusts are the most flexible devices available in estate planning, they have to be considered in every person's plan. A trust not only can shield a beneficiary from third parties, but can provide characteristics that may not exist in the beneficiary, i.e., secure a beneficiary against his or her improvidence.

❖

CHAPTER 7

The Role of Trusts in Estate Planning

*M*ore than 125 years ago, Oliver Wendell Holmes was aware of the value of trusts when he said, "Put not your trust in money, but put your money in trust."

Trusts are the most useful and unique devices that are available in the field of estate planning. They can be used not only to span the gap between life and death, but to avoid and defer estate taxes.

There are a multitude of reasons why we create a trust. This chapter explains the different kinds of trusts and when they should be used. For example, in order to defer estate taxes when a noncitizen spouse is a surviving beneficiary, a trust must be used. Later on, I will focus on the creation of a trust for particular purposes, such as for asset protection purposes or for children with special needs.

Today, trusts have become the superstars of estate planning. They are usually created either for the benefit of the grantor or for the benefit of another person. They can be used to fund a child's education, provide for a spendthrift beneficiary, provide for a spouse that cannot manage or assume responsibility of property, provide for continuity in the event of incapacity, provide unusual tax benefits, provide for disabled persons in order to protect their entitlements, avoid probate, and hold property for elderly persons who cannot manage their own affairs. An important feature of a trust is the ability of its grantor to maintain postmortem financial control (ruling from the grave). The ability of a trust to span the void between life and death is probably its most extraordinary characteristic. Most states have laws placing limitations on the duration of such control. As a general rule, a trust may only last as long as any beneficiary named in it remains alive and for a certain period of time thereafter (twenty-one years after the last beneficiary dies).

A trust affords unique tax and management benefits to both its creators and its beneficiaries. The property of an elder person's estate and his or her spouse's assets have to be integrated in the planning strategy for both lifetime management and transfer at death. In addition, consideration of potential needs like nursing home care and the support of children must be factored into the process. In the field of elder law, trusts are probably the most important devices employed.

Estate Taxes

The critical issue regarding trusts and estate taxes is whether the trust property will be includable in the gross estate and therefore subject to being taxed. It will be included in your estate for estate tax purposes in the following cases:

- If any power of revocation is retained
- If you hold a reversionary interest beyond a permissible amount (where the initial market value of the reversionary interest exceeds 5 percent of the value of the trust's assets, the trust would be considered a "grantor trust" for federal tax purposes)
- If you retain a power to direct the distribution of the assets of the trust or retain any enjoyment over the benefits of the trust

If, as the grantor, you retain simply administrative powers, the assets of the trust will normally not be included in your gross taxable estate. In a 1993 case, the United States Tax Court ruled that a grantor could replace a corporate trustee with another independent successor corporate trustee (even though the trustee's power to distribute income and principal was generally discretionary), and by doing so, the grantor did not retain any right of the enjoyment of the property. The Tax Court indicated that under the law of trusts, a trustee's primary obligation is to the interests of the beneficiary of a trust.

Particular Kinds of Trusts

There are various kinds of irrevocable trusts that may be employed in your estate plan. Each serves varied functions and has special income, gift, and estate tax impacts. One of the main purposes of these trusts is the saving of taxes. However, for many people, avoiding probate is a desired goal as well.

The Irrevocable Inter Vivos Trust

The main estate planning device to save estate taxes is the irrevocable inter vivos trust. In order to be able to benefit from this device, you must irrevocably transfer your property to the trust and must not retain any rights over it. Such a transfer could be subject to gift taxes and can be made available for the annual gift tax exclusion. If the grantor's spouse has a qualifying income interest in the trust, the marital deduction will be available.

The Pour-Over Trust

The pour-over trust is a trust into which assets are poured or added from another source. The addition could come from the estate owner's will or from a source completely outside the estate. It is useful as a receptacle for benefits from a qualified employee benefit plan or life insurance proceeds. Also, it may receive assets from other trusts or estates, such as from relatives.

The pour-over trust may be either revocable or irrevocable, having all the advantages and disadvantages of either type of trust. If the trust is revocable, as grantor, after watching it operate and seeing changes in circumstances, you may make whatever modifications are necessary. If it is irrevocable, later changes may be barred and as grantor you should initially provide provisions that are flexible enough to permit the trustee to deal with changed situations. However, in irrevocable form, the trust enables you to avoid probate of the trust property.

When benefits are payable to several beneficiaries, the trust form is usually the most effective way of making distributions in accordance with the wishes of the grantor and the needs of the beneficiaries.

The pour-over trust is helpful not only where there are multiple beneficiaries, but also where there are multiple assets. It permits the bringing together of these assets in one place and the development of a plan that coordinates and makes use of them in a way that will further the objectives of the grantor and the interests of his or her family.

When used with a will, the pour-over trust may be viewed as involving a testamentary disposition of property. It has long been recognized that a will may incorporate another document by reference. The courts have been able to sustain pour-overs on the basis of incorporation by reference, but implicit in the incorporation-by-reference theory is a requirement that the trust be in existence when the will is executed.

Since pour-overs may not have been fully tested in a particular jurisdiction, it may be advisable to include a fail-safe provision in a will to provide for an alternate disposition of the estate if the pour-over trust is invalidated. If such a provision mirrors the distribution provisions of the trust, one benefit of the pour-over will—avoidance of disclosure of the dispositions to be made—will be lost.

Coordination of revocable pour-over trusts and wills can be risky. There is the danger that the trust may not be in existence at the testator's death, having been revoked without any subsequent change to the estate owner's will. An intestacy problem may arise, perhaps with respect to the taxpayer's entire residuary estate. To avoid such a potentially disastrous result, the will might contain either: (a) an express incorporation by reference of the provisions of the revocable trust, which would keep the trust "alive" (at least as part of the will) even after its revocation, or (b) some form of contingent testamentary bequest that will ensure that a will disposition preferable to intestacy can be made if the pour-over trust is revoked. These fail-safe provisions provide a degree of insurance in the event of lapse of omission in an estate plan.

The Pour-Up Trust

In a pour-over trust, assets are usually poured into a living trust. In another alternative, the assets of a living trust are poured into a testamentary trust or an estate, reversing the flow found in a pour-over trust. This form of trust is sometimes referred to as a "pour-up trust." A pour-up trust might be useful in the following situations:

- An elder family member has created a living trust with the prime purpose of achieving family income tax savings by removing income-producing property from his or her high tax bracket to the lower tax bracket of the trust or beneficiaries. On his or her death, the income-splitting advantage is lost.
- An individual has created a trust for the support of his or her parents (or other aged relatives). On the death of the beneficiaries, the trust will have served its purpose, whether these deaths occur before or after the death of the grantor.
- An individual has created a "standby trust" to manage his or her assets while he or she is traveling or disabled. On his or her death, such trust will have served its purpose.
- An individual has created a living trust to manage a portion of his or her estate with a view to observing how the trustee manages it before the individual dies and the trust becomes irrevocable.

In these and possibly other situations, a pour-up trust may prove appropriate. At the time of setting up a trust, you may not be in a position to determine the precise disposition of the trust assets. You may prefer to leave that determination to your living trust or will.

Providing for the Elderly

A trust may prove useful if you contribute substantial amounts to the living expenses of an elderly parent. Aside from whatever income tax benefit is available for claiming one's parent as a dependent, these contributions are expensive because they are made on an after-tax basis. An irrevocable trust with income payable to an elderly parent for life with remainder to your children can be used to save estate taxes and support a parent.

The use of a trust of this kind will succeed in shifting income, but it has disadvantages, the main one being that the trust property may not return to you. If you, as grantor, retain a reversionary interest in the trust, all of the trust income will be taxed to you unless, at the time of creation, your interest in the trust is worth less than 5 percent of the total initial value of the trust property. There are other powers you cannot retain if you want to avoid tax on the trust's income. You may not control the beneficial enjoyment of principal or income, such as by adding beneficiaries or varying the distribution of income. A third-party trustee, however, is permitted to exercise certain powers without tax jeopardy to the grantor. As grantor, you also may not retain any administrative powers exercisable primarily for your own benefit, such as the power to deal with the trust for less than adequate and full consideration or the power to borrow trust funds without proper interest or security.

A trust of this type may have other disadvantages as well: (1) potential gift tax liability may reduce the total tax benefits and may impact on the unified credit; and (2) start-up and administration costs of the trust may also reduce any potential tax savings.

It is possible for you to retain a testamentary power of appointment over the trust principal without having the income of the trust taxed to you. However, retention of this power will cause the trust to be included in your gross estate and may eliminate one of the advantages of creating this type of irrevocable trust. As long as the trust is not subject to inclusion in your gross estate, all future appreciation in value of the trust property will pass to the remainder beneficiaries free of estate tax.

The Revocable Living Trust

The use of the living trust for estate planning purposes is discussed in detail in chapter 8.

Testamentary Trusts

A trust may be created in accordance with instructions contained in your will. Such trusts are known as testamentary trusts. They are used when you are unwilling to part with certain property during your lifetime, not even in a living trust, but want the control that a trust can provide, which you perceive as being in the best interests of your beneficiaries.

While the testamentary trust does not result in any immediate estate or income tax savings, when the will is executed or takes effect, it may. The trust can protect the trust property from successive estate tax levies as it passes from one beneficiary to another. It may be characterized as a case of "pay now, save later." It may not always work out as planned, but if the trust can initially be funded with property of relatively low value but with strong appreciation potential, the savings for the family can be enormous.

The most common example of an estate tax–skipping trust that can be created in a living trust or will is a "credit shelter" or "by-pass trust," which is used in conjunction with the unlimited marital deduction. The credit shelter trust may pay your surviving spouse income for life and possibly permit use of the principal for his or her defined and ascertainable needs. But it carefully avoids giving the survivor too much control over or rights in the trust property. In this way, the property will not be includable in the survivor's gross estate and can pass estate tax–free to the remainder beneficiaries.

The trustee may be authorized to accumulate income for specific purposes spelled out in the trust. Flexibility can be most important in a testamentary trust, and consideration should be given to the use of a number of special provisions designed to meet changes in the circumstances of the beneficiaries.

One of the most important things to consider in connection with testamentary trusts is that provisions can be made for a beneficiary that could not be made, if you were to set up a trust for yourself, without encountering income and estate tax complications. For example, if you created a trust and retained the income rights for yourself, the trust property would be includable in your gross estate under the Internal Revenue Code. If, under the terms of the trust, income could be used to pay insurance premiums on your life or that of your spouse, the income would be taxable to you under the Internal Revenue Code and you would be treated as the owner of the policy and the proceeds would be includable in your gross estate. However, neither of these results would occur if you were the beneficiary of a testamentary trust.

The Support Trust

In a support trust, the trust provides that the beneficiary is only to receive as much of the income or principal as is necessary for support and education. This will ensure that the funds will be used to provide for the beneficiary in a sensible manner. Although the corpus of the trust may be invaded as necessary if the trust instrument contains such provision, it will also be controlled by necessity, not by the whim or desire of the beneficiary.

The Discretionary Trust

The discretionary trust places more responsibility upon the trustee in connection with the distribution of the income and principal of the trust. Under this type of trust, the trustee distributes to the beneficiary as much of the income or principal as he or she deems proper. However, in this type of trust, the trustee can be given the discretionary right to distribute the benefits of the trust to a number of beneficiaries, not just the primary beneficiary. This is the "sprinkling" or "spray" provision under which the trustee can make distributions to a number of beneficiaries without regard to equality as to amounts or as to times. However, the trustee may not avoid the fiduciary obligations imposed on trustees by distributing the funds improperly. In some instances, a court may step in to control a trustee if there has been a failure to observe the intent of the grantor. Improper distributions might be those favoring one beneficiary over another, unreasonably refusing to distribute assets, or failing to adequately provide for the beneficiary according to the wishes of the grantor.

The Grantor Trust

A grantor trust is one in which the income is taxable to the grantor because the grantor retains substantial control over the trust assets or retains certain prohibited administrative powers. An example of this would be a revocable inter vivos trust. By retaining the power of revocation, the grantor can terminate the trust at any time and reclaim the trust assets. When the purpose of setting up the trust is to benefit the grantor, directly or indirectly, and the grantor has control or advantage with regard to the trust assets, the grantor is taxed on the trust income.

Retirement Benefits

A trust can be designated as a beneficiary of a retirement benefit. This can be an important tool in estate planning in the case of a subsequent marriage. For a detailed explanation of this subject see chapter 22.

Qualified Domestic Trust

The tax law that created the unlimited marital deduction for United States citizens created the qualified domestic trust (QDOT) for a noncitizen spouse. This type of trust defers estate taxes in the estate of a citizen until the death of the noncitizen surviving spouse. However, the terms of a trust of this kind is not as advantageous as a QTIP trust available for citizens. Under a QTIP trust, when the second spouse dies, the remainder in the trust is taxed in the second spouse's estate. Under a QDOT trust, the first estate is left open and when the second spouse dies, the assets in the QDOT trust are taxed in the estate of the first spouse to die.

In order to qualify as a QDOT, the trust must meet certain requirements of the Code:

- At least one trustee must be a U.S. citizen or a domestic corporation.
- A principal distribution cannot be made without being subject to the right of the U.S. trustee to withhold the amount of the tax due on the distribution. However, distributions to a surviving spouse of principal on account of hardship are exempted from tax. Hardship is considered a need of immediate and substantial financial assistance relating to the noncitizen spouse's health, maintenance or support, or that of any person the spouse is legally obligated to support.
- The executor of the estate has to make an election to have the trust treated as a QDOT.

The trust must also satisfy the same conditions as a trust for a U.S. citizen spouse to qualify for the marital deduction.

Federal Legislation Update

On November 27, 1996, final regulations on a qualified domestic trust (QDOT) were issued by the Internal Revenue Service that (among other things) provide:

If the fair market value of the assets of the QDOT at the death of the first decedent exceeds $2 million, the trust instrument must require that: (1) at least one U.S. trustee be a bank or (2) the U.S. trustee furnish a bond or security to the IRS in an amount equal to 65 percent of the fair market value of the trust corpus, determined as of the decedent's date of death. The regulations further provide that if the fair market value of the QDOT assets is $2 million or less, the QDOT need not meet the bank or bond requirements if, as an alternative, the trust instrument expressly provides that no more than 35 percent of the fair market value of the trust assets, determined annually, may be invested in real property that is not located in the United States.

If a QDOT has assets with a value in excess of $2 million in trust, you may use any one of the following of three security arrangements (alternating between them as long as one is in place at all times):

1. At least one trustee is a U.S. bank
2. The U.S. trustee furnishes a bond to the Internal Revenue Service in an amount equal to 65 percent of the value of the trust corpus (as of the date of the decedent's death)
3. The U.S. trustee furnishes a letter of credit to the Internal Revenue Service under the same terms as the bond

For the purpose of the security arrangement, the value of a personal residence is excluded if its value is less than the exemption amount.

Estate tax is not imposed on distributions to the surviving spouse for "hardship" reasons. Hardship includes distributions in response to an immediate and substantial financial need regarding the spouse's health, maintenance, education, or support, or that of any person the spouse is legally obligated to support.

The Taxpayer Relief Act of 1997 provides that in countries that do not permit a trust from having a U.S. trustee, the Treasury Department has the authority to waive the "U.S. trustee" requirement, if certain conditions are met.

The Dynasty Trust

A dynasty trust can be a unique device in estate planning. By transferring property to a trust and taking advantage of the unified credit and generation-skipping tax exemption (GST), you and your descendants could defer payment of any transfer tax (gift/estate) on the property in the trust for at least 90 years and possibly more.

A dynasty trust creates life income interests in successive generations of your family. Although the initial creation of the trust could be taxable (if the value of the property exceeds the exemptions), no estate or GST will be payable at the death of any of the succeeding beneficiaries during the term of the trust. Assuming no distributions of trust principal are made during the term of the trust, no transfer tax will be payable until the beneficiaries who receive the assets upon the trust's termination transfer those assets by gift or death.

To provide flexibility during the term of the trust, the beneficiaries can be given special powers to permit them to appoint trust principal to family members either during their lives or upon their deaths. The trustee can be given the right to distribute or apply the principal in order for the beneficiaries to accomplish lifetime goals and for their support, maintenance, and care.

CHAPTER 8

The Living Trust

*T*here is no better method for you to hold assets than in a living trust. After reading this chapter, it will be clear to you that the living trust is the answer to just about every estate planning program. This chapter tells how it works and all of the advantages. The first living trust was written in this country approximately 230 years ago, and this chapter tells you its origin and how it arrived on our shores. Proper estate planning requires you to include other documents in your plan besides a living trust, which are the pour-over will and the power of attorney.

Where Did It Come From?

The origin of the living trust is rooted in English Common Law. In England, people used it to protect their assets from the Crown. By placing their assets in a trust, the general population prevented the English king and the lords from unjustly taking property away. The trust held title to land and thereby permitted land to pass from one generation to the next. The English courts upheld the validity of the trust, which thereafter became a part of English Common Law. The trust was then brought to this country by colonists. Today, the living trust is recognized in all fifty states as well as throughout the world.

Downsides to a Living Trust

There are no disadvantages to creating and using a properly prepared living trust. The incorrect perception that there is a downside to a living trust can result from preparing the living trust improperly or failing to properly fund it. A living trust that fails to consider all of the life situations of the grantor and the required tax concerns could be disastrous to a family. Furthermore, if you fail to fund your living trust, you have created an incomplete transaction and you leave your estate vulnerable to the probate process.

What is a Living Trust?

The living trust is probably the most important legal device used in estate plans that are administered by banking institutions and trust administrations. The cost of creating a living trust may exceed that of creating a will but should be substantially less than that arising from a probate proceeding.

The living trust not only allows you continued total control over your affairs during your lifetime but also provides continuity in management and supervision in the event of your incapacity. This remarkable and unique device gives you the opportunity of seeing your "will" in operation while you are alive. It offers the avoidance of multiple probate proceedings where property is claimed in more than one state, as well as stronger insulation against attack on the basis of personal or undue influence or lack of capacity. The living trust insures that after your death your survivors will have total control over your property, without depending on the sanction of the courts.

In the vast majority of estate plans, the living trust should be designated as its cornerstone. The lifetime trust, as it sometimes is called, is named as such because it is created during your lifetime. You can amend or revoke the trust at any time. It can be funded by the simple transfer of property or can remain unfunded until a specific event, e.g., your incapacity, at which time an attorney-in-fact, provided with the right, will transfer your assets. Thereafter, the assets will be managed by your trustee for your benefit.

Certain states do not allow the creation of a "springing" power of attorney (one that takes effect only upon the occurrence of a certain event, such as your incapacity). In such states, a living trust could be created with a provision that the successor trustee will act only in the event of your incapacity.

The living trust avoids many of the administrative procedures that are required in a guardianship proceeding, such as accountings, court permission to buy or dispose of the ward's property, and the posting of a bond.

How a Living Trust Works

Most people understand the significance of a will, but very few have any knowledge about trusts. A will is a legal document that transfers assets to heirs at death. A trust does the same thing. A will names an executor or personal representative to do this. A trust names a trustee to do the exact same thing—and that's where the similarity ends.

The living trust works as follows: You (the grantor/settlor) establish a written revocable trust agreement, naming yourself as the beneficiary (or one of the beneficiaries) while you are alive and family members or others as beneficiaries after your death. As such, you maintain full and absolute control over your assets and can revoke or change the trust at any time. The trust is funded during your lifetime by the transfer to it of your assets. Almost any kind of property you own can be placed in the trust—bank accounts, stocks, bonds, and real estate. You simply place the property in the trust by changing the name or title of the asset to the name of the trust. As such, no control is lost since you designate yourself as the trustee and therefore continue to manage and handle your property as before. Assets that have their own beneficiary designations, such as employee benefits, life insurance, IRAs, and the like are not transferred to the trust, but the trust can be named as the beneficiary of such items. However, before making any designations of such benefits, you should ascertain both income and estate tax impacts on each.

As a general rule, you name yourself as the trustee or co-trustee of your living trust and you designate a successor trustee to take over upon your incapacity or death, at which time the trust becomes irrevocable. After your death, the trust makes provisions for the distribution of its assets to the beneficiaries you have designated, either outright or through the creation of further trusts that can qualify for the maximum estate tax benefits.

The living trust, therefore, is in effect a contract that is self-efficient and requires no approval by any third party to carry out its provisions after your death.

Formats

A living trust can take various forms, such as the following:

- A trust that is fully funded with assets, wherein you retain full authority until your incapacity or death, at which time its management is taken over by the successor trustees.
- A trust that is fully funded with assets, wherein you designate an additional or cotrustee until your incapacity or death, with full powers vested in the cotrustee.
- A trust that is fully funded with assets, wherein your sole authority is the right to amend or revoke the trust agreement. The trustee

is not you (the trustee is a relative or a bank), and the trustee is given the full discretion to pay or apply the income and principal to or for your benefit.

- A trust that is totally unfunded (has no assets), sometimes called "standby trust," with a durable power of attorney authorizing the agent to transfer property to the trust in the event of incapacity.

Pour-Over

Provisions should always be made for a "pour-over" of your assets at the onset of your disability or death. The ability to transfer upon incapacitation is effectuated by a provision in the durable power of attorney. The power of attorney should be created at the time the living trust is created. Upon death, the transfer is completed with a pour-over will. The estate plan must coordinate both the nonprobate and probate devices to permit an orderly distribution of all of your assets at death. A pour-over will can cover those assets that are not transferred to the living trust during your lifetime and will therefore provide for the orderly administration of all of your affairs. Where there is a combined will and trust in the estate plan, the will normally provides for the probate estate to be poured-over, or added to the living trust when the administration of the estate has been completed. The entire estate is thereafter held and administered in accordance with the provisions of the living trust, allowing all assets to be distributed through the living trust after the death of the estate owner.

Incapacity

Since one of the important purposes of the living trust is to avoid court proceedings in the event of incapacitation, the trust must provide specific guidelines and conditions to determine the incapacity of the grantor. The determination procedure might be on the basis of either of the following methods:

- Certifications by two physicians (who are not on the team of the grantor's treating physicians) who could certify as to the lack of capacity of the grantor
- The existence of a court order certifying the incapacity of the grantor

Advantages of the Living Trust

Following is a list of advantages gained by using a living trust. The extent of all of these advantages will vary from state to state, depending on the laws of the applicable jurisdiction. The living trust will:

- Avoid the publicity, expense, and delay of probate.
- Avoid the interruption of income for family members on the death of the head of the family or on his or her becoming disabled or incompetent.
- Allow the grantor to view the trust in operation and to make changes as experience and circumstances suggest.
- Serve as a receptacle for estate assets and for death benefits from qualified employee benefit plans and insurance on the life of the grantor.
- Bring together assets scattered in two or more states or jurisdictions and place title in the trustee, thereby avoiding additional administrations of the estate owner's estate, particularly real estate, in places where such property is located.
- Make it easier to select the law that is to govern the trust than if this were attempted by will.
- Enable a going business to continue without interruption.
- Facilitate gifts to charities in states where there are restrictions on charitable gifts by will.
- Relieve the grantor of the burdens of investment management.
- Authorize the trustee to advance funds to the grantor's executor for certain purposes or to buy assets from the executor at a fixed price; thereby, it will avoid the forced sale of estate assets at depressed prices.
- Be less vulnerable to attack on the grounds of the grantor's lack of capacity, fraud, or duress than a will or a will-created trust would be.
- Require less accounting, administration, and judicial supervision than a trust created by will.
- Bar a surviving spouse's statutory right in some states to share in the deceased spouse's property.
- Place the property beyond the reach of the grantor's creditors, in some states.
- Assist in the management of assets for a young adult or spend-thrift.
- Assist in the management of assets for an elderly or incapacitated person. Rather than necessitate the appointment of a guardian, a trustee or successor trustee can immediately step in and manage the assets of the trust.
- Permit the purchase of U.S. Treasury bonds (flower bonds) when the grantor has or may become incompetent, provided that the trustee is required to use the bonds in payment of estate tax or that the trust terminates in favor of the grantor's estate.

- Permit trust property to be withdrawn by the grantor during his or her lifetime for the purposes of making gifts without making the gifted property includable in the grantor's estate.

The living trust may be amended at any time during your lifetime and before incapacity. This is usually accomplished by executing a written amendment setting forth the desired changes.

Avoiding Probate and Its Expenses

Assets held in the living trust at the time of your death are not subject to probate because they are not legally owned by you.

As has been discussed, probate is the process whereby a will is validated by a court (admitted to probate) and an executor or personal representative is appointed to conduct the affairs of the estate. The affairs include paying estate bills and collecting estate receivables; filing the income, estate, and other tax returns; paying any taxes due; and finally distributing the remaining estate assets according to the provisions in the will. This process can take years and can be costly. One of the main advantages of the living trust is that it passes assets on to your survivors without the involvement of this procedure. Probate fees can amount to anywhere between 1 and 9 percent of the total assets of the estate, which is substantially more than the cost of establishing a living trust.

The probate process covers only those assets that are solely in your name. It does not cover assets held in joint name, insurance payable to a named beneficiary, pension funds, IRA's, or assets held in trust. Thus, transferring assets into the living trust mainly avoids probate, the expenses of probate, and, in simple situations, the delay between the date of death and the final distribution of assets.

Trust Administration Expenses

By transferring assets into the trust, you will avoid the legal expenses of probate; the administration of a trust, however, involves some legal expenses, which should be minimal in amount. These could include the cost of transferring your property to the living trust. If stocks, bonds, and cash in a bank are involved, these assets can be transferred to the trustee by you without any cost.

Transferring real property requires the preparation and filing of a new deed. If the property is subject to a mortgage, the mortgage instrument must be examined to see if the property can be transferred without adverse consequences, such as the acceleration of the mortgage indebtedness. In some situations, consent of the mortgagee may be required.

Title insurance policies also should be examined to determine if there are any title insurance consequences due to the transfer.

Avoiding probate does not mean that your estate will avoid the administrative process of preparing and filing your final income tax return or filing and paying your estate taxes. In many instances, it does not avoid preparing an inventory and accounting. In addition, someone has to collect any outstanding assets, pay your debts (if any), and finally make distribution to the beneficiaries. But his process is usually preferred by the successor trustees.

Multiple Probate Proceedings

Avoiding probate is particularly important if you live and own real property in more than one state. Each state exercises its own jurisdiction over its real estate. In these situations, each state where you live could claim that you were a domiciliary, or permanent resident, of that state and not only impose estate taxes but also make a claim against your estate for past-due state resident income taxes. If an additional or ancillary administration is required in the state where real property is located, the risk of income tax liability could be increased, since the income tax commission of the state is usually notified of the probate proceeding.

Each state has the power to determine the domicile status of its citizens. The fact that you claimed domicile and lived in another state or that your will is being probated in that other state is not determinative of your final domicile. Even if you acknowledged that you were a domiciliary or resident of a state, in an affidavit of domicile, voting in a particular state and other indications would not be in and of themselves binding in determining your domicile.

Avoidance of Publicity

When a will is admitted to probate, it becomes a public record and your assets become known to the public. In addition, the beneficiaries of your estate are made public as well as is what they have inherited. Trusts generally remain private and their terms secret. However, if in addition to the living trust, there is a will that is being probated and the will provides for a pour-over of assets into the living trust (which is common), the probate court may require that the living trust be filed with the court as part of the probate proceedings. In such an instance the provisions of the trust may not remain secret.

Conversely, there are situations in which the probate court will seal the probate records so that even though there is a probate, publicity is avoided and the estate assets remain secret. Thus, it is possible for a person to establish a living trust for the purpose of secrecy and still have the trust instrument filed as public record, and for a person who has a will and not a trust to have the will terms remain secret.

Under the probate system, anyone can review the records of the probate court (the inventory and the estate tax proceedings), thereby knowing the assets of the estate, the identity of the beneficiaries of the estate, and the dispositions of the assets. No such opportunities are available when a living trust is established.

Protection against Incapacity

The living trust is an excellent method for protecting your assets in the event of incapacity. The trust can make specific provisions for the continuity of your affairs in the event of disability. The living trust can also be a "springing trust." Under such circumstances, the management of the living trust will only shift to the successor trustee when the incapacity occurs, as defined in the trust. Incapacity should only be determined by a certification method of independent individuals or by a court order and left to the judgment of the successor trustee or beneficiaries.

Many senior citizens place their assets into a living trust because they want to avoid court intervention if they become unable to manage their affairs. Court proceedings are both expensive and time consuming.

In the event of incapacity, the choice of the trustee becomes of vital importance. The trustee should not only be able to manage your assets but also have a sincere concern for your personal care.

Trusts that provide for incapacity should be supplemented by a durable power of attorney. That gives the attorney named power over any assets that are not held in trust even if the person granting the power becomes incapacitated. Such powers should provide for the ability of the agent or attorney-in-fact to transfer any of your assets not previously transferred by you to the trust. In many states, the durable power of attorney will become effective only in the event of your incapacity (a springing power of attorney), so that you retain all powers and authority until you become incapacitated.

Avoidance of Family Disputes

The establishment of a living trust should be considered if you believe that there may be a dispute among family members after death. In this instance, the living trust has several advantages over a will. No notice is required to be given to family members upon the death of the grantor, so they may not even be aware of—or ever become aware of—the existence of the trust. Even if they learn of the trust, the assets of the trust may in fact be distributed long before the heirs realize that a trust exists. Such a distribution would make a challenge more difficult.

Where there is a will, and therefore a probate proceeding, notice must be given to the heirs either before the will is admitted to probate or after the appointment of a personal representative, depending upon the laws of the state of domicile. The heirs would then have a chance to challenge the will before any assets were distributed. A challenge would also tie up the assets, with the result that no assets could be distributed until the challenge is resolved. Since there is no statutory method in existence for the challenge of a living trust, it's very difficult to challenge such an instrument.

A trust that operates and exists for some period during your lifetime is more difficult to challenge than a will, which takes effect after death. It is more burdensome to prove incapacity, fraud, or undue influence in the establishment of a trust if the trust was being managed during the lifetime of the grantor, especially where the grantor was a trustee. The courts of this country have fairly consistently protected living trusts from challenges by claimants.

In some states, "in terrorem clauses" (forfeiture in the event of a contest) are voided by statute, so that an individual cannot protect his or her estate plan by providing for forfeiture of a bequest in the event of a challenge by an heir.

Common circumstances in which a will contest is likely are the following:

- Favoring one child. If a will gives one child a significantly larger legacy than other children, a contest may ensue.
- Favoring a second spouse. If a will gives a second spouse a share that seems disproportionate, the children of a prior marriage may be disposed to contest.
- Favoring children of a prior marriage. If a will favors the children of a prior marriage over those from a second marriage, the latter may be inclined to contest.
- Substantial charitable bequests. If there are large charitable bequests, heirs may be disposed to challenge.
- Bequests to a lover. Bequests to a mistress of the testator or to a male companion of the testatrix may evoke challenge.
- Bequests by homosexuals or lesbians. Bequests by homosexuals or lesbians to those with like preferences may be challenged as the product of undue influence.

If a will contest seems likely, consideration must be given to a revocable living trust as an alternative to a will.

Protecting Assets from Creditors

If you do not designate specific trust property in your living trust to pay your debts and taxes when you die, the trustee has the authority to designate which trust property will liquidate those obligations. The question of whether the trust assets are protected from the claims of creditors depends upon local law.

If the living trust is revocable by the grantor, most states will allow the creditors access to the trust assets while the grantor is alive. In addition, if a conveyance is made to a living trust and there are unpaid creditors, the transfer can usually be voided as a fraudulent conveyance, and the creditors can reach the assets.

In some states, the rules are more lenient and the courts look into the financial status of the person at the time the property is put into the living trust. The questions usually posed surround whether there is actual or unintentional fraud. Was the transferor solvent at the time the property was put into trust? Was the transfer made to avoid the payment of debts? If the answers are no, the trust is prepared to protect against the unexpected, and a "spendthrift" provision may in fact provide protection against creditors.

After the grantor dies, the trustee is not liable for distributions made prior to the time that the trustee is notified of the creditors' claims. With respect to federal taxes, however, the trustee would be liable for the taxes due if distributions were made prior to the payment.

Spouses

Most states give a surviving spouse elective rights or "common law dower" or "courtesy" (a right to a life estate), which is a statutory right to inherit a certain portion of the estate of the deceased spouse. For a more detailed discussion of this subject, see chapter 16. The question of whether the elective rights of a surviving spouse can be defeated through the use of a revocable living trust depends upon state law.

The Uniform Probate Code, which is applicable in many states, requires the elective right of a surviving spouse to apply the deceased's "augmented estate," which represents not only the property owned at the time of his or her death but the value of any property transferred during his or her lifetime, without consideration (gifts). For example, the New York rule (adopted in many states), holds that the elective right of the spouse cannot be defeated by a transfer to a revocable living trust or similar transfer over which the grantor retains control.

New York has included revocable lifetime transfers as part of the "net estate," which is counted in calculating a surviving spouse's share of the estate. Subject to certain exceptions, New York also includes as part of the net estate any transfer made without consideration within one year from the date of death and made in contemplation of death.

The Massachusetts rule holds that the elective right of the spouse can be defeated if the transfer to the trust is legally binding, regardless of whether the transfer was made to limit the spouse's elective share.

Uniform Probate Code

The Uniform Probate Code does not allow a spouse's right of election to be defeated. Its provisions do not limit a forced or elective share to the traditional probate estate, but instead extend the election to the "augmented estate," which includes the living trust's assets. Other states have limited the use of a living trust to defeat a spouse's share by court rules that have treated the trust as fictitious on the grounds that, when property is placed in a living trust, it has not been divested. In either type of state, the property in the living trust will be subject to the spouse's forced or elective share.

Spendthrift Trusts

Assets may also be protected from the claims of future creditors by transferring them to a trust established by a third party—for example, a spouse. Such a trust, however, is usually irrevocable and includes a spendthrift clause that insulates the beneficiaries' interests from being assigned to or attached by creditors. The law of the situs of the trust will determine the rights of the parties.

In all situations in which there is a transfer without consideration, the question of a fraudulent transfer always exists.

Interruption of Business

The death of an estate owner is a big blow to any business he or she may own or have an interest in. Probate delays could compound the issue and cause liquidity and management problems for the business. Proper structuring of the business and the use of key-man insurance can minimize the problem, but a living trust is another way to provide for the efficient continuation of the business. It allows the trustee to act in the deceased's stead without court approval and provides for a smooth transition to the survivors, the partners, or whoever inherits the business.

Special Assets

You may be better off not including certain assets in a living trust. It may be difficult to transfer an automobile into the trust since an insurance company may balk at insuring the beneficiaries of a trust. Similarly, you may not wish to transfer jewelry into a trust, which would require a listing of the jewelry and could give rise to insurance problems or questions in the event of a tax audit if the jewelry is disposed of.

There is also a question of whether a married person would want to transfer the family residence into a living trust, rather than have it pass to a surviving spouse. If the residence were transferred to a living trust, the trust provisions must provide for its maintenance and permit the surviving spouse to reside there rent-free. This would make the surviving spouse dependent upon the trustee's discretion in maintaining the residence, which may be an undesirable situation, especially where the trustee is a residuary beneficiary.

Further, you should consider that certain benefits might be lost after the death of the grantor, when the living trust becomes irrevocable. For example, in Florida and certain other states, a residence can qualify for the homestead exemption, which exempts a portion of the real estate taxes and immunity from creditors' claims, only if it is owned by a revocable trust.

In addition, many married people feel, for psychological reasons, that if one of them dies, the residence should pass to the survivor, rather than be held in a trust. In these situations, a joint tenancy with right of survivorship (which also avoids probate) might be a better alternative.

New York State Law

Most states specifically authorize by statute the creation of a revocable living trust agreement in which the grantor is the sole trustee and beneficiary during his or her lifetime. Prior to June 25, 1997, New York had no such statutory authority and only recognized living trusts through its case law.

On June 25, 1997, the Governor of New York, George Pataki, signed into law a bill permitting the creation of a revocable living trust agreement in which the grantor is the sole trustee and beneficiary during his or her lifetime. The new law does require that after the current beneficiary's interest in the trust ceases, there must be provisions providing for the assets to pass to the next estate.

The bill requires that the trust be in writing, signed by the creator, and acknowledged in the presence of a notary public. This is the same formality that has to be observed for the recording of a deed. If the creator of a trust is not the sole trustee at least one trustee must join in the execution. Any amendment or revocation must be signed in the same manner, and the trustee must be notified in writing. However, the law permits that, in place of the acknowledgment, a trust will be valid if it is signed in the presence of two witnesses. If a trust is a pour-over receptacle of a will, it must be acknowledged. The alternate method of legal execution of the trust instrument will facilitate families in situations where the creator may not be ambulatory or it is difficult to bring in a notary public to take the acknowledgment.

The new law makes express provisions concerning the funding of the trust by providing that the trust will be subject to and valid as to only those assets that have been actually transferred to it. This mandates that an asset transfer must be completed in order for it to be considered part of the corpus of the trust. However, for assets that are not registered, such as tangible personal property, the new law provides that an instrument of assignment setting forth a description of the assets will suffice for transfer purposes. As such, a provision in the trust instrument assigning to the trustee "the assets set forth in Schedule A appended hereto" is insufficient and does not accomplish the transfer of those assets.

The new law allows the creator of a living trust to revoke or amend it by a specific express provision in his or her will. As a result of the new law, there should be an increased usage of the revocable living trust as a will substitute.

The Successor Trustee

The selection of a successor trustee is an important planning decision. The successor trustee is the person or institution who normally succeeds after your death or incapacity. The trustee must, in addition to understanding the structure of the family, be qualified to handle all the management and financial-accounting duties necessary to properly administer the assets of the trust. You may decide to name a professional trustee. Banks and trust companies are the most typical sources of professional trustees. They offer stable, albeit conservative, money management. However, such trustees may not be aware of the various needs of the beneficiaries of the trust; as such, where possible, a cotrustee should be named. Most elder family members will name a spouse or, if none exists, one or more children to serve as the successor trustees.

Income Tax Consequences of a Living Trust

There are no income tax savings to the grantor in establishing a living trust. The income generated by the trust assets will be taxable under the grantor-trust rules of the Internal Revenue Code. These sections provide that if the grantor retains the right to revoke, the power to control beneficial enjoyment, or the right to receive the trust income, then he or she is taxed as if the trust does not exist.

If the grantor is a trustee or cotrustee, the trust does not need a separate taxpayer identification number, nor must a separate federal income tax return be filed for the trust. If the grantor is not a trustee or cotrustee, then a separate taxpayer identification number is needed, and a separate federal tax return (1041) must be filed if the trust has taxable income, gross income of $600 or more, or a beneficiary who is a nonresident alien. All items of income, deduction, and credit, however, should be reported directly on the grantor's individual federal income tax return.

The Tax Reform Act of 1997 added Section 645 to the Internal Revenue Code, which permits an executor and a trustee to elect that a qualified revocable trust be treated and taxed as part of a decedent's estate for income tax purposes. Section 645 therefore makes available to trusts some of the income tax advantages traditionally available only to estates. If the election is made, only one Form 1041 (fiduciary income tax return) is filed, rather than separate returns for the trust and the estate. The return is filed under the name and identification number of the estate. All items of income, deduction, and credit are combined. If there is no estate representative, the trustee files the Form 1041. Electing trusts may select a fiscal year. The election is made in a written statement attached to Form 1041 filed for the first taxable year of the related estate.

Income Tax Benefits

As grantor, you will also maintain certain income tax benefits, even if assets are transferred to the trust. Some of these benefits are as follows:

- Series EE bonds can be transferred to the trust without gain.
- The trust can hold S corporation stock because grantor trusts can be stockholders of S corporations.
- If the grantor owns a residence, all benefits of the income tax laws are available.
- A transfer of an installment obligation to the trust will not be deemed a disposition.
- The transfer of depreciable property to the trust will not cause depreciation recapture.

Cautions

There are several traps that have to be avoided with regard to certain special assets. If the living trust owns S corporation stock and if there is a litigated dispute that keeps the estate from being settled for more than two years after the grantor's death, the S corporation election may be lost. An estate has no such limitation.

With respect to passive activities for income tax purposes, after the grantor's death there is no provision to allow the $25,000 deduction for active participation in passive rental activities. An estate can claim such a deduction for a two-year period (subject to certain rules).

An executor can file a joint final income tax return with the surviving spouse, but a trustee cannot.

A trust must file calendar-year returns, while an estate can elect a fiscal year.

Trusts are subject to the throwback rule, estates are not. If property is distributed to a beneficiary and the distribution results in a loss, the loss could be disallowed. This does not apply to estates.

Gift Tax

If the trust is revocable, there are no gift taxes upon its creation because, as grantor, you maintain dominion and control over the trust.

However, a taxable gift can inadvertently be made if you become legally incapacitated during the term of the trust. In such event, the living trust then becomes irrevocable. The trust agreement can guard against this happening by providing that any power of revocation will continue to be exercisable after your disability by the holder of your power of attorney; or you can retain a special power of appointment that is set forth in the living trust. Further, it can provide for you to reserve the right to dispose of providing for your assets by your will.

Estate Tax

The gross estate includes all assets in which you have an interest, whether beneficial or otherwise. Upon your death, the fair market value of the assets in the living trust will be included in your estate for estate tax purposes.

If you have made a gift of trust property within three years of the date of your death, the question of whether these assets are included in your gross estate depends upon the terms of the trust. Gifts made by you from your living trust in which you were the sole beneficiary are not included. The theory is that since the trustee could only distribute assets to you, the assets would be considered distributed to you, who then transferred them to the recipient of the gift. If you are not the sole beneficiary of the living trust, however, gifts made by the trust within three years of your death could be included in your estate for estate tax purposes.

Professional Asset Management

A lifetime advantage of a living trust is that it allows you to retain professionals to manage its investments. Although a professional trustee is not required, the option is open. If the beneficiaries are young or financially naïve, the attraction of professional management is even greater because, after your death, the trustee will be there to protect the assets until the beneficiaries are able to exercise responsible judgment on their own. Designating a professional trustee also gives you the opportunity to see how they will manage the living trust. If you do not like how it is being managed, changes can be made.

IRA as a Beneficiary

The living trust has no life expectancy since it is not a person but a trust. Therefore, when an IRA owner dies, if all the benefits are paid into the living trust, as the beneficiary, the total amount of the plan immediately becomes subject to income tax. However, on December 30, 1997, the Department of the Treasury issued a proposed modification to Proposed Regulation Section 1.401(2)(a)-1, D-5, which would allow a revocable living trust to be used in the same manner as irrevocable trusts—to be the beneficiary of a retirement plan if the requirements of the proposed regulations, as modified, are met. The proposed regulations require that:

- The trust becomes irrevocable upon the IRA owner's death.
- A copy of the trust must be provided to the plan administrator.
- The IRA owner must agree to provide the plan administrator with any future trust amendments.
- A certified list of all trust beneficiaries must be provided to the plan administrator. The IRA owner must also agree to provide any corrected certification when changes occur and must agree to provide a copy of the trust instrument if requested by the plan administrator. If there is more than one beneficiary, the life expectancy of the oldest beneficiary is used to calculate required minimum distributions. For further discussion on this subject, see chapter 22.

Funding the Living Trust

Title to property has to be transferred to the trust in its name. In other words, assets should not be transferred to the trustee but to the "trust." Trustees can change, which would require the reregistration of the property, whereas the trust continues its existence until it terminates according to its terms.

Property such as tangible personal property can be transferred by either listing it in a schedule attached to the trust or by executing a separate assignment of such property to the trust.

To transfer real property to a living trust, a deed has to be recorded setting forth the trust as the grantee of the property. To transfer securities, living interests, partnership interests, bank accounts, and other assets that have a title, specific documentation and instructions are required for each item.

Remember that any property you fail to transfer to your living trust, other than property held in joint tenancy or property that already has a designated beneficiary, will be probated. If your aim in setting up the living trust is to avoid probate, do not defeat yourself by omitting the crucial step of transferring your property to the living trust.

Marital Living Trusts

Since a living trust is revocable, it can be amended at any time by written document. A joint marital living trust created by both spouses can only be amended by both spouses. This is to safeguard each spouse against any wrongdoing by the other. In a joint spousal living trust, when one spouse dies, the deceased spouse's portion becomes irrevocable, while the surviving spouse's portion of the trust remains revocable, and he or she can amend such share as if it were a single person's trust.

A marital joint living trust can be revoked by either spouse at any time. Revocation restores both spouses to the same position they were in prior to the creation of the document.

Joint or Shared Ownership Property

In the eight community property states, where property is owned by spouses jointly or on a shared-owner basis, both spouses are equal owners of all property acquired after marriage.

Having separate living trusts for each spouse for joint or shared ownership property is generally not preferable. This is because each owner can transfer only his or her share of the property to his or her separate trust. To accomplish this, ownership of the joint property must be divided. Dividing shared marital property in half could lead to unfair and undesired imbalances; for example, one spouse's share could appreciate and the other's could depreciate.

As such, there is no need for spouses to divide property ownership as long as one trust is created to handle both spouses' shared interests. This can be done using a marital living trust. In it, each spouse has full authority to designate the beneficiaries of his or her portion of the property. When the first spouse dies, the jointly owned or shared marital property is divided. The deceased spouse's portion of the property is transferred to the beneficiaries. One beneficiary is commonly the surviving spouse, but children, friends, and charities may also receive property. If the surviving spouse inherits property, he or she normally transfers it to his or her living trust, which continues in effect in its revocable form.

Beneficiaries and Trusts for Children

Beneficiaries are the persons or organizations that will receive the assets of the living trust after your death. In a joint marital living trust, each spouse can name his or her own beneficiaries.

Trusts for children who are beneficiaries under a living trust can be created as part of the living trust. In doing so, you can designate when the child will receive the trust property, who will manage it for the child, and what benefits the child will receive from his or her trust during its term. In such an instance, the trustee should be given broad powers to use the assets of the trust for the support, maintenance, and welfare of the child.

Using a Living Trust and a Will

In many instances, proper estate planning requires the creation of both a living trust and a will. This is especially true if not all assets can be placed into a trust or if there are special situations such as minors who need a guardian or litigation involving the estate owner.

To maximize estate tax planning goals, reduce transfer costs, fund a child's education, provide for an elderly parent, provide for a spendthrift beneficiary, provide for a spouse who cannot manage or assume the responsibility of property, avoid a contest, and provide for a continuity in your affairs, the living trust is the best means available.

Coordination between a living trust and a will is particularly important in situations involving payment of debts, taxes, and distribution. If a single bequest is to be made to a beneficiary, the living trust and the decedent's will must be coordinated so that the instrument making the payment has sufficient assets and that only one payment is made. Care must also be taken so as not to eliminate the bequest through cross-references between the trust provisions and the will provisions. If a marital deduction clause is used together with the establishment of a family trust, the will and trust documents must be coordinated so as not to eliminate or duplicate the amounts left to such trusts.

Questions about Living Trusts

Should everyone have a living trust?

Yes. However, certain young people who are really not thinking about their mortality and who will not die for a long time are really not interested in focusing on their form of estate planning. The main considerations of these people are the care of their minor children and an adequate distribution stream to their family. Financial security for their family is of permanent significance and usually a will and a life insurance plan are the primary devices put into place. Probate avoidance and a continuity in the event of incapacity is not a current concern.

Where there are no estate tax concerns and the assets can be passed on by the use of other nonprobate techniques such as joint ownership, life insurance, or pay-on-death accounts, the estate owner may not resort to the creation of a living trust. However, this can deny the estate owner the other features of the living trust such as providing continuity in the event of incapacity.

If, however, your estate is burdened with creditors, then you should consider the probate process. This is because the rules of the courts provide a cut-off time for creditors to file claims. If creditors fail to act, the beneficiaries can receive their property without concern about future claims. The living trust does not offer this kind of protection and the assets could therefore be subject to future claims of creditors for a longer period of time.

If you anticipate receiving property in the future, a living trust will really not be beneficial to you. This is because a living trust is effective to receive property you presently own. If your circumstances are as such, then you must create a backup will at the same time you make your living trust so that the assets to be received will flow to your beneficiaries through your living trust.

Where a guardian of a minor child is necessary, a will is required for this designation in most states. You can still have a living trust that would operate together with your backup will containing the designation. People with little or no estates need not be concerned with testamentary dispositions. They can implement the transfer of their assets by other devices.

How do you create a living trust?

A living trust is created by a written instrument that is often referred to as a trust agreement, trust indenture, or declaration of trust. The measure of the understanding necessary to execute a trust agreement is whether you understand the nature of the transaction.

How do you create a will?

A will must be written, witnessed, and executed with the formalities set by state law. The standard of capacity for signing a will is less than required for signing a trust agreement. When you make a will, you are only supposed to know who your heirs are and the nature of your assets. Legal cases have held that less capacity is required for you to make a will than for you to execute any other legal document.

If you have a living trust will there be any court proceedings when you die?

No. You will, however, have to seek the help of the courts for the appointment of a trustee if no successor to yourself is designated in the trust instrument or where the terms of the trust agreement are in dispute.

Should you have a durable power of attorney in addition to a living trust?

Yes. The agent can be given the right, among other things, to transfer to your trust any property you may not have transferred, both before and after, if you should become disabled.

During your lifetime, what taxes will a living trust avoid?

None. A living trust will not save any taxes. Since the trust is revocable, the assets of your trust are included in your federal gross estate. The fact that they are to be included in the estate for tax purposes does not mean they are taxable upon your death. If the trust has provisions taking effect at death that either avoid (unified credit) or defer (marital deduction) taxes, the assets will not be subject to estate taxation at that time. Income taxes are required to be paid on assets that are transferred to your living trust. For income tax purposes, under the "grantor trust" income tax rules, you are treated as the owner of the trust.

If you are the sole trustee or cotrustee, your living trust is not required to obtain a separate taxpayer identification number from the Internal Revenue Service (you can use your social security number). If you are not a trustee, besides obtaining an identification number, an annual fiduciary income tax return for the trust must be filed. No gift tax return will have to be filed nor will gift taxes have to be paid when you create your living trust.

If you should become mentally incapacitated, a gift tax question might arise, due to the fact of the irrevocability of the trust. This would only arise if your beneficiaries were other than your spouse and their shares were in excess of the unified credit. The rationale behind this is the fact that your power to revoke the trust may no longer exist. This could cause all the transfers to take place after your death under the terms of the trust to be subject to gift tax. However, the use of a durable power of attorney, which survives your disability and authorizes and directs your agent (attorney-in-fact) to act on your behalf, with regard to a partial or complete revocation of the trust, will avoid this problem. This is yet another reason for you to engage only a professional advisor who is experienced in this field.

Can the living trust make distributions to persons other than the grantor?

Yes. The trustee can be authorized to make discretionary distributions to other persons.

Is the living trust valid in other states?

Yes. The living trust is used in every state and in many foreign countries as well.

If a residence is owned and thereafter sold by the living trust, are all income tax benefits available to the grantor?

Yes. The living trust can make use of the exemption provisions of the Internal Revenue Code.

Will the homestead exemption be lost if a home is transferred to a revocable living trust?

Usually, no. State homestead exemptions, which protect a homeowner's equity interest in a home from creditors, will not be lost because the house is transferred to a revocable living trust.

A "homestead exemption" is a legal device, available under the laws of most states, to protect the equity in a home from creditors, up to an amount set by the laws of each state. If you qualify for a homestead, the home is protected against forced sale by creditors (other than mortgage holders) if the equity in the home is below the statutory limit. If the equity is larger than the amount protected by the homestead law, the home can be sold, but in many states the protected amount is permitted to be invested in another home.

Is it expensive to transfer property into a living trust?

No. Except for deeds to real estate, which should be at minimal expense, transferring assets into a living trust should have no cost whatsoever. Your attorney should prepare the documents necessary to transfer your real property. All other assets can be transferred by letter of transfer, and no fee should be charged. Stocks and bonds should be transferred by your stockbroker, as a service to you, without fee. As a general rule, the cost of transferring your assets into your living trust should be nominal.

Must you go to court to amend a living trust?
    No. If the trust so provides, you can revoke or amend your living trust simply by the preparation of a written instrument.

❖

CHAPTER 9

Understanding and Minimizing Estate Taxes

*T*he body of the tax law that covers estates is complex, and the tax imposed is the severest levied in our country. Because the tax rates are so high, estate planning has become a necessity. Proper planning for the orderly transfer of assets will produce effective tax savings.

The federal estate and gift tax systems were unified for taxing transfers of property that take place both during your lifetime and upon your death. The Tax Reform Act of 1976 joined the two separate systems and established a unified rate schedule and one unified credit. The rates of taxation for gifts made during one's lifetime and for testamentary transfers are the same. A single progressive tax rate schedule is therefore applied to cumulative lifetime gifts and testamentary transfers. A stopgap or additional tax was also created; this is designated as the generation-skipping transfer tax that precludes property from passing over a generation without transfer taxes being imposed. For a detailed discussion of this tax system, see chapter 12.

This chapter discusses what an estate is, what its components are, how it is valued, what deductions and credits are allowed, and how the tax is calculated. The various methods of how you can pay estate taxes are explained, as is the postmortem period, one of the most important phases of estate planning, when options are available to both the surviving spouse and the legal representatives of the estate.

The private annuity, a rarely discussed estate planning strategy, is probably the most underemployed device available in the estate planning field. The private annuity arrangement can remove an asset from your estate and permit you to keep the annual cash benefits during your lifetime. This technique is discussed later in this chapter.

81

The second edition of this book contained a new section which discussed federal legislation enacted in August 1997, which made a number of changes in the gift and estate laws. Included was an overview of the dramatic changes in the New York State gift and estate tax laws, signed into law on August 7, 1997, which put New York State on par with most of its sister states. This edition addresses the changes brought about by the Economic Growth and Tax Relief Reconciliation Act of 2001. Among other things, this act includes the repeal of the estate tax. For a complete discussion of the revisions to the transfer tax system set forth in this act and signed into law on June 7, 2001 by George W. Bush, see the end of this chapter.

Since the United States imposes an estate tax on all assets of both its citizens and its residents, international estate planning is very important. The ins and outs of this area of estate planning are discussed within this chapter.

An Overview

The estate tax is inclusive; in other words, estate taxes are imposed on the very property that will be used to pay the tax.

All citizens of the United States, and any person owning property situated in the United States, are subject to federal estate tax. Your estate is liable for the tax on the entire taxable estate. The beneficiaries of the estate may have to pay the tax if the estate does not pay it when it is due. The rate of taxes depends upon the size or value of the taxable estate. Many states impose estate taxes as well. There are several exemptions available which permit your property to pass free of estate taxes. The significant exemptions are the unified credit or lifetime exemption; the unlimited marital deduction, which permits benefits left to a surviving spouse to be transferred free of taxes; and property given to recognized charities.

Practically speaking, it is almost impossible to eliminate estate taxes. The goal of the estate owner should be to minimize or reduce the estate taxes imposed on transfers from one generation to the next.

The Gross Estate

All property in which you have an interest at the time of your death is included in your gross estate. This includes the following:
- One-half interest in community property.
- Joint interests.
- Annuities.
- Property subject to general power of appointment.

- Life insurance proceeds.
- Life interest in property for which QTIP marital deduction was elected.
- Property gifted during your lifetime. The gross estate does not include interests in property that terminate at the time of your death, as do some life estates.

The gross estate includes the full value of all property of a U.S. citizen or resident no matter where the property is situated. If property is taxed by a foreign country, a credit for foreign death taxes may be available to reduce the federal estate tax.

Certain income is included in the gross estate, such as dividends, interest, rents, and compensation, including contingent fees. Income accrued prior to death but not reportable on your final income tax return is known as "income in respect of a decedent" (IRD). There is a special income tax deduction for estate taxes attributable to the inclusion of IRD in the gross estate.

Community Property

In community property states (Arizona, California, Idaho, Louisiana, Nevada, New Mexico, Texas, Washington, and Wisconsin), all property acquired by the spouses during their marriage is regarded as owned in equal shares by the spouses, and, therefore, each spouse has a vested interest in one-half of the shared property. The one-half interest is acquired while the spouses are domiciled in a community property state and continues even if the couple subsequently moves to a non–community property state. However, each spouse may also acquire property separately by gift or inheritance. At the death of one spouse, therefore, only one-half of the community property and all of the separately acquired property are included in that spouse's gross estate.

Joint Interests

Included in the gross estate is the entire value of property held by you and any other person as joint tenants with a right of survivorship at your death. The value of your interest in the property, however, will be reduced to the extent that your estate can show that the surviving joint tenant: (1) had an original ownership interest never transferred for full consideration to the decedent; or (2) made an original contribution to the cost of acquiring the property, unless this contribution came from your own funds.

If the joint tenants are spouses, unless one of the spouses is not a U.S. citizen, only half the value of the asset is included in the deceased spouse's gross estate at his or her death, regardless of who furnished the original consideration. There is an exception to this provision involving real property acquired by a married couple as joint tenants. Pursuant to a 1981 amendment to the Code, the estate of a decedent who died after 1981 is entitled to a full-basis step-up in entireties for real property purchased before 1977 and for which the surviving spouse supplied none of the consideration. Significant tax planning opportunities are therefore available for married individuals with pre–1977 jointly held real estate.

Annuities

The gross estate includes the value of an annuity that still has residual value after your death; for example, one which is payable to a beneficiary who survives you. Also included in the gross estate are payments from qualified pension, stock bonus, or profit-sharing plans; tax-deferred annuities; individual retirement accounts (IRAs); and certain military retirement plans. The amount included in the gross estate is the proportion of the annuity attributable to your contributions to the purchase price. Contributions made by your employer or former employer are deemed to be contributed by you if made by reason of your employment.

Powers of Appointment

Any property over which you have a general power of appointment at the time of your death is included in your estate. A general power of appointment allows you to appoint property to yourself or your estate, your creditors, or the creditors of your estate. A power of appointment is not general, and as such is not included in your estate, if it can be exercised only in favor of specific persons or a limited class of persons.

Proceeds of Life Insurance

Generally, the proceeds of an insurance policy on your life, whether payable to your estate or to other beneficiaries, are included in your gross estate. This rule does not apply, however, if at the time of your death you retained no incidents of ownership in the insurance policy and the proceeds were not payable to your estate or to be used for the benefit of your estate. For avoidance of estate taxes on life insurance, see chapter 14.

QTIP Marital Deductions

A marital deduction is allowed for the value of all property in which a surviving spouse receives a lifetime "qualifying income interest." This property is known as a "qualified terminable interest property" (QTIP) and is includable in the gross estate of the surviving spouse if the estate of the first spouse takes a marital deduction with respect to this property.

Property Transferred during Decedent's Lifetime

The gross estate includes: (1) transfers effective at decedent's death; (2) transfers with a retained life estate; and (3) revocable transfers. These types of transfers, together with gifts of life insurance and all gift taxes paid within three years of death are included in gross estates, as well.

Gifts Made within Three Years of Death

Generally, the value of property transferred as a gift prior to your death is not includable in your gross estate but may be subject to the gift tax. However, certain gifts, such as a gift of life insurance, a transfer effective at your death, a transfer with a retained life estate, or a revocable transfer, are included in your gross estate.

Transfers Effective at Death with Reversionary Interests

The gross estate includes the entire value of property transferred by you as a gift if you retained a "reversionary interest" in the property (a right to receive the property back at some future date). This is so if the value of such right is in excess of 5 percent of the value of the entire property immediately before your death. For example, you create a trust to pay income to your brother for his lifetime. Upon your brother's death, your brother's son is to receive the principal of the trust. If the son is not living at the time of your brother's death, the trust principal reverts back to you. If there is a greater than 5 percent chance that you will outlive your brother's son, the trust principal is included in your gross estate. In order to determine the potential "chance," the ages and health of all of the significant parties is evaluated actuarially.

Transfer with a Retained Life Estate

The gross estate includes the value of all property to the extent of your interest therein, which you have transferred at any time, by trust or otherwise (unless by a sale for full consideration) and in which you have retained an interest for life or for a shorter period. These retained interests are the possession, enjoyment, or right to the income of the property, or the right to designate the persons who will possess or enjoy the property or the income from it.

For example, say you create a trust to pay income to your descendants during your lifetime and you retain the power to determine from year to year which of your descendants will actually receive the income and in what proportions. This retained power will cause the entire trust property to be included in your gross estate.

Revocable Transfers

The gross estate includes the value of any interest in property transferred by you to another for less than full and adequate consideration if you possess at the time of your death the power to alter, amend, revoke, or terminate the transfer in favor of anyone, such as the power to change a beneficiary.

How Is the Property of the Estate Valued?

The property included in the gross estate is valued as of the date of your death, unless your legal representative elects a date six months after the date of your death (the "alternate valuation date"). The alternate valuation date may be chosen only when it reduces both the value of the gross estate and the federal estate tax liability. The alternate valuation applies to all the includable assets of your estate. The amount of the marital and charitable deductions, which depend on the value of property passing to a spouse or charity, must also be adjusted to the alternate value. The value of property that is sold between the date of death and the alternate valuation date is, for estate tax purposes, its sales price. There is usually a trade-off between estate and income tax savings when choosing the alternate valuation date. The estate tax values of estate assets become the inherited cost basis for income tax purposes. The alternate valuation should only be used if the reduction in estate tax exceeds the present value of the additional income tax. The decision regarding the alternate valuation election depends upon many factors, including the estate tax rate, the income tax rates of the beneficiaries, and their investment goals.

Fair Market Value

The values of assets includable in the estate is their fair market value on the valuation date. Fair market value is the price at which the property would change hands between a willing buyer and a willing seller, neither being under any compulsion to buy or sell, and both having reasonable knowledge of relevant facts. If the item is one generally sold at retail, the fair market value is the price at which the item or a comparable item would be sold.

A special-use valuation election, available to those whose estates consist largely of a farm or other closely held business, allows the property to be valued at its farm- or business-use value rather than at its fair market value. The reduction in value as a result of this election cannot exceed $820,000.

What Are the Deductions Allowed?

Once the value of the gross estate is determined, the next step is to subtract from it a number of allowable deductions. The difference is the taxable estate. The two most significant deductions are the marital and charitable deductions. They are important because they can be planned for in advance and can substantially reduce or eliminate the estate tax altogether.

In addition, the following deductions are also allowable:

- Funeral expenses, including the costs of a tombstone, monument, or mausoleum; funeral services; and a burial plot for the decedent or his or her family, including the reasonable cost of its future care.
- Administration expenses actually incurred in administering the estate, i.e., collecting assets, paying debts, and distributing property among the people entitled to it. These expenses include executor's commissions, attorneys' fees, court costs, accountants' and appraisers' fees, and the like.
- Claims against the estate that were allowable and enforceable as personal obligations of the decedent under local law. A pledge to a charity is deductible if it would have qualified as a bequest and is enforceable against the estate. Accrued but unpaid taxes may also be deducted. State and foreign death taxes and the federal estate tax are not deductible.
- Unpaid mortgages and debts, such as the expenses of the decedent's final illness.
- The value of losses incurred during the settlement of the estate from fires, storms, shipwrecks or other casualties, or from theft, to the extent that they are not compensated by insurance or other sources.

Charitable Deduction

A bequest to a qualifying charity is deductible from the gross estate. There is no limit on the amount of this deduction. An estate will pay no estate tax if it is all left to charity. A charitable deduction is also available if a charity is an income or remainder beneficiary of a trust. See chapter 11 for a discussion on charitable trusts.

Marital Deduction

An unlimited marital deduction is allowed for property included in a gross estate that passes outright to your spouse. Transfers of terminable interests or interests that terminate upon the happening of a certain event, such as the remarriage of a surviving spouse, or with the passage of time, do not qualify for a marital deduction. Exceptions to these include qualified terminable interest property (QTIP), power-of-appointment trusts, and if the period of time that a spouse must survive the deceased spouse does not exceed six months.

Property passing to the surviving spouse as a joint tenant by right of survivorship, through dower or curtesy interests, under powers of appointment, and by transfers made during your lifetime that are included in your gross estate, all qualify for the marital deduction. The deduction also applies to life insurance proceeds paid outright to the surviving spouse or to a trust which itself qualifies for the marital deduction.

A transfer of property to a trust under which all beneficial interests pass to the surviving spouse may also qualify for the marital deduction.

No marital deduction is allowed for property passing to a surviving spouse who is not a U.S. citizen unless the property passes in the form of a qualified domestic trust (QDOT). For a discussion of this type of trust, see chapter 7.

QTIP Transfers

Transfers of a life estate in qualified terminable interest property (QTIP) to a spouse is an exception to the terminable interest rule and qualifies for a marital deduction. Your spouse must have a "qualifying income interest" for the property to be so designated. This means that he or she must be entitled to receive all the income from the property at least annually, and that no person can appoint the property during your spouse's lifetime to anyone other than your spouse. The transfer may be in the form of a life estate for your spouse or a trust. You may retain or create powers over part or all of the QTIP corpus, but only if they are exercisable on or after your surviving spouse's death. Thus, your surviving spouse need not be given a general power of appointment. In order to qualify a transfer as QTIP, an election to take the marital deduction for a QTIP transfer is made by your legal representative on the estate tax return and is irrevocable. Property thus qualified is subject to a gift tax, if transferred during your spouse's lifetime, or subject to an estate tax upon your spouse's death as part of his or her estate.

International Estate Planning

Federal estate taxes are imposed on all property owned by U.S. citizens worldwide and by residents of the United States whether they are citizens or not. The United States does have estate tax treaties with various countries, which, in some instances, provide for full credits for estate taxes paid to another nation. If no treaty exists, the foreign country could tax its citizen and if that citizen resided here, the United States could tax the same assets as well. A foreign citizen who may not reside here could be subject to U.S. estate tax laws if he or she owns property here. Property is considered located here if it is:

- Real property located in the United States
- Tangible personal property located in the United States—this includes clothing, jewelry, automobiles, furniture, or currency
- A debt obligation of a citizen or resident of the United States, a domestic partnership or corporation, any estate or trust (but not a foreign estate or trust), the United States, a state or a political sub-division of a state, or the District of Columbia
- Shares of stock issued by domestic corporations

Property Not Located in the United States

Notwithstanding the above rules, property of a nonresident, noncitizen decedent is not considered located in the United States if it is:

- A deposit with a U.S. bank, if the deposit was not connected with a U.S. trade or business and was paid or credited to the decedent's account.
- Stock issued by a corporation that is not a domestic corporation, even if the certificate is physically located in the United States.
- An amount receivable as insurance on the decedent's life.

If you are a foreign citizen residing outside of the United States and if you own shares of stock in a domestic corporation such as Ford Motors, you would be subject to federal estate taxes on those shares. These estate taxes might be avoided by the creation of an offshore entity.

There are certain government securities that are exempt from federal estate tax, such as Treasury bonds that mature longer than six months from inception. The rationale for making them estate tax free is to encourage their purchase by foreign nationals.

Expatriation

There are certain estate planners who advocate expatriation to a country that does not impose estate taxes. (Canada, Ireland, and the Bahamas do not impose estate taxes.) However, our laws impose a ten-year rule. This rule provides that, if you die within ten years of changing citizenship, all property owned through foreign corporations, directly or indirectly, is added back into your estate. This means that if you expatriate, you have to liquidate and remove all of your property from this country.

Under the present rules, a person who was a noncitizen permanent resident (i.e., a "green card" holder) of the United States in at least eight of the fifteen taxable years immediately preceding leaving the United States, a U.S. citizen who expatriates, or a long-term resident who leaves the United States will automatically and irrebuttably be presumed to have expatriated or left for tax purposes. Therefore, he or she will be taxed under the ten-year tax regime of the Internal Revenue Code if the individual's average annual U.S. income tax liability for the past five years is more than $100,000 or whose net worth is $500,000 or more (both adjusted for inflation).

The new automatic irrebuttable presumption rule will not apply to a former U.S. citizen who otherwise meets the income or assets test if that person falls into one of the following categories: (1) the person was born with dual citizenship; (2) the person becomes a citizen of the country in which the person, his or her spouse, or one of his or her parents was born; (3) the person was present in the United States for no more than thirty days during any year in the ten-year period immediately preceding the date of his or her loss of citizenship; (4) the person relinquishes citizenship before reaching age eighteen and a half; and (5) any other category of individual prescribed by Treasury Regulations.

To avoid the application of the automatic irrebuttable presumption rule, such persons must apply within a year of the expatriation for a ruling that they did not have avoidance of U.S. tax as a principal purpose. There are no comparable exceptions for long-term residents who leave the United States, although the IRS is permitted to issue regulations exempting certain categories of long-term residents from the rule. Furthermore, U.S. source income on which the expatriate (or former long-term resident) will continue to be taxed includes items of gain or income from the sale of U.S. assets (e.g., U.S. stocks). Congress has also passed a measure that, in effect, prohibits former U.S. citizens who renounced their U.S. citizenship for the purpose of avoiding U.S. taxation from entering the United States (Health Insurance Portability and Accountability Act). The decision as to whether renunciation was for tax avoidance is to be made by the INS rather than the IRS.

Disclaimers

If your surviving spouse disclaims a bequest, it is treated as if it did not pass to him or her and therefore does not qualify for the marital deduction. Similarly, an interest disclaimed by a beneficiary that passes to a surviving spouse does qualify. A disclaimer is not the same as acceptance of the property and subsequent disapproval of it. A formal "qualified disclaimer" must be executed in writing and communicated to the legal representative within nine months after the transfer or, in the case of a minor, by the age of twenty-one.

Credits Allowed against the Estate Tax

Discussed below are the various credits allowed against the estate tax.

Unified Credit

Each of us is allowed a unified credit, which in 2002 is $345,800, against the estate tax and is equivalent to $1,000,000 in property value. The tax credit exempts the transfer of property from estate tax. The amount of the credit that is not used will be lost.

For a married couple, the way the exemption is utilized can have a positive result of estate tax savings. This tax can be avoided by creating a trust in the amount of the exemption for the benefit of the surviving spouse, who would receive all income therefrom and the principal, if necessary. Upon the death of the second spouse, the property in the trust will pass to the next generations, estate tax free. The benefits from the trust can also be sprinkled or sprayed among children and grandchildren in addition to the surviving spouse. If both spouses create such a plan, then upon the death of the survivor of them, they can effectively pass property having a value equal to both exemptions to their heirs, estate tax free. An example of the use of both the credit and unlimited marital deduction is discussed in detail later in this chapter.

You should consider leaving more than the exemption amount in a by-pass trust if: (1) there are enough liquid assets to pay some tax at the first spouse's death; (2) the spouse can afford to pay some tax at the first death (i.e., the entire estate is not needed to support the surviving spouse); and (3) the surviving spouse will have a taxable estate greater than the exemption amount credit equivalent.

Credit for State Death Taxes

A credit is allowed against the federal estate tax for any inheritance, estate, legacy, or succession tax paid to any state or the District of Columbia. At the end of this chapter is a schedule setting forth how the death tax laws of each state are classified. As you can see from the schedule, many states impose a "credit estate tax." This tax is equal to the credit for the state death taxes computed in calculating the federal estate tax. This type of estate tax is commonly referred to as a "sponge tax" or "pickup tax." This means that the state does not have an estate tax per se, but simply receives the amount of the credit calculated in a federal taxable estate as its state death tax. The states with only pickup taxes are Alabama, Alaska, Arizona, Arkansas, California, Colorado, Delaware, District of Columbia, Florida, Georgia, Hawaii, Idaho, Illinois, Kansas, Maine, Massachusetts, Michigan, Minnesota, Mississippi, Missouri, Montana, Nevada, New Hampshire, New Jersey, New Mexico, New York, North Carolina, North Dakota, Oregon, Rhode Island, South Carolina, Texas, Utah, Vermont, Virginia, Washington, West Virginia, Wisconsin, and Wyoming. Toward the end of this chapter is a chart outlining the state death tax laws.

Credit for Gift Tax
A credit against the estate tax is allowed for gift taxes paid on gifts made prior to 1977, for any portion of such a gift that is later included in a decedent's gross estate.

Credit for Tax on Prior Transfers
A credit against the estate tax is allowed for federal estate tax paid on the transfer of property to the present decedent from a person who died within ten years before or after the present decedent's death. The original transferred property need not be identified in the present decedent's estate nor be in existence at the time of his or her death. It suffices that the prior transfer of property was subject to federal estate tax in the prior person's estate and that the prior person died within the prescribed time. If the transferor died within two years before or within two years after the transferee's death, the credit allowed for the tax on the prior transfer is 100 percent of the maximum amount allowable. If the transferor predeceased the transferee by more than two years, the credit allowed is a reduced percentage of the maximum amount allowable. The percentage allowable may be determined by using the following table:

PERIOD OF TIME		
EXCEEDING	NOT EXCEEDING	% ALLOWABLE
—	2 years	100
2 years	4 years	80
4 years	6 years	60
6 years	8 years	40
8 years	10 years	20
10 years	—	none

Credit for Foreign Death Taxes
A credit against the federal estate tax is allowed for any estate, inheritance, legacy, or succession taxes actually paid to any foreign country on

property located in that country that is included in the decedent's gross estate. The credit cannot exceed the federal estate tax attributable to such property. The credit must be claimed within four years after the filing of the estate tax return.

Computation of the Estate Tax

The federal estate tax is computed as follows:
1. Determine the gross estate.
2. Subtract from the gross estate the permissible deductions.
3. Add the value of taxable gifts made after 1976.
4. Apply the unified rate schedule to the taxable estate

The result is the tentative estate tax. Next:

5. Subtract from the tentative estate tax any gift taxes payable (not actually paid) on post–1976 gifts.
6. Deduct the following applicable credits:
   - The unified credit
   - The credit for state death taxes
   - The credit for gift tax on pre–1977 gifts included in the gross estate
   - The credit for tax on prior transfers
   - The credit for foreign death taxes

The result is the net estate tax.

Federal Estate and Gift Tax Rate Schedule

For decedents dying and gifts made in 1993 and thereafter, the federal estate and gift tax rate schedule currently is as follows:

IF THE AMOUNT WITH RESPECT TO WHICH THE TENTATIVE TAX TO BE COMPUTED IS:	THE TENTATIVE TAX IS:
Not over $10,000	18 percent of such amount.
Over $10,000, but not $20,000	$1,800, plus 20 percent of the excess of such amount over $10,000
Over $20,000, but not $40,000	$3,800, plus 22 percent of the excess of such amount over $20,000
Over $40,000, but not $60,000	$8,200, plus 24 percent of the excess of such amount over $40,000

IF THE AMOUNT WITH RESPECT TO WHICH THE TENTATIVE TAX TO BE COMPUTED IS:	THE TENTATIVE TAX IS:
Over $60,000, but not $80,000	$13,000, plus 26 percent of the excess of such amount over $60,000
Over $80,000, but not $100,000	$18,200, plus 28 percent of the excess of such amount over $80,000
Over $100,000, but not $150,000	$23,800, plus 30 percent of the excess of such amount over $100,000
Over $150,000, but not $250,000	$38,000, plus 32 percent of the excess of such amount over $150,000
Over $250,000, but not $500,000	$70,800, plus 34 percent of the excess of such amount over $250,000
Over $500,000, but not $750,000	$155,800, plus 37 percent of the excess of such amount over $500,000
Over $750,000, but not $1,000,000	$248,300, plus 39 percent of the excess of such amount over $750,000
Over $1,000,000, but not $1,250,000	$345,800, plus 41 percent of the excess of such amount over $1,000,000
Over $1,250,000, but not $1,500,000	$448,300, plus 43 percent of the excess of such amount over $1,250,000
Over $1,500,000, but not $2,000,000	$555,800, plus 45 percent of the excess of such amount over $1,500,000
Over $2,000,000, but not $2,500,000	$780,800, plus 49 percent of the excess of such amount over 2,000,000
Over $2,500,000	$1,025,800, plus 50 percent of the excess of such amount over $2,500,000

Method of Paying Estate Taxes

Without question, the largest burden that can be placed on your estate is paying the federal estate taxes, usually due within nine months from the date of your death. As indicated by the chart above, the rates begin at 37 percent on property valued in excess of the unified credit (the current exempt amount is $1,000,000). If your estate is not liquid, it could encounter adverse financial effects to meet these obligations. This could even erode or reduce the value of the potential inheritances of your survivors. Of course, as you have read elsewhere in this chapter, with proper planning, married couples can completely avoid and postpone all estate taxes until the surviving spouse dies. In addition to death taxes, your death triggers other obligations, such as funeral expenses and professional fees for attorneys, accountants, and appraisers where necessary. If property passes through probate, the court fees and expenses of probate will be incurred.

If the state of your domicile imposes a death tax, this will have to be paid as well, and usually within the same time frame. Some states do not even have the same estate tax structure as the federal government. This is often found in the area of the unlimited marital deduction. In such an event, the state may impose a state inheritance tax even though there may be no federal estate tax.

A sound estate plan must not only include strategies for reducing the amount of estate tax ultimately payable by the beneficiaries, but also should include techniques for providing for the payment of the tax that will be due.

Generally, funds to pay the estate tax can come from:
- The maintenance of liquid investments by the decedent.
- The sale of assets to raise the funds necessary. This may not be advantageous due to the possibility that a forced sale may generate lower prices. If you have an interest in a closely held business, a buy-sell agreement could ease a liquidity problem. In such a case, usually the business or the co-owners would purchase the interest. In many instances, the purchase is funded with life insurance proceeds on the life of the deceased owner.
- The purchase of life insurance. Life insurance, besides providing liquidity for the payment of estate taxes, is also a method of reducing estate tax, since it can be kept out of the taxable estate. One of its advantages is that the receipt of the death benefits from a life insurance policy comes at approximately the same time the obligations of the estate owner accrues. For a more detailed discussion of life insurance and its vital role in estate planning, see chapter 14.
- Borrowing, including borrowing from the federal government under Section 6166 of the Internal Revenue Code. Borrowing to pay estate tax is an alternative that may be available to create liquidity to pay for transfer costs. It can make economic sense if the after-tax cost of the loan is less than the return after tax on the funds. A problem that occurs sometimes with this approach is the ability of furnishing proper collateral satisfactory to the lender in order to obtain the needed financing.

Normally, estate taxes are due within nine months of death. However, if a closely held business interest is included in the gross estate and if its value exceeds 35 percent of the adjusted gross estate, the estate may qualify for a deferral of tax payments. Under this arrangement, only interest on the tax due is paid until two years after the normal due date for estate taxes on the value of the business. The estate tax related to the closely held business interest can then be paid in ten equal annual installments. As such, a portion of the estate tax is deferred for as long as fourteen years from its original due date. Interest is charged for the deferred payments but only at the rate of 2 percent on the estate tax related to the first $1,060,000 of the closely held interest. The interest rate on the remaining deferred amount is reduced to 45 percent of the rate charged for underpayment of taxes.

- Section 303 Redemption. If the value of a closely held corporation is included in the gross estate and if the value exceeds 35 percent of the adjusted gross estate, the corporation can buy from the estate its shares of stock. The distribution from the corporation cannot exceed the amount of the estate taxes and the funeral and administrative expenses. If the redemption qualifies under the appropriate section, there is no negative income tax to the shareholders (dividend) resulting from the distribution.

There are time requirements during which a Section 303 redemption can occur. Distributions by a corporation in redemption of its shares of stock must take place within three years and ninety days after the filing of the estate tax return to qualify under Section 303. If the estate has a dispute with the Internal Revenue Service in the Tax Court of the United States, the redemption must be completed within sixty days following the date on which the decision becomes final. Furthermore, if an extension of time is elected under Section 6166, the redemption must be completed during the time determined for the payments of the installments.

Tandem Use of the Unified Credit and Unlimited Marital Deduction

The unified credit is an important factor in marital deduction planning. When a person has a spouse, an estate plan should be created that makes the maximum use of the unified credit and the unlimited marital deduction. A husband and wife can shelter unlimited amounts between them and may pass up to the total amount of both of their unified credits to their children or other beneficiaries, free from federal transfer tax. For example, in 2002, if the husband has an estate of $2,000,000 and the wife has no separate estate of her own, the husband may make a marital deduction bequest of half that amount and place the rest in trust ("by-pass" or "credit shelter" trust). This trust will pay the income, and principal, if necessary, to his surviving spouse for life, giving the remainder upon her death to their children or others, and neither his estate nor his spouse's will owe any federal estate taxes (assuming no increase in value in the surviving spouse's estate).

This should be contrasted with the estate tax result if the husband had made use of the maximum marital deduction, $2,000,000. While the husband's estate would escape federal estate tax, the surviving spouse's estate would incur a federal estate tax of $435,000, assuming the $2,000,000 had remained intact and the survivor had, in the interim, sufficient additional assets to pay funeral and administrative expenses.

1. Assume a husband dies and is survived by a wife and children and his will provides that his wife is to receive his entire estate. His adjusted gross estate (gross estate less funeral and administrative expenses) is $2,000,000.

Adjusted Gross Estate	$2,000,000
Marital Deduction (Unlimited)	2,000,000
Taxable Estate	$ 0

Assuming the surviving spouse's death occurs in 2002, the estate tax is calculated as follows:

Assets Inherited from Husband	$2,000,000	
Estate Tax Before Unified Credit and Other Credits		780,800
Unified Credit		345,800
Estate Tax Before Other Credits		435,000
The Net to the Beneficiaries Is	$1,565,000	

2. If the husband's will had provided for his wife to receive one-half of his estate and for the balance to be placed in a credit shelter trust for the benefit of his wife, the following would be the result:

Adjusted Gross Estate	$2,000,000	
Marital Deduction (to Spouse)	1,000,000	
Estate Tax Before Credits		345,800
Unified Credit		345,800
Net Estate Tax		$ 0

Upon the surviving spouse's death, the estate tax is calculated as follows:

Assets Inherited from Husband		$1,000,000
Estate Tax Before Unified Credit and Other Credits		345,800
Unified Credit		345,800
Estate Tax Before Other Credits		0
Therefore, Estate Tax Savings with the Trust Structure Is	$ 435,800	
and the Net to the Beneficiaries Is	$2,000,000	

Postmortem Planning

There are often effective methods of reducing estate taxes. The estate can select a fiscal year for income tax purposes. The benefits to this are twofold: Income taxes on the income of the estate can be delayed, and the distributions received from the estate by a beneficiary will be included in that persons income tax return for the following year (as opposed to the year of receipt).

An estate can choose to deduct most of the expenses it incurs during the administration of the estate on either its income or estate tax returns. In order for the beneficiaries to get the benefit of certain losses and deductions of the estate in excess of the income for the final year, these should be paid in the year of termination.

If a noncitizen spouse receives an inheritance that is not in the appropriate form of a qualified domestic trust, she or he can create such a trust and contribute the inheritance to it and in that way preserve the marital deduction and the deferral of the estate taxes until his or her demise.

Disclaimers can be filed in order to both increase and decrease the marital share.

If a surviving spouse is entitled to the distribution of qualified retirement plan benefits and is subject to an excise tax of 15 percent, he or she can elect to roll the obligation over and postpone payment.

QTIP and QDOT treatment can be elected. If a spouse becomes a U.S. citizen before the estate tax return is filed, the QDOT format will not be necessary.

There are certain income tax elections that a surviving spouse must consider, such as:

- Not claiming any commissions (compensation) as an executor or personal representative
- Making a rollover of a lump-sum retirement plan distribution
- Electing to file a joint final income tax return for federal and state purposes with the deceased spouse

In connection with generation-skipping trusts that are subject to generation-skipping tax (GST), which are discussed in detail in chapter 12, distributions to a grandchild for medical expenses or to pay tuition will not be subject to this type of tax.

An election has to be made to step-up the basis of interest inherited in a partnership.

A beneficiary who might inherit property subject to GST could renounce an amount over the exemption level ($1,100,000 in 2002).

An election can be made to report interest on government savings bonds on the final income tax return of the deceased person.

Private Annuities

A private annuity, as distinguished from a commercial annuity, is an arrangement between an individual owner (annuitant-transferor) and another person or entity (obligor-transferee) whereby property is transferred in exchange for cash and an unsecured promise to pay a fixed amount for the annuitant's life.

The Internal Revenue Service has approved a cost-of-living adjustment that was an integral part of the private annuity agreement. Thus, a private annuity can not only ensure a lifetime arrangement of income but also guard against the ravages of inflation. As a general rule, the private annuity works best as an estate-freezing device when the annuitant is in poor health. However, in view of present Revenue rulings and case law, a private annuity arrangement can be created even when an individual is afflicted with an incurable condition, so long as the condition has not proceeded to the point where death is (1) imminent within a year and (2) predictable.

Estate and Income Tax Advantages of Private Annuities

If you own property that has high appreciation potential, such as your own business or undeveloped real estate, you should consider steps that you can take today to reduce the future tax cost of transferring such property to your children or other beneficiaries. If you retain the property until your death and the property appreciates substantially, there will be a corresponding increase in the size of your taxable estate.

The private annuity is one alternative to head off a significant estate tax increase. It also offers a number of income tax and practical advantages. The strategy is this: You transfer to a child (or other individual) in exchange for the child's promise to make annual payments to you for your life. There is no gift tax on the transfer provided that the value of the property does not exceed the present value of the payments, as determined under the tables in the Code. The interest factor used in applying the Code tables changes monthly. Thus, the present value of an annuity fluctuates with interest rate movements. When interest rates are relatively low, property can be transferred, without gift tax costs, for smaller payments by the younger family member than would be required when interest rates are higher.

Estate Tax Advantages

Transferring property in exchange for annuity payments removes the property from your taxable estate for estate tax purposes. Unless your death is imminent at the time of the transfer, this result will be achieved even if you die shortly after the transfer.

The annuity payments that you receive will be included in your taxable estate. You can avoid this result, however, by using the payments to make tax-free annual gifts to children, grandchildren, and other beneficiaries.

Income Tax Advantages

A private annuity offers an income tax advantage if you are transferring a capital asset that already has increased in value from the time you acquired it. Unlike an ordinary sale, with an annuity you do not pay tax on the entire capital gain in the year of the transfer. Instead, your gain is spread out over your lifetime. This may reduce your taxes in other ways, such as by keeping your income below a level that would trigger the reduction or loss of itemized deductions or other tax benefits or that would trigger taxation of social security benefits.

A private annuity also has an advantage over an installment sale. With an installment sale, depreciation recapture income is taxed in the year of the sale, regardless of when payments are made, and a resale of the property by the purchaser could accelerate the seller's deferred gain. With a private annuity, any recapture is taxed as payments are made, and a resale of the property by the child has no impact on the annuitant's tax situation.

Practical Advantages

Private annuities also offer practical advantages. A private annuity can relieve you of a burden of managing business or investment property. In addition, private annuities can save estate administration costs because the transferred property is removed from your probate estate.

The estate tax and other advantages outlined above can be achieved only if the property is transferred in exchange for your child's (or other individual's) unsecured promise to make the annuity payments. The estate planning benefits may be lost if you retain any interest in the property or if the payments are tied to the property's income.

The Federal Estate Tax Restated

What is the federal estate tax?

The federal estate tax is a tax imposed by the federal government on the transfer of property of a deceased person at the time of his or her death. The amount of tax depends on the value of the property transferred that is included in the estate of such person. The total value of the property transferred, less certain deductions and, in 2002, a $1,000,000 exemption equivalent amount, is subject to estate tax at graduated rates. The current rates under the Act range from 39 percent on the first $250,000 in the estate above the $1,000,000 exemption to 50 percent on amounts over $2,500,000 in the estate.

What property is included in the gross estate?

In general, the federal estate tax is imposed on any property owned or controlled by you that passes to someone else at your death.

Are there any exemptions or credits that can alter the federal estate tax?

Yes. The most important is the exemption equivalent ($675,0000 in 2001) that comes from the unified credit against federal estate and gift taxes that every person is entitled to.

Basically, every person has a tax credit ($220,550 in 2001) that can be applied against federal estate and gift taxes. If a person does not make any taxable lifetime gifts, and therefore does not use any of his or her unified credit during life, the unified credit covers the equivalent amount of property included in the decedent's estate.

The unified credit relieves people who have less than the credit value in property in their estate from paying any federal estate tax or even filing a federal estate tax return.

What happens if a person dies owning more than the equivalent amount of property?

The legal representative of your estate is required to file a federal estate tax return and pay any tax that is due within nine months following your death. An estate can file an amended estate tax return and file a claim for a refund no later than three years from the date the return was filed or two years from the date the estate tax was paid, whichever is later.

If a person has more than the exemption amount in the estate passing at death, does this mean that federal estate tax always has to be paid?

No. In this case, a federal estate tax return has to be filed, but there may not be any tax due. That is because there are deductions that may reduce the taxable estate and cause the federal estate tax that is due to be covered entirely by your unified credit.

The most important deduction is usually the marital deduction. Any amounts included in the estate that pass to your surviving spouse, or pass into certain types of trusts for the spouse's benefit, qualify for the unlimited marital deduction. This deduction basically means that no federal estate tax is due on such property at the first spouse's death.

The Taxpayer Relief Act of 1997

The Taxpayer Relief Act of 1997 (the "Act") signed by the President on August 5, 1997 is the first tax legislation in many years to enact a number of provisions involving reductions and tax credits in the areas of estates, gifts, sale of residences, and capital gains.

The following is an overview of the relevant estate and gift tax provisions:

Unified Credit

The law increased the unified credit against the estate and gift tax to an effective exemption of $625,000 for decedents dying and gifts made in 1998; $650,000 in 1999; $675,000 in 2000 and 2001; $700,000 in 2002 and 2003; $850,000 in 2004; $950,000 in 2005; and $1 million in 2006 and thereafter. Each person who has executed a living trust or will containing a credit shelter trust provision should have, at such time, reexamined it to be sure the exempt amount was not expressed in a specific dollar amount.

Cost of Living Adjustments

Four estate and gift tax provisions are indexed for inflation after December 31, 1998:

1. The $10,000 annual gift tax exclusion
2. The $1 million generation-skipping transfer tax
3. The $1 million of value of a closely held business eligible for the low interest rate in installment payments of estate tax. The Act also reduced the interest rate on the estate of a decedent dying after December 31, 1997 to 2 percent on the first $1 million of taxable value. The interest rate imposed on the amount of the deferred estate tax attributable to the business in excess of $1 million of taxable value was equal to 45 percent of the interest rate applicable to underpayments of tax.

   If the estate of a decedent who died before 1998 elected installment payments under Code Sec. 6166, the fiduciary could elect

before January 1, 1999 to have the new provisions apply to installment payments due after the effective date of the election. However, no deduction would be allowed for estate tax or income tax purposes for the interest paid on the deferred estate taxes.
4. The $750,000 special use value.

Exclusion for Qualified Family-Owned Businesses

This new exclusion permits the fiduciary of an estate to elect special estate tax treatment for qualified "family-owned business interests" if such interests comprise more than 50 percent of a decedent's adjusted gross estate and certain other requirements are met. For decedents dying after December 31, 1997, this provision, together with the unified credit, can effectively exclude the first $1.3 million of value in qualified family-owned business interests from a taxable estate. However, this exclusion is reduced by the unified credit, so it is $675,000 in the year 1998 and $300,000 in the year 2006.

To qualify for this exclusion, a family-owned business interest is any interest in a business principally located in the United States and owned at least 50 percent by one family, 70 percent by two families, or 90 percent by three families, as long as the decedent's family owns at least 30 percent of the business. Each business owned by the decedent and members of the decedent's family is subject to separate testing to determine if it is a qualified business interest. The benefit of this exclusion is generally recaptured if no qualified heir remains active or the business is disposed of within ten years of the decedent's death. This exclusion is available for estates of persons dying after December 31, 1997.

Gift Revaluation

In calculating prior taxable gifts for estate tax purposes, the Act provided that for gifts made after August 5, 1997, a gift for which the statute of limitations has passed cannot be revalued for purposes of determining the applicable estate tax bracket and available unified credit. However, the statute of limitations will not run on inadequately disclosed gifts made in calendar years ending after August 5, 1997, regardless of whether a gift tax return was filed for other transfers in that same year. The timely filing of a gift tax return starts the running of the statute of limitations for assessment of additional gift taxes. The Code provides that the amount of any tax imposed severally must be assessed within three years after the return is filed. This can be extended to six years if the gift tax return omits items that are properly included having a value in excess of 25 percent of the total amount of gifts set forth in the return.

The statute of limitations will run only if a gift tax return is filed. If no return is filed or if a fraudulent return is filed with the intent to evade tax, there is no period of limitations and a deficiency may be assessed at any time.

Revocable Trusts
A transfer from a revocable or living trust will be treated as if made directly by the grantor, for decedents dying after August 5, 1997. Therefore, annual exclusion gifts made from such a trust within three years of the grantor's death are not included in the gross estate of the grantor.

Expansion of Generation-Skipping Transfer Tax Exception
For generation-skipping transfers occurring after December 31, 1997, the predeceased parent exception to the generation-skipping transfer tax has been expanded to include transfers to collateral heirs (e.g., grand-nieces and grandnephews), provided the decedent has no living lineal descendants at the time of the transfer.

Capital Gain Rate Reduction
The Act reduced the maximum individual rate of tax on net capital gains from the then current rate of 28 percent to 20 percent, provided that any capital gain incurred by an individual in the 10 percent tax bracket is taxed at a rate of 10 percent. These rates apply for purposes of both the regular tax and the alternative minimum tax and are effective for sales, exchanges, and installment payments received after May 6, 1997. The current 28 percent maximum rate would continue to apply to sales or exchanges of property held more than one year but not more than eighteen months and collectibles held for more than one year. In addition, for tax years beginning after December 31, 2000, the maximum rate on net capital gains would be reduced 2 percent for property held more than five years. To qualify for the reduction from 20 percent to 18 percent, the property must be acquired after December 31, 2000. A gain from the sale of depreciable real property may be subject to at least three different rates: (1) ordinary rates on the accelerated depreciation, if any; (2) the maximum rate of 25 percent on straight-line depreciation; and (3) the maximum rate of 20 percent of any excess gain.

Sale of Principal Residence
Under the Act, an individual is able to exclude $250,000 ($500,000 on a joint return) of gain realized on the sale or exchange of a principal res-

idence after May 6, 1997. The reinvestment of sales proceeds and age-fifty-five exclusion are no longer considerations for excluding a gain on the sale of one's principal residence. The exclusion can be used many times but generally not more than once every two years. To be eligible, generally a person must own the residence and occupy it for at least two of the five years prior to the sale or exchange.

State Estate and Gift Tax Law

On August 7, 1997, Governor George Pataki signed into law estate and gift tax provisions (the "Legislation") placing New York on a level with the vast majority of states. Prior to this Legislation, in 1995, New York took a step toward reformation by permitting an estate a deduction for the net value of an individual's principal residence of up to $250,000. The deduction is not allowed for that part of the residence that passes to charity or for which a marital deduction is claimed.

Estate Tax

The Legislation increased New York's unified credit of $500 against the estate tax, which is equivalent to an exemption of $115,000 in property, to $300,000 in property on and after October 1, 1998 and further increases it to the equivalent of the federal unified credit on and after February 1, 2000.

The New York State estate tax was repealed in the case of persons dying on and after February 1, 2000 and replaced with a pickup or sponge tax.

New York State is therefore in the same position as the vast majority of states in the country, including the sun-belt group (Arizona, California, and Florida). The state estate tax imposed in those states is only that which equals the "state death tax credit," which means that the total federal and state estate tax payable is equal only to the federal estate tax and no more. Following the subsection on gift tax, below, is a chart that sets forth the transfer taxes imposed by the states.

Gift Tax

For gift tax purposes, the unified credit property equivalent was increased to $300,000 for gifts made on or after January 1, 1999. The state gift tax was repealed for all gifts made on or after January 1, 2000, which means that at this time, based upon current laws, the only states that have a gift tax are Connecticut, Louisiana, North Carolina, and Tennessee, in addition to the commonwealth of Puerto Rico.

	INHERITANCE TAX	ADD'L ESTATE TAX FOR FED. CREDIT	ESTATE TAX	FOR FEDERAL CREDIT ONLY	GIFT TAX
Alabama*				•	
Alaska				•	
Arizona*				•	
Arkansas				•	
California*				•	
Colorado*				•	
Connecticut*	•	•			•
Delaware	•	•			
District of Columbia				•	
Florida*				•	
Georgia				•	
Hawaii*				•	
Idaho*				•	
Illinois*				•	
Indiana*	•	•			
Iowa*	•	•			
Kansas*	•	•			
Kentucky	•	•			
Louisiana	•	•			•
Maine				•	
Maryland*	•	•			
Massachusetts*				•	
Michigan*				•	
Minnesota				•	
Mississippi				•	
Missouri*				•	
Montana*	•	•			
Nebraska*	•	•			
Nevada*				•	
New Hampshire	•	•			
New Jersey	•	•			
New Mexico				•	
New York*		•[1]	•[1]	•[2]	•[3]
North Carolina*	•	•			•
North Dakota			•		
Ohio*		•	•		
Oklahoma		•	•		
Oregon				•	

	INHERITANCE TAX	ADD'L ESTATE TAX FOR FED. CREDIT	ESTATE TAX	FORFEDERAL CREDIT ONLY	GIFT TAX
Pennsylvania	•	•			
Puerto Rico			•		•
Rhode Island*				•	
South Carolina*				•	
South Dakota	•	•			
Tennessee*	•	•			•
Texas*				•	
Utah				•	
Vermont				•	
Virginia*				•	
Washington*				•	
West Virginia				•	
Wisconsin				•	
Wyoming				•	

*This state also imposes a generation-skipping transfer tax equal to the federal credit

[1]Repealed 2/1/2000   [2]Effective 2/1/2000   [3]Repealed 1/1/2000

The Taxpayer Relief Act of 1997: Tax Exclusions, Credits, and Exemptions

	APPLICABLE UNIFIED GIFT AND ESTATE TAX EXCLUSION	APPLICABLE UNIFIED GIFT AND ESTATE TAX CREDIT	QUALIFIED FAMILY-OWNED-BUSINESS EXCLUSION	ANNUAL GIFT TAX EXCLUSION INDEXED AT ASSUMED 3% INFLATION	GST EXEMPTION INDEXED AT ASSUMED 3% INFLATION
1998	$ 625,000	$202,050	$675,000	$10,000	$1,000,000
1999	$ 650,000	$211,300	$650,000	$10,000	$1,030,000
2000	$ 675,000	$220,550	$625,000	$10,000	$1,060,000
2001	$ 675,000	$220,550	$625,000	$10,000	$1,090,000
2002	$ 700,000	$229,800	$600,000	$11,000	$1,120,000
2003	$ 700,000	$229,800	$600,000	$11,000	$1,150,000
2004	$ 850,000	$287,300	$450,000	$11,000	$1,190,000
2005	$ 950,000	$326,300	$350,000	$12,000	$1,220,000
2006	$1,000,000	$345,800	$300,000	$12,000	$1,260,000

Legislative Update

The Economic Growth and Tax Relief Reconciliation Act of 2001 ("the Act") revised certain estate, gift, and generation-skipping transfer tax provisions of the Internal Revenue Code as follows:

Repeal of Estate and Generation-Skipping Transfer Taxes
The Act repeals the estate tax for decedents dying after 2009. The Act also specifies that the generation-skipping transfer tax is repealed for transfers made after 2009. The Act does not repeal the gift tax.

Along with the repeal of the rest of the estate tax in 2010, the Act repeals the provision imposing an estate tax on the value of the property remaining in a Qualified Domestic Trust at the death of a noncitizen surviving spouse beneficiary. However, the Act retains, through December 31, 2020, the provision imposing an estate tax on lifetime distributions to a surviving spouse from a Qualified Domestic Trust created by a decedent dying before 2010.

Reductions of Estate and Gift Tax Rates
Beginning in 2002 and continuing through 2009, the Act reduces the maximum estate and gift tax rates. For decedents dying in and gifts made in 2002, the Act eliminates the two highest rate brackets 50 percent for transfers over $2,500,000 and eliminates the 5 percent surtax (which phases out the graduated estate and gift tax rates) applicable to transfers over $10 million. For subsequent years, the Act specifies that the maximum rates for decedents dying and gifts made in a particular year are: (1) 49 percent in 2003; (2) 48 percent in 2004; (3) 47 percent in 2005; (4) 46 percent in 2006; and (5) 45 percent in 2007–2009. The tax rate used for generation-skipping transfers prior to repeal is reduced as the highest estate tax rate declines.

After 2009, The Act sets the highest gift tax rate at 35 percent. Applicable to gifts made after this date, the Act provides that a transfer in trust is a taxable gift unless the entire trust is treated as a grantor trust for income tax purposes as to the donor or the donor's spouse and except as provided by regulations.

Increase in Exemption Equivalent of Unified Credit, Lifetime Gifts Exemption, and GST Exemption Amounts
The Act increases the unified credit effective exemption amount (the applicable credit amount) to: (1) $1,000,000 for estates of decedents dying in 2002–2003; (2) $1,500,000 for estates of decedents dying in 2004–2005; (3) $2,000,000 for estates of decedents dying in 2006–2008; and (4) $3,500,000 for estates of decedents dying in 2009. For gifts made after 2001, the Act establishes an effective lifetime exemption amount for gift tax purposes equal to $1,000,000. The Act continues the GST exemption amount as under present law through the end of 2003. For 2004-2009, the Act specifies the GST exemption amount as the same

amount as the unified credit exemption amount applicable to decedents' estates in those years.

The Act also repeals the deduction for qualified family-owned business interests for estates of decedents dying after 2003.

Reduction of Credit for State Death Taxes
For estates of decedents dying in 2002, the Act provides that the state death tax credit allowed cannot exceed 75 percent of the credit otherwise determined. For estates of decedents dying in 2003, the Act specifies that the applicable percentage of the credit is 50 percent of the state death tax credit. For estates of decedents dying in 2004, the Act provides that the applicable percentage of the credits is 25 percent of the state death tax credit.

Credit for State Death Taxes Replaced with Deduction for Such Taxes
In 2005, the Act replaces the §2011 credit state death taxes with a deduction for death taxes (i.e, estate tax, inheritance, legacy, or succession taxes) actually paid to any state or the District of Columbia pertaining to property included in a decedent's gross estate. To qualify for the new §2058 deduction, the Act provides that the state death taxes must be paid and claimed before the later of: (1) four years after the decedent's estate tax return is filed; or (2) (a) sixty days after a decision of the Tax Court redetermining an estate tax deficiency becomes final; (b) the expiration of a §6166 or §6161 extension period for paying the estate taxes; or (c) the later of the expiration of sixty days from the date the Internal Revenue Service mails a notice disallowing a refund claim, sixty days after a court decision regarding a refund claim becomes final, or two years after a waiver of a notice of disallowance for a refund claim is filed. For estates of decedents dying after 2004, the Act also repeals the credit for certain state death taxes allowable against the GST tax.

Termination of Step-Up Basis at Death
The Act provides that the present rules relating to the basis of property acquired from a decedent, which provide for a stepped-up basis for such property, will not apply to decedents dying after 2009.

Treatment of Property Acquired from a Decedent Dying after 2009
The Act provides that beginning in 2010 property acquired from a decedent will be treated as if acquired by a gift, and recipients of such property will receive a basis equal to the lesser of the decedent's adjusted basis in the property or the fair market value of property on the date of the decedent's death.

The Act includes as property acquired from the decedent: (1) property acquired by bequest, devise, or inheritance or by the decedent's estate from the decedent; (2) property transferred by the decedent to a qualified revocable trust or to any other trust with respect to which the decedent reserved a power to alter, amend, or terminate the trust; and (3) other property passing from the decedent without consideration.

The Act permits a decedent's estate to increase the basis of assets transferred, as determined on an asset-by-asset basis, by up to a total of $1.3 million and to further increase the basis of assets by the amount of the decedent's unused capital losses, net operating losses, and certain built-in losses. The Act also permits an additional $3 million increase to the basis of outright transfer property and qualified terminable interest property transferred to a surviving spouse. The Act permits nonresidents who are not U.S. citizens to increase the basis of property by up to $60,000. In no case, however, may the basis of an asset be adjusted above its fair market value. The Act provides that these amounts be adjusted for inflation after 2010.

The Act allows the basis of property to be increased above the decedent's adjusted basis only if the property was owned or treated as owned by the decedent at the time of the decedent's death. The Act applies special ownership rules to property the decedent held jointly with another, treats the decedent as owning property transferred by the decedent during his or her lifetime to a qualified revocable trust, and treats the decedent as owning the surviving spouse's one-half share of community property if at least one-half of the property was owned by, and acquired from, the decedent.

The Act provides that a decedent is not treated as owning property solely by holding a power of appointment with respect to that property. In addition, the Act provides that property is not eligible for a basis increase if acquired by the decedent by gift during the three-year period ending on the date of the decedent's death, if the property constitutes a right to receive income in respect of the decedent or if the property consists of stock or securities of certain foreign and international companies.

The Act provides that gain will not be recognized at the time of death if the estate or heir acquires from the decedent property subject to a liability greater than the decedent's basis in the property, and no gain will be recognized by the estate on the distribution of such property to a beneficiary by reason of the liability.

The Act extends to the estate and heirs the income tax exclusion of up to $250,000 of gain on the sale of a principal residence, such that if the decedent's estate or heir sells the decedent's principal residence, $250,000 of the gain can be excluded on the sale of the residence, provided the decedent and/or the heir used the property as a principal residence for two or more years during the five-year period prior to the sale.

The Act provides for the recognition of gain or loss on the transfer of property in satisfaction of a pecuniary bequest only to the extent the fair market value of the property at the time of the transfer exceeds the fair market value on the date of decedent's death, not the property's carry-over basis.

For transfers at death of noncash assets in excess of $1.3 million and appreciated property the value of which exceeds $25,000 received by the decedent within three years of death, the Act requires the executor of the estate to report certain information to the Internal Revenue Service and to the beneficiary; any failure to report the required information will result in monetary penalties. No penalty will be imposed if the failure to report the information is due to reasonable causes, but further penalties will result if the failure to report is due to an intentional disregard for the rules.

Expansion of Availability of Installment Payment for Estates with Interests in Qualifying Lending and Finance Businesses

The Act expands availability of the installment payment provisions by providing that a decedent's estate with an interest in a qualifying lending and financing business is eligible for installment payment of estate tax. The Act also provides that an estate with an interest in a qualifying lending and financing business that claims installment payment of estate tax must make all installment payments (including principal and interest) over five years. These provisions are effective for decedents dying after 2001.

Generation-Skipping Transfer Tax

Deemed allocation of the generation-skipping transfer tax exemption to lifetime transfers to trusts that are direct skips. Under the Act, the generation-skipping transfer tax exemption will be allocated automatically to lifetime transfers that are "indirect skips." An indirect skip is any transfer of property (that is not a direct skip) subject to the gift tax that is made to a generation-skipping transfer trust, according to the Act. The Act also defines a generation-skipping transfer trust.

In addition, the Act provides that, if any individual makes an indirect skip during the individual's lifetime, then any unused portion of that individual's generation-skipping transfer tax exemption is allocated to the property transferred to the extent necessary to produce the lowest possible inclusion ratio for that property.

Sunset Provision

In order to comply with the Congressional Budget Act of 1974, the 2001 Act provides that all provisions of, and amendments made by, the 2001 Act shall not apply to estates of decedents dying, gifts made, or generation-skipping transfers after December 31, 2010 (Act. Sec. 901(a)(2)). The IRC (Internal Revenue Code) will thereafter be applied and administered as if these provisions and amendments had not been enacted.

Apparently, this provision was included to insure compliance with the federal budget law. It is anticipated that this provision will be removed in later legislation.

The Act
Exemption Equivalent Rates of Tax

YEAR	EXEMPTION EQUIVALENT (APPLICABLE EXCLUSION AMOUNT)—ESTATE AND GST AT DEATH	MAXIMUM ESTATE AND GIFT TAX RATE
2002	$1,000,000	50%
2003	1,000,000	49%
2004	1,500,000	48%
2005	1,500,000	47%
2006	2,000,000	46%
2007	2,000,000	45%
2008	2,000,000	45%
2009	3,500,000	45%

Beginning with gifts made in 2002, the Applicable Exclusion Amount for gift tax purposes will be increased to $1 million (2002–2009). For gifts made after the estate tax repeal (2010 and thereafter), the amount of the credit allowed against the gift tax will be equal to (1) the amount of the tentative tax reduced by (2) the sum of the amounts allowable as a credit for all preceding calendar periods.

For gifts made after December 31, 2009, the gift tax will be computed using a rate schedule having a top marginal rate of 35 percent. The top rate will apply to amounts over $500,000. The 2001 Act also reduces the top marginal income tax rate to 35 percent, effective in the year 2006.

Gift Tax Rates—2010

IF THE AMOUNT IS: OVER (1)	BUT NOT OVER (2)	TAX ON (1)	RATE ON EXCESS OVER (1)
$ 0	$ 10,000	$ 0	18%
10,000	20,000	1,800	20
20,000	40,000	3,800	22
40,000	60,000	8,200	24
60,000	80,000	13,000	26
80,000	100,000	18,200	28
100,000	150,000	23,800	30
150,000	250,000	38,800	32
250,000	500,000	70,800	34
500,000	—	155,800	35

Observations

- If there is no further legislative action by Congress, the law in effect on May 26, 2001 would return on January 1, 2011. The Act repeals the estate tax but retains the gift tax. Since the gift tax will be retained, it looks like Congress wants to discourage income shifting that might otherwise be possible. However, the gift tax plays an important part in shifting income.
- The state death tax credit currently in effect under the Code Sec. 2011 remains in effect through December 31, 2004, subject to reduction by the applicable percentage. For estates of decedents dying after December 31, 2004, the state estate tax is treated as a deduction rather than a credit. Therefore, the state death tax credit is eliminated prior to full estate tax repeal. The majority of the states that have the "sop," "sponge," or "pick-up" tax may need to consider enacting estate, inheritance, and/or succession taxes to make up for the revenue loss due to the elimination of the credit.
- Life insurance will still play a role in estate planning after full estate tax repeal, as a family may wish to insure against the potential capital gains tax resulting from the carryover basis provisions.
- Decreasing term life insurance is a possibility as estate tax repeal approaches. However, if the estate tax is not repealed, it could be more costly or impossible to purchase replacement insurance.
- In light of the repeal, the reduction of the estate and gift tax rates and the increase in the estate, gift, and generation-skipping transfers tax exemption, planning strategies may depend in large part on your circumstances. The elder generation who may not live to see repeal should continue to reduce their estates, for estate tax purposes, by employing the typical leveraged techniques.

- Pending repeal, the surviving spouse should be the main beneficiary to permit the deferral of the estate tax, where the spouse may survive until after repeal (if in fact repeal ever really occurs).
- The increases in the applicable exclusion amount should be utilized. However, any state gift tax that may be imposed (as of now only Connecticut, Louisiana, North Carolina, Tennessee, and Puerto Rico) needs to be taken into account.

The following significant events will take place in the year 2010:
- The estate and generation-skipping tax will be repealed.
- The step-up in the basis will be limited for assets transferred at death.
- The maximum gift tax rate will be reduced to 35 percent.
- Life insurance will continue to be a valuable asset, but its emphasis for use will be shifted to liabilities for income tax as opposed to estate tax.
- At the death of the first spouse, $1.3 million of gains can be passed on to heirs and $3 million of gains can be passed to the surviving spouse. The surviving spouse can pass $1.3 million of capital gains upon his or her death. Therefore, married persons will be able to transfer at death the aggregate of $5.6 million at a stepped-up basis.
- If you plan to survive the repeal of the estate tax, under the Act it would be appropriate to die, not anytime after December 31, 2009, but between January 1, 2010 and December 31, 2010, since the "sunset provision" provides for the law as it was in effect on May 26, 2001, to return on January 1, 2011.

Federal Gift Tax Rate Schedule Under the Act

TAXABLE AMOUNT OVER	TAXABLE AMOUNT NOT OVER	TAX ON AMOUNT IN COLUMN 1	RATE OF TAX ON EXCESS OVER AMOUNT IN COLUMN 1 (PERCENT)
$ 0	$ 10,000	$ 0	18
10,000	20,000	1,800	20
20,000	40,000	3,800	22
40,000	60,000	8,200	24
60,000	80,000	13,000	26
80,000	100,000	18,200	28
100,000	150,000	23,800	30
150,000	250,000	38,800	32
250,000	500,000	70,800	34
500,000	750,000	155,800	37
750,000	1,000,000	248,300	39
1,000,000	1,250,000	345,800	41
1,250,000	1,500,000	448,300	43
1,500,000	2,000,000	555,800	45
2,000,000	2,500,000	780,800	49
2,500,000		1,025,800	50

CHAPTER 10

Gifts

$\mathcal{E}$very complete estate plan should include a lifetime gift giving program. The end result of making gifts while you are alive, and the use of the various strategies that are available, is the potential savings of substantial amounts of estate taxes. Gift planning during your lifetime requires a multitude of considerations, the first of which is the tax consideration. Gift taxes, both federal and state, may be levied on certain transfers. The form of the intended gift is equally as important. Whether the gift should be outright or placed in trust should be considered. Choosing which property to give away is another important consideration.

This chapter outlines this information in extensive detail, including what are allowable gifts, and when you can make tax-free gifts. Charitable gifts and gifts between spouses, which are discussed at length, have important impacts because of their tax deductibility. Gifts to a noncitizen resident spouse require special planning in order to be effective.

The making of a gift and the establishment of a gift-giving pattern involve income, gift, and estate tax considerations. All of these are explained in this chapter, in addition to the ability of a person to renounce a gift.

The federal tax rate on gifts is the same as the estate tax rate on property transferred at death. The federal estate and gift tax systems are "unified," so that if you make taxable gifts totaling $400,000 while you are alive, only property equivalent to the balance of the exemption amount can be transferred to those other than your spouse, free of federal estate tax when you die. Gift taxes aren't actually paid until the credit is used up—that is, until you've given away the amount of the exemption.

Definition of Gift

A gift is a transfer of property without adequate and full consideration in money or money's worth. To be considered a gift, the transfer is complete when it leaves the person who makes the gift, and that person retains no power to change the disposition of the property, either for his or her own or another's benefit.

Exclusion

Gifts made in a given calendar year are taxable minus the allowable exclusions and exemptions. The exclusions are: (1) the annual exclusion; and (2) amounts paid on behalf of another person for certain educational expenses and for medical care.

The annual exclusion permits you to exclude up to $11,000 in gifts to each separate recipient each year, or $22,000 if a husband and wife elect to split the gift. Generally, if a gift is split, a lower gift tax bracket is applicable to the total taxable gift. In addition to the annual exclusion, the unified credit of each spouse applies to a split gift. If the gift is made in trust, you are entitled to the annual exclusion for each trust beneficiary. Where one spouse makes a gift, the spouses may treat the gift as having been made by both, and each may then claim the annual exclusion for that gift.

A gift of a "future interest" does not qualify for the annual exclusion. Any gift of an immediate interest in trust income is a gift of a "present interest." If, however, the power to divert the trust income to other beneficiaries or to accumulate or distribute the income is at the trustee's discretion, the gift is one of a future interest. Giving the beneficiary of a trust a "Crummey Power," i.e., the right to withdraw property from the trust when it is contributed to the trust, is considered a general power of appointment, and this thus gives a beneficiary a present interest in the trust. A contribution to a trust containing this provision would then qualify the gift for the annual gift tax exclusion.

Gifts to minors will also qualify for the annual exclusion, provided that all of the following apply:

- The custodian may expend principal and income for the benefit of the minor prior to the minor's reaching age twenty-one.
- The unexpended principal and income pass to the minor at age twenty-one.
- If the minor dies before age twenty-one, the property passes to the minor's estate or to persons appointed by the minor under a general power of appointment.

The exclusion may still be claimed if minors attain majority at age eighteen under state law. Gifts to minors made pursuant to the Uniform Gifts to Minors Act or the Model Gifts of Securities to Minors Act qualify for the annual exclusion as well.

An unlimited gift tax exclusion is allowed for tuition payments made directly to educational organizations and for unreimbursed payments made directly to health care providers for medical services, where these payments are made on behalf of another person. These exclusions are allowed in unlimited amounts in addition to the annual exclusion.

The Unified Credit ("Exemption Equivalent")

Each person has a unified credit for transfer taxes that may be applied against gift or estate taxes. The unified credit, therefore, describes the amount of property that can be sheltered or protected from gift taxes in addition to the gift tax exclusions that are available. In 2002, the federal unified credit is $345,800, which is the equivalent of the value of $1,000,000 in property. New York State's unified credit of $500 was equivalent to $300,000 in property. (For a detailed discussion of the far-reaching expansion of the unified credit, see chapter 9.) The use of the unified credit permits you to avoid gift tax. This means that you can give property equivalent to the exempt amount to persons other than your spouse and incur no liability for federal gift tax purposes. If gifts are split between spouses (made on the basis of electing one-half each), no federal gift tax will be imposed until the entire worth of both exemptions have been used. The amount of the unified credit that you use up during your lifetime reduces, on a dollar equivalent basis, the amount you have available for estate tax exclusion when you die.

Charitable and Marital Deductions

The gift tax charitable and marital deductions have the same basic requirements as their estate tax counterparts. The gift tax charitable deduction is also unlimited and available for gifts to the same recipients as would qualify as a bequest for the estate tax deduction. The same restrictions apply to gifts of property to charity where some of the interests in the property are noncharitable. These gifts must take one of a number of prescribed forms, such as a charitable remainder annuity trust or unitrust. For a more detailed discussion of charitable gifts, see chapter 11.

There is an unlimited marital deduction for gifts made between spouses. In other words, one spouse may transfer unlimited amounts of assets to the other spouse without worrying about gift tax liability as long as the transfer meets the requirements of the Code for deduction; i.e., an outright gift or, if in trust, in the form of a QTIP trust or an estate trust in which the recipient beneficiary spouse is given the right to direct the disposition of the principal upon his or her death. A gift tax return need not be filed if a donor's gift qualifies for the marital deduction.

Disclaimers

A person may refuse to accept a gift by executing a qualified disclaimer, thereby causing the interest in the gift to transfer to another person. That transfer will not be considered as a gift if the formalities for a qualified disclaimer are followed. A qualified disclaimer must meet all of the following requirements:

- The disclaimer must be in writing—it must describe the interest disclaimed and must be signed by the disclaimant or his or her legal representative.
- The disclaimer must be received by the maker of the gift or executor (in the case of disclaimers of bequests) within nine months of the creation of the property interest (usually at the death of the estate owner) or nine months of the date the recipient of the gift turns twenty-one.
- The disclaimant must not have accepted the interest or any of its benefits.

Computation of Gift Tax

The rate of tax is determined by the total amount of all gifts you make during the calendar year in question and in all the preceding years since June 6, 1932. The rates range from 37 percent to 50 percent plus any state gift taxes.

The maker of the gift is responsible for paying the gift tax. If he or she dies before doing so, the executor or administrator of the estate must pay it out of the estate, or if there be no such person, the heirs are liable.

Considerations in Making Gifts

Strategies should be developed for lifetime giving. You may have a variety of personal and financial reasons for making gifts. You may want to experience the pleasure of sharing accumulated wealth with family members or a favorite charity. You may wish to assure that certain persons receive particular gifts now rather than risking uncertainty in distribution after your death. You may want to see firsthand the way a recipient handles a gift.

In order to select the most efficient and cost-effective way, you need to pose certain questions, such as the following:

- What should be given to one recipient rather than another?
- What is the most appropriate vehicle or instrument for making the gift?
- What time schedule for the gift is desirable?
- What are the financial and tax consequences of these choices?
- Are there less expensive alternatives available?

Net Gift Technique

The net gift technique involves a gift made on condition that the recipient of the gift pay the gift tax. However, it cannot be employed until the donor's unified credit has been used up. In addition, when the person who receives the gift pays the federal gift tax, the maker of the gift might be required to pay income tax if the gift tax required to be paid by the donee exceeds the donor's cost basis in the gifted property.

Gifts to a Spouse

Gifts to a spouse may be made outright, in joint ownership, or in trust. Apart from your personal motives in making gifts to your spouse, the owner will find both advantages and difficulties in each of these respective methods of gift giving.

Income Tax Considerations

Gifts between spouses consisting of income-producing property generally offer no income tax savings to the spouses. A couple filing a joint return is taxed at a lower rate than married persons filing separately with the same aggregate income. Moreover, the filing of separate income tax returns by an elderly couple might lead to additional tax liability with respect to half of their social security benefits. Those who file separately do not enjoy the "modified gross income" exemptions of $25,000 afforded to elderly single individuals filing individually and $32,000 for couples filing jointly. The only situation where tax savings can be realized by separate filings is where both spouses have taxable income and one has very high medical expenses, a substantial portion of which is not covered by Medicare or other health insurance.

A different picture, however, emerges in some states (e.g., New York) where tax rates for married spouses filing separate returns may be lower in the aggregate than the rate for a joint return. An elderly couple residing in such a state, particularly if its rates are high, might, therefore, reap some tax savings by transferring income-producing property to a spouse with a lower taxable income.

Gift and Estate Tax Savings

Gifts to a spouse may create a limited opportunity for estate tax savings for some elderly persons, but obviously not for persons having estates not subject to the estate tax. The estate of an estate owner who has made no taxable gifts after 1976 will not be subject to federal estate tax if he or she dies with an estate equal to the exemption amount or less.

Marital Deduction

Gifts between spouses enjoy an unlimited marital deduction for gift tax purposes and do not reduce the estate tax marital deduction. In most cases, there is no tax advantage in a transfer of property to a spouse during lifetime as compared with a transfer to that spouse at death. In either case, there will be no tax liability for the spouse making the gift. Instead, the transferred property will be taxable as part of the other spouse's estate.

Unified Credit

Gifts made to your spouse during your lifetime may produce estate tax savings if your spouse dies before you do and if you own substantially more property than your spouse does. This is particularly so if the estate of your spouse is less than the amount protected by the unified credit. Interspousal transfers may enable the estates of both spouses to take full advantage of the unified credit. By making gifts to your spouse, you can assure that you both will be able to fully utilize the unified credit. Such transfers would not be taxable, as they are covered by the unlimited gift tax marital deduction. By utilizing the unified credit in the combined estates of both spouses, the value of both exemptions can be bequeathed to others, free of federal estate tax.

In addition, if your spouse dies before you do and if the transferred property has a fair market value greater than the cost basis, the basis will be "stepped up" to market value sooner than if it had been retained by you. The basis of transferred property will not be stepped up if you gift the property to your spouse and he or she bequeaths the property to you and dies within one year of the gift transfer.

There are some risks and disadvantages in this arrangement. The spouse who has received the gift might squander it. Divorce is sometimes a possibility. If you die first, your spouse's cost basis in the gifted property will continue to be your original basis, rather than the basis at your death had you retained the property. Some risk can be reduced by making a QTIP gift in trust (see below) with the children receiving the remainder after the death of your spouse, or by purchasing life insurance on the life of your spouse with the children designated as both beneficiaries and owners of the policy.

QTIP Gifts to Spouse

With certain exceptions, if you give your spouse a gift of anything other than an outright gift, the value of the gift will not qualify for the marital deduction. The one exception to this rule allows you to control who will receive the property when your spouse's interest terminates and permits a marital deduction for the property that is a gift of qualified terminable interest property (QTIP). QTIP is property that you transfer to a trust created by you in which your spouse has a qualifying income interest for life and with respect to which you make an election that the property in trust be treated as QTIP. A qualifying income interest for life gives your spouse the right to all income from the property for life, payable at least annually, and prohibits distributions of the property held in the trust to anyone other than your spouse during his or her lifetime. A QTIP gift to a spouse has the same advantage as any other spousal gift, in that it may augment your spouse's estate so as to take advantage of the unified credit, while taking the property out of your estate.

At the death of your spouse, the balance of property remaining in the trust will pass to those persons you name in the trust agreement. You may name yourself as the remainder beneficiary. If you do, the property will be eligible for the marital deduction in your estate. If the trust property has a basis less than its fair market value at your spouse's death, it will receive a step up in basis. If, however, the objective of the gift was to assure that your spouse has sufficient property at his or her death to utilize fully his or her unified credit, retaining a reversionary interest would defeat the objective. This is so because in passing the property back to you, your spouse would not have used his or her credit to protect the property. The property would be covered by the marital deduction and would be fully subject to tax as part of your estate. If the property has appreciated beyond the unified credit amount at the time of your spouse's death, the following could be considered:

- The amount of property in the trust at the time of your spouse's death equal to the credit amount could be passed on to remainder beneficiaries other than yourself.

- The balance could be retained in a marital deduction (QTIP) trust for your benefit without paying any estate taxes on it at the time of your spouse's death. Upon your death, this portion of the trust would be includable in your estate for estate tax purposes.

A QTIP election is not always beneficial. It may be advantageous not to elect marital deduction treatment for lifetime gifts of a terminable interest. This alternative involves the donor's use of his or her unified credit to shelter the gift to the spouse and ultimately to permit the transfer of any appreciation in the property tax free to his or her children or grandchildren.

Example: In 2002, Robert has an estate of $2,000,000. He makes a gift to his wife, Mary, in trust, of the income on certain property valued at $1,000,000, with the remainder to their children after his spouse's demise. If Robert elects not to use the marital deduction for this gift, his unified credit equivalent amount of $1,000,000 is sufficient to avoid gift tax on the gift of $1,000,000. When his wife dies, this property will pass to their children estate tax free and would not be part of her estate.

Robert dies thereafter and leaves to his wife, outright, the balance of his estate, valued at $1,000,000. The property previously gifted in trust is now worth $1,250,000. His wife subsequently dies with the estate intact and worth $1,000,000. Her estate escapes estate tax by virtue of her unified credit of $1,000,000. The property gifted in trust previously is still worth $1,000,000 and passes estate tax free to the grandchildren. If Robert had not previously used his unified credit, in order to avoid estate tax in his estate, he would have had to leave his wife at least $1,000,000 in a form eligible for the marital deduction, which would have consequently been includable in her estate. At her death, her estate would then pay a federal estate tax of approximately $75,000.

Gifts Made by an Attorney-in-Fact

As previously explained, through the use of the annual gift tax exclusion, your estate can be substantially reduced during your lifetime without paying any transfer tax costs.

If you were to become incapacitated, your ability to continue this kind of gift giving would be severely restricted unless a properly prepared durable power of attorney were in effect. This document specifically authorizes your attorney-in-fact to make gifts on your behalf. Without this specific language, the Internal Revenue Service would not recognize any such gifts and would include any gifts made by your attorney-in-fact after the occurrence of your disability, in your gross estate.

The ability of an attorney-in-fact to make gifts, without specific authorization, depends upon state law. Only the state of Virginia authorizes an agent to perform any act that a principal could do, without specific express authorization.

A Gift by a Nonresident Noncitizen

If you are neither a citizen nor a resident of the United States, the federal gift tax only applies to a transfer, by you, of property that is situated in the United States. The gift tax applies only to transfers of real and tangible property.

A Gift to a Noncitizen Spouse

For gifts made after July 13, 1988, a gift to a noncitizen spouse will not qualify for a marital deduction (regardless of the donor's citizenship). However, the first $110,000 (2002) of gifts made to a noncitizen spouse during the year will not be taxed. If gifts are made in excess of this amount, no marital deduction will apply to reduce the gift and as such, the gifts are subject to gift tax. For gifts made after June 29, 1989, the $110,000 annual exclusion for transfers by gift to a noncitizen spouse is allowed only for transfers that would qualify for the marital deduction if the recipient spouse were a U.S. citizen. Thus, a gift in trust would not qualify for the annual exclusion unless it were within one of the exceptions (QTIP) to the terminable interest rule. The $110,000 annual exclusion for gifts to a noncitizen spouse is available regardless of whether the donor is a citizen, resident alien, or a nonresident alien. On the other hand, a gift to a citizen spouse will qualify for a gift tax marital deduction regardless of the citizenship of the spouse making the gift.

Example: Don, a U.S. citizen, is married to Maria, a resident alien. In 1990, Don transfers to Maria one hundred shares of X Corporation stock valued for federal gift tax purposes at $130,000. The transfer is a gift of a present interest and is a deductible interest for gift tax purposes. Accordingly, $110,000 of the $130,000 gift is not included in the total amount of gifts made by Don during the calendar year for federal gift tax purposes. Don must include $20,000 on his annual gift tax return, Form 709, as a taxable gift.

There is no unified credit against the gift tax imposed on transfers by nonresident noncitizens. However, the unified credit is available for transfer by resident noncitizens.

Deathbed Gifts

Generally gifts made within three years of death are not includable in your gross estate for estate tax purposes. The only gifts that would be includable in your estate would be the gift of a life insurance policy and gifts wherein certain rights or powers have been reserved by the donor. If the retained interest or power is transferred within three years of death, the property will be includable in the estate.

State Gift Taxes

Presently, there are four states and one U.S. possession that impose state gift taxes: Connecticut, Louisiana, North Carolina, Tennessee, and Puerto Rico. In these jurisdictions, the gift tax regulations are generally similar to the estate tax regulations.

Gift Tax Advantages

Even though the gift tax and estate tax rates are the same, there are tax advantages to making gifts during life. A gift of property with potential appreciation will be removed from future appreciation in your estate, and gifts of income-producing assets remove future income from your estate.

Another advantage is that the gift tax is calculated only with regard to the value of the gift made and not the amount of the gift tax (provided that the gift is made more than three years before the donor's death). If property is transferred at death, the estate tax is calculated with regard to both the value of the property transferred and the property used to pay the estate tax.

For example, assume that you have made prior gifts that have used up your transfer tax credit and, as a result, place you in the 37 percent transfer tax bracket. If you now make an additional taxable gift of $100,000, the gift tax on this gift is equal to 37 percent of $100,000, or $37,000, and the total cost of the gift is $137,000. On the other hand, if you do not make the gift and the $100,000 is transferred at your death, the estate tax on the $100,000 is equal to 37 percent of $137,000 ($100,000 plus $37,000), or $50,690, and the cost of the transfer would have been $150,690. Thus, the lifetime gift would save $13,690 in transfer taxes.

Lifetime gifts can achieve many planning objectives, such as the following:
- Reduction of your taxable estate and therefore reduced estate taxes.
- Shifting of future appreciation of assets to the next generation.
- Shifting of future earnings on property.
- In those states that do not have a capital gains tax (e.g., Florida), a sale by the gift recipient would reduce income taxes.

- By making large intrafamily gifts, the transfer costs are less than passing the same property upon one's demise.
- Taking advantage of the current acknowledgment by the Internal Revenue Service that permits minority interests to be discounted for gift tax purposes.
- Control can be maintained by the donor through the creation of Value Reduction Devices.
- Any portion of a gift that is deferred until January of the following year permits the donor to have the use of the gift tax until April 15 of the year following the year of gifting. However, any gift tax paid within three years prior to the demise of the donor will be included in the donor's estate for estate tax purposes.

A sale of property is another method of removing future appreciation from the estate of the owner. A sale also accomplishes the transfer of property while maintaining financial security to the former owner of the asset. The costs of such a transaction are: (1) the income tax consequences to the seller; (2) the loss of control over the property sold; and (3) cash burden on the purchaser.

Bargain Sale

Property may be sold for less than its actual value. If the sale is bona fide, at arm's length, and there is no gift intention, there will be no gift. However, if property is sold at a price below fair market value, such a sale will be treated as part sale and part gift under the Code. To the extent that the consideration received in money or money's worth is less than the fair market value of the property sold, there is a gift. A bargain sale that results in gift tax liability may also arise where the purchase price is equal to the fair market value of the property sold, but the notes given in exchange are worth less than their face amount, as where they provide for low or no interest.

Payment of Gift Tax

Gift tax must be paid and reported on Form 709 on or before April 15 of the year following that in which the gift was made.

Custodial Accounts For Minors

Under most state laws permitting the creation of custodian accounts of securities and other property for minors, the custodian generally has the discretionary power to distribute (apply), or withhold (accumulate) income, and to accelerate the distribution of principal for the minor's benefit. This is the kind of power that, if reserved by the grantor of a trust, could lead to the inclusion of the trust funds in the grantor's gross estate. The Treasury Department has ruled that this rule is applicable to custodial accounts in the custody of the one who makes the gift (donor) if the donor is the custodian or successor custodian and dies while acting in that capacity before the minor attains majority. The same rule is applied by the Treasury Department to gifts under the Uniform Gifts to Minors Act and the Model Gifts of Securities to Minors Act. In other words, giving securities and other property to children through a custodial account may result in the transferred property being included in your gross estate, unless someone other than you is named as the custodian of the gift.

Trusts for Minors

Trusts can be created for minors to take advantage of the gift tax annual exclusion. In order to accomplish this, the trust must provide for the following:

- The income and principal of the trust may be used for the benefit of the minor until the minor reaches age twenty-one.
- Any income and principal not used for the minor will pass to the minor upon reaching twenty-one years of age.
- If the minor dies before reaching twenty-one years of age, the trust fund must be payable to his or her estate or to such persons appointed by the minor under a general power of appointment.

Revaluation of Gifts

Prior to enactment of the Taxpayer Relief Act of 1997 (the "Act"), as a result of federal court decisions (two of which were handed down in 1994), it could not be assumed that the statutory three-year limit protects a gift from being revalued by the Internal Revenue Service. This assumption was repudiated by these decisions. In those cases, the federal government was permitted to revalue gifts for estate tax purposes in spite of the fact that the three-year statute of limitations for reviewing a gift had long expired. The rationale of the courts was that if the value of the gifts affected the calculation of the estate taxes in the estate of the maker of the gift, the value of the gift originally made can be reviewed in the subsequent estate tax proceeding.

In the reported cases, the value of the gifts set forth in the filed gift tax returns did not result in the payment of any gift taxes because the value of the gifts did not use up the donor's unified credit. The makers of the gifts had made gifts of mineral rights, land, and/or closely held shares of stock to family members a few years before the respective donors died.

After the deaths of the donors, the Internal Revenue Service audited their respective estate tax returns and the government took the position that the gifts, as reported by the taxpayers, were substantially understated. The estates subsequently challenged the government's contention on the grounds that the three-year statute of limitations barred the review of these gifts. The courts, in handing down decisions in favor of the government, concluded that a revaluation could be made, even after the statutory limitation period, if it affected the calculation of the estate taxes in the estate of the maker of the gifts.

The Act provides that gifts made after August 5, 1997 cannot be revalued for estate tax purposes if the gift tax statute of limitations has expired. See chapter 9 for a detailed discussion of new provisions of the Code.

❖

CHAPTER 11

Charitable Contributions

$\mathcal{G}$ ifts to charitable organizations are eligible for income and estate tax deductions. The benefits of a charitable gift can be divided between a beneficiary and a charity through the creation of a trust. This chapter describes the various forms in which charitable contributions can be made and the sophisticated strategy of combining the use of a charitable trust with an irrevocable life insurance trust.

Besides the use of the unlimited marital deduction, the charitable estate tax deduction is really the only effective deduction that can completely shelter an estate from estate taxes.

The Estate Tax Deduction for Gifts to Charity

Charitable contributions can generate not only income tax deductions but also estate tax deductions. The same contribution, if made during your lifetime, can generate both if it is includable in your estate by reason of your retention of a lifetime interest or powers over it. If the contribution is made by a living trust or a will, an estate tax deduction may be taken, and distribution by the estate to the charity may qualify as a distribution deduction on the estate's income tax return. This, in effect, would amount to the estate receiving both an income tax deduction and an estate tax deduction for the same charitable contribution. In any case, whether by living trust, will, or by a lifetime transfer, the charitable contribution is allowable only if the property is includable in your gross estate.

In many ways, the estate tax rules parallel the income tax rules for charitable contributions. This is generally true as to qualified recipients, the rules governing gifts of charitable remainders, and the valuation of gifts. There are, however, some differences. Most significant is the absence of the percentage limitations found in the income tax rules.

Charitable Trusts

Charitable trusts may be either inter vivos or testamentary in nature and may be set up to select charities as either income and/or remainder beneficiaries. For a charitable trust to be valid, it must serve some charitable purpose. Legitimate purposes include, but are not limited to, certain types of assistance for the financially disadvantaged, to advance a social interest of society, or assistance to help legally bring about a change in the law. The size of the group designated to benefit from the trust may vary. However, the larger the group of beneficiaries, the more flexibility there is.

One of the great differences between a charitable and noncharitable trust is that the former is not subject to the rule against perpetuities. This means that charitable trust arrangements may be perpetually in existence.

Charitable Remainder Trusts

If a person wishes to split the benefit of a bequest between a charity and a beneficiary, a trust will solve the problem. A charitable remainder trust will pay income to the beneficiary for a certain period and the assets remaining in the trust will pass to a charitable organization. The Code defines the charitable remainder trust as one that provides periodic distributions to one or more noncharitable income beneficiaries for life or a term of years.

There are three types of charitable remainder trusts:
- Annuity trusts
- Ordinary unitrusts
- Income-only unitrusts

Charitable Remainder Annuity Trust (CRAT)

An annuity trust pays a fixed annual sum to the noncharitable income beneficiary without regard to current income yields of the trust. The amount to be received should not be less than 5 percent of the original value of the trust in order to preserve certain tax benefits to the creator of the trust. The present value of the donee's remainder interest, less the fair market value of the property placed in the trust, is the charitable deduction to the donor for federal income, gift, and estate tax purposes, i.e., the actuarially calculated dollar value of the benefits of the trust to the noncharitable beneficiary as of the date the trust is created. The amount of the deduction would be less if the gift provides for a successor beneficiary to receive a benefit from the trust before the charity receives the remainder interest.

The annuity trust provides the income beneficiary with the greatest protection against loss in the value of the trust's principal. The beneficiary is not at the mercy of market or general economic fluctuations, since the fixed amount of the annuity must be paid even if the corpus of the trust must be consumed to satisfy the commitment.

The Charitable Remainder Unitrust (CRUT)

A charitable remainder unitrust pays out each year an amount generally equal to a fixed percentage (at least 5 percent), as selected by the donor, of the value of trust assets for the tax year. The trust assets are usually valued, as provided in the trust agreement, on the first business day of each taxable year.

This type of trust may also be designed to pay out either its net income for the year, or the specified fixed percentage amount, whichever is less. This arrangement is commonly called a "net income" unitrust. With a net income unitrust, the trust agreement may provide that for the years in which trust income exceeds the specified unitrust amount, the excess income may be used to make up for past years in which the trust's net income was less than that amount. This type of net income unitrust is known as one with a "make-up" or "catch-up" provision.

The charitable remainder unitrust has the benefit of providing a hedge against inflation. In an inflationary economy, the value of the trust assets increase along with prices in general, thereby providing higher annual payments to the income beneficiary; on the other hand, when the market goes down, the payments decrease.

This trust is also flexible, since it can receive additional transfers of property subsequent to the initial transfer. Therefore, the same trust can be used for multiple charitable gifts, thus eliminating the costs of creating multiple trusts.

A possible disadvantage of the unitrust is the uncertainty of the amount of the annual payment to the income beneficiary. Accordingly, a donor whose primary concern is the certainty of the amount of income distributed to the income beneficiary should not utilize the unitrust for making a charitable remainder gift.

In such event, the donor's estate would receive a deduction for the value of the trust that will be received by the charity. The amount of the deduction would be determined by the size of the trust, the trust's terms, and the income to be paid to the charitable lead trust beneficiary.

Charitable Lead Trust

The scenario can be reversed by providing in the first instance for a charitable organization to receive income for a certain period with the remainder passing to the donor's beneficiaries after the set period. This is called a charitable lead trust (CLT). The CLT is an invaluable estate-planning tool because it affords the estate owner the opportunity to shift substantial assets out of the gross estate, at a significant discount, to individual beneficiaries with potentially little or no transfer tax.

The charitable lead trust is principally an income-shifting device, designed to provide an income yield to charitable organizations. It has the following features:

- A charitable lead trust may be created by any taxpayer, individual, or corporation for the purpose of distributing an income yield to a qualifying charitable beneficiary.
- The trust may be created during the grantor's lifetime (inter vivos) or upon his or her death (testamentary).
- The instrument must be irrevocable and contain a payout obligation based upon a fixed percentage of the annual fair market value of the trust ("unitrust") or a fixed dollar amount or percentage of the initial fair market value of the assets conveyed to the trust ("annuity trust").
- The trust may last for any specified duration. There is no minimum or maximum period, although tax consequences will vary with duration.
- The charitable beneficiary may be designated in the instrument or be determined annually by the trustee or grantor.
- The remainder interest may revert back to the grantor or pass to a noncharitable third party.

The lead trust is really a combination of two gifts: an income interest and a remainder interest. The value of the annuity conveyed to a charity is determined with reference either to the gift tax or estate tax regulation, depending upon how the trust is designed and when it becomes effective. Such a consequence will entitle the donor to an income tax deduction, a gift tax deduction, or an estate tax deduction.

If the remainder interest is conveyed from the grantor to a noncharitable beneficiary—for example, children or a trust for their benefit—a taxable gift will have occurred at the time of creation, valued as the difference between the fair market value of the property transferred in trust and the value of the charitable annuity conveyed. Therein lies the estate-planning benefit of the lead trust. The Treasury tables that establish the value of the annuity interest are computed on the basis of the present worth of an annuity interest at a discount rate which floats from month to month, for trusts created after April 30, 1989.

Example: Mr. Jones transfers $100,000 into a trust for fifteen years, requiring 10 percent or $10,000 to be paid to a public charity during the trust term. At the end of the trust's duration, the remainder will be distributed to his children. Assuming a 10 percent discount rate, the present value of the charitable gift is $76,061. Thus, the present value of the remainder interest passing to the children is $23,939 ($100,000 less $76,061).

Charitable Remainder Trust (CRT) Strategy

Combining the use of a CRT with an irrevocable life insurance trust can provide for the replacement of an asset lost through the charitable gift. Removing an asset from an estate, replacing it with an asset outside the estate, and paying the insurance premiums with income tax savings is a positive strategy. If the CRT continues for the joint life of both spouses, then this plan would favor the use of an insurance policy payable on the death of the second spouse. If the CRT terminates on the death of one spouse, then the insurance would be placed on that individual's life. The insurance proceeds will replace the loss of the asset passing to the charity.

CRT Tax Savings

Example: John owns an asset worth $100,000 with a cost basis of $20,000. He wishes to leave the asset or its value to a child and wants to leave a bequest to charity.

John establishes a CRT using the asset worth $100,000, which produces a current income tax deduction of $40,000 (this varies with the age of the donor). The tax deduction produces current income tax savings of $13,200 (assuming 33 percent total tax brackets), plus avoidance of income tax in capital gains of $22,400 ($80,000 x .28).

Total tax savings:	$ 35,600
The trust pays John an 8 percent annual annuity	$ 8,000

John gifts the $8,000 annually to his child, who purchases a $100,000 life insurance policy on John's life with the child as the beneficiary; or John establishes an irrevocable trust funded by an insurance policy on John's life for the benefit of his child.

Under the plan: the child receives	$100,000
What would the child receive if the asset had been in John's estate at	
50 percent federal estate tax?	$ 50,000
How much does the charity receive at John's death?	$100,000
How much tax did John and his estate save?	
Current income taxes	$ 35,600
Estate taxes	$ 50,000
Total	$ 85,600

By transferring low-basis, low-yielding assets to a CRT, which in turn sells the assets and acquires high-yield assets, you can obtain a current charitable income tax deduction, increase current income, and avoid incurring tax on capital gains. The income tax savings and increased income stream can be used to purchase life insurance to replace the assets eventually passing to charity. You should not overlook, however, that in addition to estate tax planning, CRT's can play a supporting role or even take center stage in retirement planning.

Who Should Consider a Charitable Remainder Trust?

Often, an individual holding highly appreciated assets will fund a charitable remainder trust during his or her lifetime. If these assets were sold by the individual, a capital gains tax would be imposed upon the proceeds, often significantly reducing the remaining base of wealth. However, when appreciated assets are contributed to a charity and the assets are sold by the trustee, usually no tax will be imposed on the trust's gain, and a much larger base of wealth will be available to generate payments for the noncharitable beneficiaries of the trust. The Internal Revenue Service, in some circumstances, will impute the gain experienced by such a trust directly to the grantor (for example, where there was an understanding that the appreciated assets contributed to the trust would be sold by the fiduciary). Therefore, it is important if you are creating a charitable remainder trust with appreciated assets to seek the services of an experienced tax counselor to reduce the risk of having the gain attributed back to you.

Estates That Include Significant IRD

The exemption from taxation of the trust also can enhance wealth for those who inherit certain property when the property owner dies. Although most property is entitled to an income tax–free stepped-up basis when the owner dies, some assets (usually referred to as "income in respect of a decedent" or "IRD") are not. Virtually every estate includes IRD, such as, for example, interests in pension and profit-sharing plans, IRAs, accrued interest on bonds, certain dividends, and certain interests in partnerships. (A proposed new law would extend IRD to certain interests in S corporations as well.) These assets can be subject to both estate tax and income tax, resulting in an erosion of 90 percent or more of their worth. By having those items paid at death to a charitable remainder trust, the income tax on them can be avoided or postponed, often resulting in a tripling or quadrupling of the value of the assets for the eventual remainder beneficiaries.

❖

CHAPTER 12

Generation-Skipping Tax

$\mathcal{I}$n order to prevent you from passing your property to persons two or more generations below you without the imposition of a transfer tax, a tax is imposed called a "generation-skipping tax" (GST). This chapter will detail the different types of transfers that can result in the imposition of this tax and what you can do to minimize it.

The generation-skipping tax is assessed in addition to any gift or estate tax required to be paid on all transfers. Each of us has a $1,110,000 GST exemption (2002), which, in many estates, shelters such transfers against this kind of tax. There are methods for maximizing the use of this exemption that will also be discussed.

Since the GST is frequently misunderstood, familiarizing yourself with the series of questions and answers at the end of this chapter will afford you a better understanding of the GST and its implications.

The Generation-Skipping Tax

In addition to federal estate and gift taxes, a tax is imposed on transfers for the eventual benefit of persons two or more generations below the donor (a "skip person"). Presently, the rate of tax is 50 percent of the value of the property transfer. Every individual has a $1,100,000 generation-skipping tax exemption.

The generation-skipping transfer tax (GST) is designed to eliminate most tax advantages that resulted from transfers of property that skipped a generation. The tax is imposed, in addition to the estate and gift tax, on direct or indirect transfers to beneficiaries who are at least two generations younger than the transferor.

Examples of generation-skipping transfers include:
- A lifetime gift to a grandchild
- A bequest by will to a grandchild
- A gift, either during your lifetime or at death, to be held in trust for the lifetime of your child with the remainder interest passing to your grandchild. The generation-skipping transfer will occur when your child's interest terminates or when assets are distributed to your grandchild.

The tax allows the government to collect transfer tax as if the property had not skipped a generation. For example, if a grandparent bequeaths property to a grandchild rather than a child, there is an estate tax on the transfer, as well as a GST tax. The end result is as if the property had passed from grandparent to child to grandchild, incurring two separate transfer taxes.

The applicable rate for the GST tax is the maximum federal estate tax rate in effect at the time of a transfer.

Exemptions

Exemptions from the tax have been provided. A $1,100,000-per-transferor exemption from the generation-skipping transfer tax will protect many estates from these provisions. The exemption amount may be allocated to any property with respect to which you are the transferor.

Married couples can elect to "split" the use of their exemptions, much like the case of the gift tax, so that a married couple has a $2,200,000 combined GST exemption. The $1,100,000 exemption per transferor applies to both lifetime and death transfers. Like the unified credit, the exemption is not transferable between spouses, but the statute makes provision for gift-splitting. The Internal Revenue Code provides that a gift will be treated as if made one-half by each spouse if the spouses elect such treatment. This means that a spouse can make the gift out of his or her property and the other spouse can elect to treat the gift as being made one-half by him or her.

A complicated set of rules governs the election of property to be covered by the exemption, the allocation of the exemption if the transferor does not elect to apply it, and the taxation of property that is only partially covered by the exemption.

The GST tax is levied upon "taxable terminations," "taxable distributions," and "direct skips" to "skip persons" (a party, two or more generations below the generation of the transferor).

Taxable terminations

Taxable terminations occur when, immediately after the happening of an event, a skip person has an interest in property; and at no time after such event may a distribution be made to a person who is not a skip person. As an example, where a parent creates a trust for a child, with remainder to a grandchild, a taxable termination will occur on the event of the child's death and the termination of the trust.

Taxable distributions

Taxable distributions occur when distributions that are not taxable terminations are made to skip persons. For example, a taxable distribution will be made when a trust permits distributions of income and principal to any descendant of a parent during the lifetime of his or her child, such as a distribution of income to a grandchild or great-grandchild. GST tax on taxable distributions is levied (after a deduction of expenses) on the full value of the property received and is payable by the beneficiary receiving the distribution.

Direct skips

Direct skips are transfers to skip persons, subject to estate or gift tax. For example, a direct skip will occur where a parent makes a gift or leaves a legacy to a grandchild of $2.5 million. The transfer will be subject to both the gift tax or estate tax and to the GST tax. Subject to an exception explained below, GST tax on direct skips is levied on the full value of the property received by the beneficiary on a tax-exclusive basis (the base for computation does not include the GST tax to be paid).

Transfers to a trust in which all the income beneficiaries are skip persons is deemed to be a direct skip, even if the remainder beneficiaries are nonskip persons. For example, the entire value of real property is subject to GST tax if you leave a life estate in property to a friend who is forty years younger (a "skip" person) with the remainder in the property to your daughter (a "nonskip" person).

An important way to maximize the use of the $1,100,000 GST exemption is to create multiple trusts to insure that at least one of the trusts will be completely free of GST tax.

Three-Trust Estate Plan

The typical marital deduction format provides the division of a spouse's estate into two parts: a credit shelter share and a marital deduction share.

A technique for maximizing the use of the GST tax exemption for married couples is the use of a three-trust plan. Under this scenario, a unified credit trust is created to which the unified credit portion of the GST tax exemption is allocated. This trust should be structured to last as long as possible within the framework of the rule against perpetuities and to ultimately pass to skip persons. A second trust is created to use the balance of the GST tax exemption. This trust should qualify as a QTIP, and the executors should make the reverse QTIP election, so that the predeceased spouse would be treated as the transferor for GST tax purposes. The final beneficiaries of this trust should be skip persons, as well. The third trust (holding property in excess of the $1,100,000 GST exemption) would also be a QTIP trust and would not be covered by any GST exemption. Any necessary principal invasions for the spouse should come out of the third nonexempt trust. The original $1,100,000 in the two GST tax-exempt trusts, plus any appreciation, could therefore pass to "skip persons" free of any GST tax.

An example of the savings that can be generated by the creation of trusts follows:

Assume John dies in 1997 with a $6 million estate, no spouse, two children, and four grandchildren:

1. All to children:

Estate	$6,000,000
Federal Estate Tax	($3,000,000)
Amount to children	$3,000,000
Estate Tax at children's level (50%)	$1,500,000
Amount to grandchildren	$1,500.000

2. Use of $1 million GST Exemption (in 1997)

$1 million to family trust (children and grandchildren) balance to children

Federal estate	$3,000,000
Amount to children	$2,000,000
Estate Tax at children's level (50%)	$1,000,000
Amount to grandchildren from children's estates	$1,000,000
Amount available in family trust	$1,000,000
Total amount to grandchildren	$2,000,000 or
	$ 500,000 more*

*If these assets appreciate—even greater results.

Questions and Answers

What is the generation-skipping transfer tax?

It is a tax levied in addition to federal estate or gift taxes. In many cases the same transfer, such as a lifetime gift, can be subject to both federal gift tax and generation-skipping transfer tax.

What are examples of generation-skipping transfers?

A generation-skipping transfer is usually either a lifetime gift or an amount passing to a beneficiary at death that skips a generation. Classic examples are lifetime gifts by a grandparent to a grandchild or outright bequests by a grandparent to a grandchild under a will. Such transfers "skip" the middle generation (the child of the grandparent who is the parent of the grandchild).

Why is a special tax needed for such transfers?

In the absence of a generation-skipping transfer tax, there is a loophole in the federal estate and gift tax system for wealthy individuals. The estate and gift tax system is intended to impose a tax on the transfer of wealth from one generation to the next. People of "normal" wealth usually abide by traditional rules and leave their property outright to their children in a transfer subject to gift or estate tax. The children either spend it or add to it during their lifetimes, and then pass it to their children, subject to another gift or estate tax, and so on.

The tax policy concern has been that the very wealthy have the means to avoid these rules. Instead of passing their wealth outright to their children, they set up trusts for their children, even grown children. These trusts are large enough that the income from them is sufficient to provide comfortably for the children's generation. At the children's death, however, the trust assets are not included in the children's estate for estate tax purposes. These trusts can stay in existence from generation to generation, subject only to the rule against perpetuities, and thereby avoid transfer taxes at the intervening generational levels.

The purpose of the generation-skipping transfer tax system, therefore, is to impose a special tax when a transfer is made that skips a generation in order to "make up" for the tax that would have been paid at the skipped generational level or levels.

What is the definition of a skip person?

The Internal Revenue Code defines a direct skip as a transfer, subject to federal gift or estate tax, to a "skip person." The requirement that the transfer be subject to gift or estate tax essentially means that the generation-skipping transfer tax applies only to gratuitous transfers and not to sales or exchanges or compensation payments or other types of transfers.

A skip person can be either a natural person or a trust. A natural person is a skip person if he or she is two or more generations below the transferor. Thus, a grandchild is a skip person to a grandparent because the grandchild is two generations below the grandparent. A child is not a skip person to a parent because the child is only one generation below the parent.

A trust can be a skip person under some circumstances. These include situations where the only beneficiaries of the trust are skip persons.

A grandparent sets up a trust in which a grandchild is the sole beneficiary. Gifts to such a trust constitute direct skips and are potentially subject to generation-skipping transfer tax at the time they are made.

What is a taxable termination or taxable distribution?

This essentially deals with distributions from a trust to skip persons, whether while the trust is in existence (a taxable distribution) or at its termination (a taxable termination).

You cannot, therefore, avoid the generation-skipping transfer tax through the use of a trust. That is because either the transfer to the trust will itself be a generation-skipping transfer or, if not, subsequent transfers from the trust to skip persons will be.

Example: Grandmother sets up a trust in her will for her only son. Under the terms of the trust, upon the son's death, any remaining trust property will pass to the son's surviving children. The transfer to the trust upon grandmother's death is not a direct skip because the testamentary trust is not a skip person (that is because the son is a nonskip person beneficiary of the trust). When the son dies, the transfer of the remaining trust property to the grandchildren is a taxable termination which is a generation-skipping transfer potentially subject to generation-skipping tax liability.

What is the generation-skipping transfer tax rate?

The generation-skipping transfer tax rate is set at the highest marginal federal estate tax rate, presently 50 percent, subject to adjustment based on the portion of the transfer that qualifies for the $1,100,000 GST exemption.

Example: Grandfather makes a $100,000 lifetime gift outright to a grandchild after having previously made a $10,000 gift to the grandchild in this year. Grandfather had already used up his $1,100,000 GST exemption. The generation-skipping transfer tax would equal 50 percent of $100,000 or $50,000. This would be over and above any federal gift tax due, if any, on such a gift. If Grandfather was in the 50 percent federal gift tax bracket, the combined gift and generation-skipping transfer tax liability on the $100,000 gift could actually be $110,000.

Are all transfers to grandchildren subject to the generation-skipping transfer tax?

No. There are two important exceptions

1. The first exception is that any lifetime gift that is a direct skip and that is not a taxable gift for gift tax purposes is essentially nontaxable for generation-skipping transfer tax purposes as well.

    This means that annual gifts to grandchildren that qualify for the $11,000 annual per donee gift tax exclusion (which can increase to $22,000 per donee if a husband and wife join in the gift under the gift splitting rules) are also exempt from the generation-skipping transfer tax.

    Example: Grandmother, a widow, gives $11,000 each year to each of her six grandchildren. These gifts are exempt from both federal gift tax and the generation-skipping transfer tax. Neither her unified credit for gift and estate tax purposes nor her $1,100,000 generation-skipping transfer tax exemption need to be applied to such gifts.

2. The second exception is, as previously mentioned, for transfers that qualify for the $1,100,000 GST exemption. For example, if the transferor's GST exemption is allocated to a direct skip, there is no generation-skipping transfer tax liability for the transfer.

    Example: Grandfather, a widower, makes a $100,000 gift outright to a grandchild. Grandfather has not allocated any of his GST exemption in prior years. He also has made no prior gifts to the grandchild this year. The first $11,000 qualifies for the annual per donee gift tax exclusion and is basically exempt from generation-skipping transfer tax as a nontaxable direct skip. If grandfather allocates $89,000 of his GST exemption to the balance of the gifts, that balance also will not be subject to generation-skipping transfer tax.

Are there any planning ideas that can maximize the amounts that can be transferred to grandchildren and later generations using the $1,100,000 GST exemption?

Yes. It is possible to "leverage" the $1,100,000 GST exemption and thereby transfer significant additional amounts to those generations. One of the most effective methods of doing so is with an irrevocable insurance trust.

The key concept is that the generation-skipping transfer tax is based on the inclusion ratio of the trust. The inclusion ratio defines what percent of the property in the trust is subject to the GST tax (after applying the exemption). As long as that inclusion ratio can be kept at zero, there is no generation-skipping transfer tax on any amounts, regardless of how large, distributed from the trust.

The way to keep the trust's inclusion ratio at zero is to make sure that all contributions to the trust have the $1,100,000 GST exemption allocated to them. This means that as long as total contributions to the trust do not exceed $1,100,000 and as long as the grantor's $1,100,000 GST exemption is allocated to those contributions, all amounts distributed from the trust are exempt.

Example: Grandfather and grandmother establish an irrevocable insurance trust which owns a life insurance policy on their lives (second-to-die) for the benefit of their six grandchildren. They make annual contributions to the trust in an amount sufficient to pay the annual premiums on a second-to-die policy insuring their lives. As long as the annual premiums over their joint lifetimes do not exceed $1,100,000 each and assuming that they allocate their GST exemptions to those premium contributions, the entire death proceeds under the policy, regardless of amount, can be distributed to the grandchildren without incurring a generation-skipping transfer tax.

Another exemption applies to a direct skip if the member of the skipped generation is deceased at the time of the transfer. In determining whether a transfer is a direct skip, a grandchild of the transferor, whose parent (the child of the transferor) is deceased, will be treated as if he or she were a child of the transferor in lieu of the *pre*deceased parent. In such a case, the grandchild and all succeeding lineal descendants of the grandchild are moved up a generation.

The Taxpayer Relief Act of 1997 extended the "predeceased parent exception" of the generation-skipping transfer tax to include collateral heirs, such as grandnieces and grandnephews, provided the transferor has no lineal descendants at the time of the transfer.

It is very important in the estate-planning process for your professional advisors to review every trust that is being administered or that (revocable or irrevocable) you have created to identify any possible GST problems. If there is any exposure to GST, because the trust does not provide the ability to amend it to divide the trust into separate parts, the aid of the courts can be sought. The courts will permit a reformation so that the trust may not only be divided and the exemption allocated to a particular part, but in certain cases, permit the utilization of a spouse's exemption.

GST Trap

There are gifts that do not count toward the gift tax annual exclusion ($11,000) and do not count for GST tax purposes: direct payment of a grandchild's tuition and direct payment of a grandchild's medical expenses or medical insurance premiums to an insurance provider.

In some instances, the gift tax annual exclusion applies as well to a generation-skipping transfer, i.e., grandparent writes a check to grandchild in the amount of $11,000. However, with a trust, the gift tax exclusion and the GST tax annual exclusion do not overlap. Transfers to trusts that qualify for the gift tax annual exclusion do not automatically qualify for the GST tax annual exclusion. In order for a transfer to a trust to qualify for the GST tax annual exclusion, the following circumstances must exist:

- The transfer is a direct skip.
- The trust can have only one beneficiary during the beneficiary's lifetime.
- The assets of the trust will be included in the gross estate of the beneficiary upon his or her death, if the trust is still in existence at such time.

Dynasty trusts and most life insurance trusts do not meet the above requirements. As a result, gift tax returns are required covering the transfers to such trusts with allocations taken for GST exemptions equal to the amount of the entire gifts.

CHAPTER 13

Grits, Grats, and Gruts

*W*hen a grantor retains certain interests in a trust for a period of time, the tax law sets forth special valuation rules at the time the trust is created. These devices are for gift tax purposes and leveraged gift transactions, and should be considered in every sophisticated estate plan.

By establishing a trust, you can make a gift of the remainder interest to your beneficiaries with the value of the gift being discounted, because the value of your retained interest reduces the value of the remainder gift. For example, a $1 million dollar house can be valued, for gift tax purposes, at approximately $333,333 and given away at that value.

Since there is no step-up in basis in this type of gift, proper tax planning must be made. Presently, however, the maximum income tax bracket is less than the maximum estate tax bracket.

Grits, grats, and gruts are acronyms for grantor retained income trusts and grantor retained annuity and unitrusts. The concepts of all these devices are quite simple. The idea is that the value of a gift can be lessened by retaining or keeping an income interest, for a certain period of time, in the property gifted away. If all goes according to plan, the income interest expires before the donor or gift giver's death. As such, there is nothing left to include in the donor's estate. If the donor dies before the expiration of the income interest period, the value of the gifted property will be included in the donor's estate with a credit for any gift taxes that may have been paid.

Retained Interests

For gift tax purposes, any retained interest other than a qualified retained interest will be valued at zero. Therefore, any gift of the remainder interest would be valued at the full value of the property transferred to the trust. For example, if a parent transfers $1 million of cash in trust for his children and retains the right to receive the income from the property for a period of years, the entire $1 million is subject to present gift tax. The grantor is not able to subtract the value of his retained income interest from the value of the gift. However, if the grantor retained, instead of mere income, a "qualified interest," then the value of his retained interest may be subtracted from the value of the gift and the harsh gift tax valuation rules may be avoided. Grits, grats, and gruts are such qualified interests. They permit the actuarial value of the grantor's retained interest to be deducted from the actual value of the property gifted in order to arrive at the value of the net gift.

How It Works

The grantor transfers assets to an irrevocable trust for a term of years with the retention of the income rights during that period of time. When the trust is established, a gift of the remainder interest is made to the beneficiary. Since this is a gift of a future interest, the annual exclusion is not available to offset the gift tax; however, the unified credit may be used for such a purpose. If the grantor survives the period selected, the assets are transferred to the beneficiary at the end of the term with no further transfer tax (estate or gift) imposed upon the property. If the grantor dies during the term of the trust (before the period ends) the entire trust is valued in the grantor's estate for estate tax purposes. Thus, the selection of the term of the trust is very important.

For income tax purposes, the beneficiaries of the trust receive no step-up in basis for the assets placed in the trust. Their basis is the grantor's at the time of the transfer plus any gift tax paid at that time. Any gain on the sale of such property by the beneficiary will generate income tax. Presently, however, income tax brackets are still less than the higher estate tax brackets.

The tax benefit flows from the fact that, for gift tax purposes, the value of the interest retained by the grantor is deducted from the value of the asset placed in trust.

House Grit

If a $1 million residence is placed in a house grit, the value of the grantor's ten-year retained right is approximately two-thirds of the present value of the house for gift tax purposes. The value of the gift for gift tax purposes would be the remainder interest, or approximately one-third would be subject to gift tax.

The intra-family house transfer is probably most significant from an estate planning perspective if the residence is likely to appreciate over the term of the trust. What is important is that as grantor, you can manipulate the value of the remainder interest, and hence the value of the gift, by lengthening or shortening the term of the retained income interest. As the term of the income interest is lengthened, the value of the remainder interest decreases. However, there is a risk in making the term too long, since the trust property will be taxable as part of your estate if you should die before it ends.

Table A illustrates remainder values for ten- and twenty-year Grits at three different ages assuming a $1 million transfer and a 10 percent interest rate.

TABLE A: Amount of Taxable Gift on Transfer of $1 Million to Grit without Reversion

AGE	10-YEAR GRIT	20-YEAR GRIT
55	$414,126	$228,154
60	428,161	262,992
65	447,315	308,676

It is often desirable for the grantor to decrease the value of the gift of the remainder interest even further. This can be accomplished by having the grantor or the grantor's estate retain a reversionary interest in the trust property in the event of the grantor's death during the term of the trust. The trust agreement would expressly provide that the trust property revert to the grantor's estate if the grantor dies before the term of the income interest ends. Because this reversionary interest has value, the remainder interest is necessarily worth less. The reversion also gives the grantor the right to dispose of the property as part of the grantor's estate. The effect of the retention on the value of the remainder interests shown above is illustrated in table B.

When interest rates go up, the value of the remainder interest in the Grit goes down, reducing the gift tax payable and increasing the tax savings.

TABLE B: Amount of Taxable Gift on Transfer of $1 Million to Grit with Reversion

AGE	10-YEAR GRIT	20-YEAR GRIT
55	$336,489	$95,562
60	314,268	76,659
65	284,001	53,901

In the grit involving the grantor's personal residence, some important decisions will have to be made if the grantor survives the income term, which is the desired result. The grantor could certainly consider simply vacating the residence and turning it over to the trust beneficiaries. The grantor could also consider paying a fair market rent once the term has expired. The payment of rent could also be viewed as an additional way to transfer wealth at no estate or gift tax cost and might be entirely reasonable under certain circumstances.

In some cases, the grantor might even consider repurchasing the residence at the fair market value of the property at the end of the income term. The repurchase does not diminish the estate and gift tax benefits of the original transaction and amounts to nothing more than a substitution of cash for real property, leaving both the grantor and the trust beneficiaries in virtually the same position from a financial point of view. Only recently, the Internal Revenue Service has ruled that the existence of a lease or purchase residence option in the trust instrument upon the expiration of a qualified Grit will not disqualify the trust, and will not affect the value of the remainder interest.

Grats and Gruts

In a grat, the grantor transfers property to an irrevocable trust in return for the right to receive fixed payments on at least an annual basis, based upon the initial fair market value of the property.

A grut is the exact same concept, except the annual payments will fluctuate each year as the value of the property increases or decreases.

Example: A sixty-year-old grantor transfers $1 million of stock in his S corporation to a grat for the benefit of his children. The grat has a term of ten years and he retains the right to receive 12 percent of the initial fair market value of the property annually for the length of the term, a yield equal to the salary and S corporation distributions he was receiving. The grantor, therefore, must receive $120,000 each year during the retained term. As a result of the fact that retained annuity is a qualified interest, its actuarial value can be subtracted from the value of the gift for gift tax purposes. Under the Internal Revenue Service rates in effect for September 1993, the value of the retained annuity interest is 80.24 percent of the value of the whole, or $802,400. The value of the gift to the remainder beneficiaries is $197,600. In this example, if the value of the closely held business stock grew at the rate of 20 percent a year, at the end of the ten-year term the beneficiaries would receive tax-free shares of stock worth $3,000,000. However, only $1,397,600 would be subjected to the transfer tax (gift) system. The original value of the gift of $197,600 and the monies received back by the grantor for his annuity would total $1,200,000. In this example, over $3,000,000 would escape estate or gift taxation, thus creating an estate tax savings of approximately $1,500,000. This is proof of the fact that people with high net worth must have carefully designed estate plans.

By using the technique discussed in this chapter, you are in effect betting that you will survive the term selected—as opposed to a private annuity, where you are betting that you are going to die sooner rather than later. See chapter 9 for a detailed discussion on this device.

CHAPTER 14

Life Insurance

*T*he importance of life insurance in every estate plan cannot be overemphasized. In many estates, life insurance may be the largest single asset. The ability to remove the taxable aspect of property out of an estate is one of the most effective planning strategies.

Life insurance, unlike any other asset, develops its optimum value at the time of death. Therefore, any technique that permits such property to be transferred tax free has the highest of priorities and importance.

This chapter will cover these subjects as well as the reasons to consider life insurance, in what form it should be owned, and the different kinds of life insurance available.

The Need for Life Insurance in Estate Planning

Experts say that $7–$8 trillion is sitting in potential estates simply waiting to be passed on to the next generation. The amount of wealth that will be transferred in the decades to come staggers the imagination. However, as a result of the 55 percent maximum federal estate tax rate plus any state death tax, much of this property will be eroded by estate taxes.

As such, adequate life insurance coverage is one of the crucial components of a successful financial and estate plan. There are many specific reasons to acquire life insurance, including: (1) to replace income lost by the death of a wage earner; (2) to provide liquidity for an estate and thereby prevent the forced sale of assets to satisfy estate taxes; (3) to shelter assets against estate taxes and thereby maximize the transfer of property; and (4) to create assets in an estate. We often forget about the favored income tax treatment life insurance generally receives. This focuses on the deferral of tax on the internal growth that takes place with whole-life insurance. Apart from tax advantages, insurance borrowing features are usually favorable and are tax free. Normally, a loan does not have to be paid back but is, however, eventually deducted from the death benefit.

Estate Taxes

The existence of the unlimited estate tax marital deduction, in addition to the unified credit, may lead many people to believe that the creation of an insurance fund may not be necessary. This can be a harmful misconception. Complete reliance on the marital deduction and unified credit may not prove to be in the family's best interests. This is a result of the dual impact of increasing longevity of the surviving spouse and the effect of inflation. The need for adequate protection is even more important where there is a loss of the marital deduction through divorce or death.

Incidents of Ownership

Life insurance proceeds are includable in your gross estate for estate tax purposes. This is true where they are payable to the estate or a named beneficiary when you die possessing any "incidents of ownership" in the insurance policy. Incidents of ownership include such powers as the right to change the beneficiary, the right to borrow against the cash value in the policy, or the right to assign or surrender the policy. An incident of ownership does not necessarily have to be a direct ownership. For example, if an insurance policy is owned by a corporation on the sole or controlling shareholder with the beneficiary being a third party, the incident of ownership would be attributed to the shareholder and would be included in his or her estate for estate tax purposes.

Third-Party Ownership

The best way to insure that the proceeds of an insurance policy will not be includable in a gross estate is to have someone other than the insured acquire and own the life insurance policy. A spouse can own an insurance policy on the life of the other spouse. Children can own a life insurance policy on the life of a parent. The owner of an existing insurance policy can transfer ownership of it and all incidents of ownership, and it will not be included in the transferor's estate, provided that person survives the transfer by more than three years. However, any such transfer could be subject to gift taxes.

Life Insurance Trust

To avoid the three-year rule and thereby have the insurance policy not included in the estate as a gift in contemplation of death, a new insurance policy can be acquired and be owned by an irrevocable life insurance trust.

A typical life insurance trust works in this way. You, as the grantor of the trust, name the trust as the owner and beneficiary of the insurance policies on your life. When you die, the trustee will collect the insurance proceeds, which will be free of estate taxes. He or she invests them prudently and makes distributions of income and principal to your beneficiaries according to the instructions you've set forth in the trust agreement. Your beneficiaries are thus spared the burden of financial management, but they will enjoy the fruits of your planning.

With an irrevocable life insurance trust, your trustee can purchase and own the policy for you (your connection to the transaction is limited to taking the physical and transferring funds to the trustee). Thus, if properly arranged, your life insurance trust can assure that your insurance proceeds will remain free of estate taxes.

One possible way to avoid the three-year rule on an existing policy could be a sale of the insurance policy. Suppose you own an insurance policy and want to put it into a trust to avoid it being estate taxed. If you put it into a trust and die within three years, it will be includable in your estate for estate tax purposes. Suppose instead you sold the insurance policy to your wife at its current fair market value (the cash surrender value). Your wife could then transfer the policy to a trust that she creates. The three-year rule will not be applicable since the transfer to your wife was a sale and not a gift. For income tax purposes, there is no taxable gain realized for a sale between spouses. In order to protect the legality of this transaction, there should be a substantial amount of time elapsing between these steps.

A life insurance trust will also allow you to:

- Determine when, in what amounts, and in what manner distributions will be made to your beneficiaries
- Give the trustee discretionary power to invade the trust in the event of a family emergency or a special situation (to finance a child's education, for example)
- Feel secure knowing your insurance proceeds will be professionally managed and invested according to your beneficiaries' needs and your own objectives
- Avoid the complexities of court-appointed guardianship if you name minor children as trust beneficiaries

- Avoid probate and the incidents thereto
- Unify your estate plan by having your estate assets "poured over" into your life insurance trust so that all of your assets can be administered by a single trustee

By having a life insurance trust acquire the policy in the first instance, the proceeds will be secure from estate taxes in both the estates of the insured and that of the surviving spouse. The funding of the trust to pay the annual premiums is usually accomplished by making annual gifts to the trust each year. However, gifts to an irrevocable life insurance trust of the amount of the annual premium payments, for gift tax purposes, are considered as "gifts of a future interest." This is so because the beneficiary will not enjoy the use of the property until the death of the insured. Such premium payments to the trust do not qualify for the gift tax annual exclusion. In order to circumvent this problem and have them qualify, the beneficiaries of the trust are given the right to withdraw (Crummey power) their proportionate share of any property gifted to the trust, which right is typically waived by the beneficiaries, thereby permitting the property to be used by the trustee to pay the annual premium. In setting up a trust of this kind, the insured person cannot serve as a trustee, otherwise the incidents-of-ownership rule will be attributable.

Change of Circumstances

What if you want to change the terms of the irrevocable trust? For example, estrangement of a child, a child develops special needs, or the death of a child. There are methods to deal with this type of situation.

You can allow the policy to lapse and replace it with a new insurance policy which is placed in a new irrevocable trust. If you are uninsurable, the grantor of the new trust could purchase the policy from the old trust for its cash surrender value. The Internal Revenue Service has ruled that a transaction of this kind is permissible, finding, however, that the trust would have a profit on the sale of the policy equal to the amount paid.

Survivorship Life Insurance

As a result of the unlimited marital estate tax deduction, the insurance industry developed a product called second-to-die or survivor insurance. This type of policy covers two lives, and does not pay off until both insureds die. These policies, therefore, provide for lower premiums than a single life policy because they insure two persons. The proceeds of the "two life" insurance policy are traditionally used to pay the estate taxes due when the surviving spouse dies. This type of insurance policy can be held in an irrevocable life insurance trust as well.

Business Split-Dollar Plan

Despite its name, split-dollar life insurance is not a special policy, but rather a special way to purchase permanent (or whole-life) coverage. Under this approach, two parties, usually a company and a key employee, agree to "split" the payment of the insurance premiums and the benefits.

In a typical case, a corporation will pay the premiums for an insurance policy on the life of an owner or key employee. The person being insured can own the policy and name whatever beneficiary he or she chooses. This type of insurance can be owned by an irrevocable life insurance trust as well. The corporation owns the cash value of the policy and a portion of the death benefit as "collateral" to the extent of the premiums it has paid. If the insured executive dies, the corporation will recover any premiums paid from the death benefits; the remainder goes to the beneficiary.

The corporation cannot deduct its premiums, but the executive is taxed on the "economic benefit" (or cost of the pure insurance coverage) that he or she receives. One way to change this tax treatment is to have the executive pay a portion of the premium out of his or her own pocket, and have the corporation pay the rest. As a result, the executive is taxed on that part of the economic benefit that has been paid with personal funds.

If the life insurance policy is owned by an irrevocable life insurance trust, the proceeds of the policy are not includable in the employee's estate. However, a new section of the Code provides that an employee is subject to income tax for any property given to him or her or to any third party for services performed by him or her for the employer. Under a split-dollar corporate arrangement, the insurance policy will eventually build up cash values, which the Internal Revenue Service says is property received by the employee and subject to being income taxed on its value, notwithstanding that the beneficiary of it is the trust which owns the policy. In addition, the IRS says that since this additional value really belongs to the employee, the employee is deemed to have made a gift to the insurance trust each year in the amount of the increase in cash value. One of the possible ways to avoid this problem is to insert a provision in the split-dollar plan that the employee or insurance trust, under certain forfeiture circumstances, will have no interest in the cash surrender value (i.e., termination of employment).

At present, various life insurance associations are petitioning to have the Internal Revenue Service amend its position.

Family Split-Dollar Plan

What happens when a family member has a definite need for insurance protection, but there is no corporation to pay the premiums? In cases such as this, many have turned to a variation of the traditional employer-employee split-dollar plan to a "family" split-dollar plan. From a tax standpoint, family split-dollar may be one of the best-kept secrets in the entire financial planning arena. An example will demonstrate why.

Assume that a child needs financial help and the deferred tax build-up of cash value in a permanent policy could be more beneficial to the child's family over the long run, especially if they need to accumulate cash on a tax-deferred basis to pay for their child's future college expenses. Acquiring permanent coverage could take care of two needs with one policy.

Once the need is recognized for a permanent policy, the child could ask a parent to assist with the premium payments. The "split" of the family split-dollar plan would work as follows: The parent would pay the premiums, but enter into an agreement with the child under which the parent would retain the right to the policy's premium buildup of cash values. On the other hand, the child would be given the right to name his spouse as beneficiary of the balance of the death proceeds in excess of the premium buildup or cash value. Over time, the parent could give his or her interest in the policy's cash value to the child, allowing the child's family full access to the cash values to fund future college expenses.

As far as the tax consequences are concerned, the parent's premium payments under a family split-dollar plan result in no income being taxed to the child. Instead, the parent is deemed to have made a gift to the child measured not by the full value of the policy's premiums, but rather by the very low "economic benefit" cost used by the IRS to value the cost of permanent insurance protection in employer-employee split-dollar plans.

Since the parent's gifts of both the premiums and the cash values do not result in taxable income, the child should not have any reportable income from the family split-dollar plan. It is easy to see why a family split-dollar is a beneficial financial planning tool.

Living Benefit Policy

In answering the needs of terminally ill persons, insurance companies have developed products that allow their insureds to receive accelerated death benefits to pay for their medical costs. These "living benefits" permit the seriously ill to have access to life insurance benefits before death. This unusual approach has a dual role in our society. It not only helps individuals to meet these obligations but removes a portion of the responsibility of the state for whatever catastrophic long-term costs it may have to pay.

The growth of this industry has been fast moving and states are in the process of enacting legislation to regulate the companies offering this product.

Types of Insurance Policies

- *Term:* Although there are many variations on term insurance, the basic point to note is that term insurance is "pure" insurance that does not have an investment element. Its biggest advantage is its low cost; however, that is not the whole story. As an individual ages, the price of insurability goes up, and consequently, over the long run, term insurance may actually prove more costly than other investment types. It is perhaps best suited to young persons and those who need coverage for short periods of time. When you may need insurance coverage the most, it may not be there or if it is, it may be too costly to maintain.

- *Conventional Whole-Life:* Whole-life is the generic form of life insurance that adds an investment element. In a conventional whole-life policy, the death benefits are fixed, and there is a fixed maturity date, as well as fixed level premiums and a fixed progression of cash values against which you can borrow or cash in. It can cost several times more to have coverage under a whole-life policy than under a term policy, but it is a way of making forced savings. With whole-life insurance, no new physicals are required as the policy continues to be extended.

- *Variable Life:* Variable life is a variation of regular whole-life insurance that adds an element of flexibility to the choice of investment vehicles. Net premiums are invested in a fund or funds selected by the policyholder. If the fund earns more than a specified return, the death benefit and the cash value increase; the converse is true if the fund earns less, except the death benefit does not decrease below the original face amount. If financial markets decline, this form of policy can have adverse effects.

- *Universal Life:* This form of policy allows for flexibility of premium payments, as well as in the face amount of insurance. It has been a popular insurance product and combines the features of term and whole-life insurance. Part of the premiums are invested in a cash fund which is invested in fixed income assets, which means as interest rates go down the premiums may go up. The rest of the premiums are used to finance renewable term insurance. This form of insurance permits you to not only vary the premium payments, but to increase or decrease the amount of the death benefit as well. Because there is no requirement that premiums are to be paid beyond the initial premiums, these policies afford great flexibility. However, universal life policies that fail to meet certain tests will be deemed to be modified endowment contracts, which could have adverse income tax effects to you. Over the life of the policy, the net cost to the policyholder may not exceed the cost of term insurance.

- *Universal Variable Life:* In an attempt to include the best of both worlds, these policies combine the investment flexibility of variable life with the premium and insurance amount flexibility of universal life. The caveat to this flexibility is that the policyholder must exercise control with a great deal of care.

- *Annuities:* Under this form of insurance, the company agrees to pay the policy amount to a beneficiary in installments, instead of a single payment. This is, in effect, a de facto trust arrangement. Establishing a trust to do the same thing may be less costly, more efficient, and have greater flexibility. You can be the beneficiary of your own annuity and as such receive installment payments during your lifetime.

Community Property

In a community property state, without an agreement to the contrary, one-half of the proceeds of an insurance policy are owned by the surviving spouse, notwithstanding the provisions in the policy as to who the beneficiary is.

Life insurance and the life insurance trust single-handedly satisfy a multitude of estate planning objectives simultaneously. The opportunity to benefit your heirs without death tax costs is so unique that it has to be considered a no lose situation.

Transfers from Trust to Trust

The vast majority of insurance trusts are irrevocable because they are created for the purpose of eliminating estate taxes. As such, the Internal Revenue Code precludes the grantor from having any incident of ownership over the trust, including the power to make trust modifications.

Otherwise, the assets owned by the trust may be subject to transfer tax at the grantor's death.

Limited choices to alter a life insurance trust are available to the grantor who has supposedly severed all interests in the trust.

Options

The aim of each proposed choice is to transfer ownership of a life insurance policy from an existing trust to a new trust that provides current needs with the least tax risk or fiduciary exposure. Each strategy, however, except the last, results in some incidental value remaining in the existing trust, which indicates that these options are not intended to be a cure-all, but rather an exercise in damage control.

Practically speaking, the trustee of the existing trust and the new trust (which may be the same person) must be willing participants to the grantor's plans.

- *Purchase of Insurance Policy by New Trust.* Grantor establishes a new trust, funding the trust with $Y. Using the grantor's contribution of $Y, the trustee of the new trust purchases the insurance policy owned by the existing trust at its fair market value (i.e., the interpolated terminal reserve value of the policy plus the value of the unexpired premiums, assuming the insured grantor is in good health).

- *Purchase of Insurance Policy by Grantor.* Grantor purchases the insurance policy held by the existing trust at its fair market value. Grantor then gifts the purchased life insurance policy to a new insurance trust.

- *Existing Trust Lends Money to New Trust.* Grantor creates a new trust. Trustee of the existing trust cashes in the current life insurance policy and lends the proceeds to the new trust. The trustee of the new trust uses the proceeds from the loan to invest in a new life insurance policy.

- *Existing Trust Merges with New Trust.* Grantor establishes a new trust whose terms are substantially similar to the terms of the existing trust. Trustee of existing trust and trustee of new trust agree through a document of merger or by means of a court order to merge the existing trust into the new trust.

Each of these options involves a number of tax and fiduciary concerns and must be skillfully and professionally attended to.

❖

CHAPTER 15

The Significance of Your Domicile

$\mathcal{W}$ here your legal residence is can be a most significant fact in estate planning. Today, many states will reach out to claim not only death taxes, but, if they feel that you were a domiciliary there, they will review your income tax records.

This chapter tells you that you can only have one domicile (residence) and it spells out the various ways you can express your intentions so as to avoid potential conflicts. "Actions speak louder than words" is an important motto.

What Is a Domicile?

"Domicile" means whatever place you set up as your permanent residence and make the primary place for your affairs. You can have many residences but only one domicile, which is where you intend to return after you have been away. There is no single explanation that sets forth the criteria for all states. A single definition of domicile would be "a person's residence that is intended to be the permanent residence and not just a temporary one." If you own property in more than one state, you face the possibility of any of the states imposing domicile on you and the tax complications that can accompany it.

Usually, these issues are not raised during your lifetime. However, they can become a concern after your death. Problems can result in litigation and additional expenses to your estate. Once established, your place of domicile continues until your permanent residence is changed. The tax regulations of the states place the burden of proof upon the person asserting a change of domicile to show his or her intention of the change. Your actions, not your declarations, are controlling in determining the facts. The fact that you register and vote in one place is not necessarily conclusive, if in fact, this was done simply to avoid taxation in a jurisdiction. In determining your intention, the length of time spent at a location is significant but not necessarily controlling.

New York Law

The leading case in the state of New York was decided by a New York Court in 1908 and still remains the law on the subject. This case provides that a written declaration of domicile shows an intent to establish domicile if it is honest and not given with the intent of deceit.

Florida Residence

When, for example, a retiree chooses his or her Florida residence as his or her domicile, there exists a method of expressing that intention in a very clear and convincing way. A written declaration of domicile is sworn to before a notary public and filed with the Florida Circuit Court. In the declaration, the individual states that it is to be taken as his or her declaration of citizenship, actual legal residence, and domicile in Florida. The retiree certifies the intent to register at the local Florida address when the registration books reopen and to comply with all other requirements of a legal resident of Florida. He or she certifies that he or she has no intention to return to the former domicile and intends to remain in Florida permanently.

What the Courts Consider

In determining domicile, the courts will look into various factors, including:

- Ownership of dwelling
- Percentage of time spent in the state where the dwelling is
- Homestead tax exemption in states where it applies
- Other real estate holdings
- Occupation or dual occupations
- Business interests and activities
- Filing of tangible and intangible property tax returns
- Voter registration and proof of actually having voted
- Automobile registration
- Driver's license
- Location of bank accounts and safe deposit boxes
- Location of a will
- Recital of domicile in a will
- Ownership of a cemetery lot

- Statement of residence via affidavit
- Church or synagogue membership
- Civic and fraternal club participation
- Union membership
- Charitable contributions
- Children's school attendance records
- Termination of residence by notice to the local taxing office, cancellation of voting registration, change of driver's license, change of auto license plates, and any of the activities showing a legitimate relocation from one state to another

Criteria for Florida

The following is a checklist of some additional actions a person can take to establish a Florida domicile:

- Obtain a Florida driver's license
- Use Florida license plates for the car
- File Florida intangible tax returns each year
- File federal income tax returns using a Florida address
- Use a Florida address for every occasion that an address needs to be given
- Avoid resident memberships in social clubs, religious organizations, and the like in the state of former domicile (those memberships should be converted to nonresident memberships)
- Obtain resident memberships in social clubs, religious organizations, and the like in Florida
- When able, file for Florida homestead exemption
- Maintain safe deposit boxes, bank accounts, and brokerage accounts in Florida and not in the state of former domicile
- Have credit cards and other bill statements mailed to Florida address
- Have Florida address printed on checks, business cards, and letterhead
- Transfer insurance to a Florida broker
- Maintain an office in Florida
- Spend more time in Florida than in other states
- Register and vote in Florida precinct

Probate and Domicile

A layman's inaccurate notions regarding his legal residence can result in his estate being devastated in probate. When holdings are sizable and located in two or more states, you can bet each state will be trying to secure its "probate allocation," unless precautionary steps are taken. Speaking of geography, estate planners often ask clients, Why don't you move to Miami Beach? While asked in jest, there is a serious rationale behind the question, because Florida doesn't have an inheritance tax or income tax, as so many states do. Yes, state death taxes can be a critical problem, but you should not relocate to Florida, or anywhere else, solely to avoid such tax problems.

If there looms a potential conflict, you should create a record containing documentation supporting your intention. Since the states are permitted to determine your permanent residence, you could face a determination from state tax authorities of multiple domiciles. This could mean multiple payments to more than one state of income and estate taxes and potential lawsuits.

All of this means that if you have a choice, choose the state with the better tax advantages, for example, Florida versus New York. If you do, you then have to alter your presence and affiliations with each. In one instance, you have to increase your contacts, and in the other you have to reduce them with a measure of continuity in each case.

Changing your domicile is not simply a game where if you perform certain acts or make certain maneuvers you are going to succeed. Where your permanent residence is situated is a question of fact and this is why your actions and not your words are the determining factors.

CHAPTER 16

The Power of the Survivor

*W*hen it comes to an inheritance, the vast majority of our states protect a surviving spouse against receiving less than his or her statutory share of an estate. In most jurisdictions, it is difficult to disinherit a surviving spouse. Usually he or she has the right to make a claim against all of the "assets" of the owner's estate. The current trend of our states has been the widening of these rights by creating laws that add to the estate of a deceased spouse—assets that may have been transferred while he or she was alive solely for the purpose of defeating the surviving spouse's eventual statutory claim.

Today, the laws of the state of New York provide the most favorable treatment for a surviving spouse who does not receive his or her statutory share. Some states permit these rights to be defeated by the creation of certain kinds of trusts.

In order to avoid havoc, litigation, and unnecessary expenses, if you anticipate a problem, an agreement with your spouse specifically providing for his or her rights should be obtained during both spouses' lifetimes through a prenuptial or postnuptial agreement.

An important right provided for by state law available to a surviving spouse is the right to receive a statutory share of a deceased spouse's estate in lieu of, or in addition to, the provisions made in a living trust or will. Forty states and the District of Columbia grant a surviving spouse this right, commonly called the "elective right." Twenty-two of these states include some categories of nonprobate property in calculating the elective share, and twenty-five of these states permit the elective share to be satisfied in whole or in part by a trust or trust equivalent.

In addition, many states have laws that increase a decedent's estate by adding back to the estate certain lifetime transfers such as joint bank accounts, Totten trust accounts, and other revocable transfers against which a surviving spouse may elect. These forms of transfers are commonly called "testamentary substitutes," since they are transfers made during a spouse's lifetime which usually do not pass to the beneficiary of such an account until the death of the person who has created it.

The law of the particular state may exempt certain property such as life insurance proceeds or retirement benefits from the elective right. A survivor's share could be reduced if property that is not exempt is transferred into property that is exempt.

In most common law property states, a spouse is entitled to one-third of the property left by the other spouse. In a few, it's one-half. The exact amount of the spouse's minimum share often depends on whether the couple have children. In some states, the surviving spouse only has to be left a certain percentage of the estate transferred by will. In other states, property transferred by means other than a will, such as a living trust, is included when calculating whether a spouse has received his or her minimum legal share of property.

What happens if a person leaves nothing to a spouse or leaves less than the spouse is entitled to under state law? In most states, the surviving spouse has a choice of either taking what was provided or rejecting it and instead taking the minimum share allowed by state law. Taking the share permitted by law is called "electing to take against the will."

When a spouse elects to take against the will, the property taken comes out of one or more of the bequests given to others by the will (or in many states, other transfer documents such as a living trust, as well). In other words, somebody else is going to get less. So, if you don't provide your spouse with at least the statutory share under your state's laws, your gifts to others may be substantially reduced.

The Augmented Estate

As mentioned above, in many common law states, all property of a deceased spouse, not just the property left by will, is considered in determining whether a spouse has been left the statutory share. This is the concept adopted under the Uniform Probate Code. This is called the "augmented estate." It means that, in determining whether a surviving spouse has been adequately provided for in the estate of the deceased spouse, the courts in most common law property states look to see the value of the property the surviving spouse has received, specifically focusing on the following types of property:

- If a deceased spouse during the marriage transferred property to a third party, but retained a right to some enjoyment over it (possession of income/revocation)
- Property in joint name with a third party with the right of survivorship
- Gifts made in contemplation of death
- Gifts totalling more than $10,000 a year to any one person

These are the types of transfers that are added back for the purposes of calculating the elective right of the surviving spouse.

In most states, the traditional permissive method for funding the elective share is through the creation of an elective share trust. Under such a trust, the surviving spouse is entitled to the income from the trust for life based upon the minimum required amount. As such, if the will of the first spouse to die does not make at least such a provision, the surviving spouse has the right to elect to receive his or her legal portion outright.

In recognition of the rights of the surviving spouse to have direct access to a portion of the estate, many states have been modifying their laws to widen the rights of surviving spouses. In some states, such as New Jersey and Maryland, the spouse's share must be left outright. In other states, like Connecticut, Florida, and Maine, it can be left in trust. The community property states protect survivors' rights through their community property laws. The election afforded in these states centers around the right of the surviving spouse to receive his or her half of the shared property outright. The state of Georgia on the other hand has no protective provision for a spouse as it does not permit a surviving spouse to elect against the first spouse's will.

New York State

Recently, New York State changed its format. Its law is probably the most favorable to a surviving spouse and may lead the way for legislation in other states.

Prior New York law augmented an estate with testamentary substitutes, including: gifts made in contemplation of death, Totten trusts, joint bank accounts, property held in joint tenancy, and revocable transfers in which the estate owner retained the power to consume, invade, or dispose of the principal. One purpose of making these nonprobate assets subject to the right of election was to limit the estate owner's ability to nullify the survivor's rights by disposing of assets outside of probate. Another purpose was to reduce the amount of the probate estate that could pass to the survivor under the right of election, if the survivor was also the beneficiary of nonprobate dispositions.

The new law adds to the existing ones the following categories of testamentary substitutes:

- Gifts made after August 31, 1992, and within one year of death that do not qualify for a federal gift tax exclusion and are made after the date of marriage
- For decedents dying after August 31, 1992, U.S. savings bonds held jointly with right of survivorship or held individually by the decedent and payable to a beneficiary other than the decedent or the decedent's estate
- For transactions entered after August 31, 1992, e.g., interests in pension, profit-sharing, individual retirement accounts (IRAs), and other retirement plan benefits (but only one-half of joint and survivor annuity and defined contribution plan benefits)
- Property over which the decedent held a lifetime general power of appointment
- Irrevocable lifetime trusts entered into after August 31, 1992, and the date of marriage, if the decedent retained an income interest or life estate

A sizeable loophole remains, however, due to lobbying by the insurance industry: the deletion of insurance proceeds from the expanded list of testamentary substitutes.

Many experts have suggested that a life insurance investment may be a safe-haven under New York law since it is not considered a testamentary substitute. An argument may be made that, if a person obtains a life insurance policy and designates someone other than his or her estate as the beneficiary and the policy is retained until death, a distribution of property within the meaning of the law has been made (as a transfer with retained possession for life) and could be deemed to be a testamentary substitute and, as such, added back to the estate for elective rights.

Elimination of Elective Share Trusts

For decedents dying after August 31, 1992, the most significant change is that the surviving spouse may elect to take the elective share outright. An income interest in a trust or a life estate, such as the right to occupy the family residence for life, will no longer satisfy the survivor's right of election. The price of taking the elective share outright is that, unless the will or trust agreement provides otherwise, the survivor forfeits all beneficial interests in any "terminable interest" for his or her benefit to the extent that the interests exceed the amount of the elective share.

Example: Mary dies on September 1, 1994, with an estate of $900,000 consisting of: a $150,000 interest in a house held in joint tenancy with her husband Jack; a $50,000 joint checking account; a $50,000 IRA of which Jack is the beneficiary; and $650,000 of securities. The securities pass to a trust in which Jack has an income interest and the couple's adult children have remainder interests. Under Mary's estate plan, the value of the property passing outright to Jack is $250,000, which is less than one-third of her estate. If Jack elects to take an additional $50,000 outright, he forfeits his income interest in the trust, thereby accelerating distribution of the trust to their children and prompt payment of estate taxes.

Planning Implications

Elimination of the elective share trust recognizes that the surviving spouse is entitled not only to financial support but also to compensation for contributing to the marriage partnership. It puts a surviving spouse in a position similar to that of a divorcing spouse. The similarity complicates estate planning. For example, estate plans calling for QTIP trusts may create a conflict of interest on the part of the person planning the estate for the spouses. The beneficiary spouse should be informed of the option to take a share outright, and a second estate planner may be necessary. Even harmonious relationships may require negotiation between each spouse's adviser in order to draft marital agreements waiving elective share rights.

Members of New York's estate planning bar also opposed the elimination of the elective share trust because it could create havoc with many existing estate planning strategies. For example, trusts designed to provide for children of a prior marriage or to hold the decedent spouse's interest in a closely held business could be sabotaged if the survivor elects to take an outright share.

A spouse's election to take a share outright can thwart marital deduction planning. Take the case of an illiquid estate consisting, for example, of a closely held business interest that is left in a QTIP trust for the transfer of the surviving spouse, thereby deferring estate taxes on the first spouse's death. The spouses have taken out a second-to-die life insurance policy, which provides the liquidity for estate tax payments when the surviving spouse dies. If the surviving spouse elects to take his or her share of the estate outright (which he or she has the right to do), he or she will forfeit the balance of the interests in the QTIP trust. This could, therefore, accelerate estate taxes to the first spouse's death, and if the forfeited portion is in excess of the applicable unified credit ($650,000), it might require partial liquidation of the estate to meet such estate taxes. If a waiver of a surviving spouse's right of election cannot be obtained, the marital deduction can be preserved by amending a decedent spouse's plan to override the law's forfeiture provision. Thus, despite the survivor's election to take a share outright, the balance of the QTIP trust could remain in trust for the survivor's benefit.

Apparently, the state of New York did not take into consideration certain legitimate reasons for putting money in trust. Under the new law, an older couple cannot get married without a prenuptial agreement and be guaranteed that the property they bring to the marriage will pass to their own children from the first marriage. In addition, the spendthrift or incompetent spouse was not considered.

The most direct method to make sure the will of the first spouse is followed, is to have the surviving spouse waive the right of election. The right of election of a surviving spouse is personal to him or her. As such, creditors have no involvement in it. If a spouse should die before exercising the right, the spouse will not have died possessing any property that would be subject to taxation.

The most secure method of limiting a spouse's right is through a prenuptial or postnuptial agreement. Without such an agreement, the only effective way to limit the election, in addition to the creation of exempt property, is the making of outright gifts to third parties.

Some states permit the right to be defeated by the creation of a revocable trust and placing assets in it. However, in the vast majority of states this form of trust will not defeat the right since the grantor maintains possession and control over the property placed in the trust. Some states permit the right to be defeated by transferring assets to an irrevocable trust even if an income interest is retained by the grantor.

It is the law of your permanent residence or domicile at the time of your death that will determine the rights of a surviving spouse with regard to real estate and personal property. With regard to property located outside of your domiciliary state, the law of the situs of the property will govern.

However, the use of a trust may afford you the opportunity to have the law of a jurisdiction other than your domicile apply to certain of your assets. To do this, you can create an irrevocable trust in your selected state and transfer assets located and kept in that state and other states. You can also recite that the law of the designated state will be applicable to the trust.

Percentages Allowed by States

The surviving spouse receives a right to enjoy one-third of the deceased spouse's real property for life in the following states: Connecticut, Kentucky, Rhode Island, and South Carolina.

The surviving spouse receives a percentage of the estate in the following states:

FIXED PERCENTAGE

Alabama	⅓ of augmented estate
Alaska	⅓ of augmented estate
Colorado	½ of augmented estate
District of Columbia	½ of estate
Florida	30% of estate
Hawaii	⅓ of estate
Iowa	⅓ of estate
Maine	⅓ of augmented estate
Minnesota	⅓ of estate
Montana	⅓ of augmented estate
Nebraska	⅓ of augmented estate
New Jersey	⅓ of augmented estate
North Dakota	⅓ of augmented estate
Oregon	¼ of estate
Pennsylvania	⅓ of estate
South Carolina	⅓ of estate
South Dakota	⅓ of augmented estate
Tennessee	⅓ of estate
Utah	⅓ of estate

PERCENTAGE VARIES IF THERE ARE CHILDREN *(usually ½ if no children, ⅓ if children)*

Arkansas	New Hampshire
Illinois	New York
Indiana	North Carolina
Kansas	Ohio
Maryland	Oklahoma
Massachusetts	Vermont
Michigan	Virginia
Mississippi	West Virginia
Missouri	Wyoming

OTHER

Delaware	$20,000 or ⅓ of estate, whichever is less

❖

CHAPTER 17

The Subsequent Marriage: Premarital and Postmarital Agreements

*W*hen people have been involved in multiple marriages and there are either more than one set of children or children from a prior marriage, the estate plan is even more complex. In such a situation, the conflict usually centers around the protection of the children from a prior union and the protection of the surviving spouse.

This chapter comprehensively informs you as to what strategies and devices are available, what your goals should be, what the tax ramifications are, and what the rights are of all of the parties.

One of the most common forms of protection and orderly distribution is the premarital agreement, which is universally recognized and in most states requires complete financial disclosure by each of the parties to it.

In finalizing an estate plan for people involved in this kind of situation, the choice of fiduciaries (executors, personal representatives, and trustees) and the application of the tax law is extremely important.

The conflict that can be presented by a subsequent marriage is the wish to provide an economic benefit to the surviving spouse, while making sure that property is available for the descendants of a prior marriage. To solve this dilemma, assets can be left in trust for the lifetime benefit of a surviving spouse with the children receiving the ultimate distribution after his or her death. However, in some instances where the spouse may not be much older than the descendants, the value of the money over a long period of time may mandate that the beneficiaries should get their inheritance, even after the impact of transfer taxes thereon, in the first instance. In this type of situation, probably the best method is providing an inheritance for each beneficiary of a specific sum or specific property based upon his or her needs without worrying about the tax aspect of the gift or having any relationship to the percentage of the entire estate.

The Choice of Fiduciaries

The choice of the executors or personal representatives and trustees in any estate plan is usually one of the hardest decisions faced by an estate owner. Naming a surviving spouse or child by a prior marriage can create conflicts. Usually, in this situation, some independent person is asked to serve either together with the family members or alone.

The Marital Deduction

From a tax deferral standpoint, most estates are helped by the use of the marital deduction. Since 1982, the tax law has permitted a marital deduction for qualified terminable interest property (QTIP). This allows the property to be placed in a trust for the benefit of the surviving spouse, who has a qualified income interest for life, with the guaranty that the ultimate disposition of the remainder balance will pass to those designated by the estate owner. One problem related to a QTIP is that, if the property in the trust is not productive, the surviving spouse has the right to demand that it be made so. A conflict can arise if, for example, property in the trust consists of an interest in a business that does not pay any dividends. See chapter 9 for a detailed discussion of the QTIP trust.

The Tax Clause

Who pays the estate taxes when the subsequent surviving spouse dies is a very significant element in estates of this nature. This problem is obvious when different groups (spouse and descendants from a prior marriage) are sharing in the estate. Great caution must be taken to be sure that the estate taxes are apportioned among the parties properly, especially when the surviving spouse controls the situation.

The following is a hypothetical example of how a situation can create a totally different result than the estate owner intended:

The estate owner desires to favor his surviving spouse with a lifetime interest in a QTIP trust that will pass to her children upon her death.

The will or living trust of the estate owner provides for the residuary or the rest of his estate to pass to his children. The estate owner's living trust or will provides that all estate taxes will be paid out of the residuary of the estate without apportionment. If the executor or trustee does not elect to qualify the QTIP trust for the marital deduction, the property in the trust could be fully taxed in his estate and the residuary estate would bear the payment of the taxes. His children would wind up paying estate taxes on an inheritance that is to be eventually received by the children of the surviving spouse, who would inherit the same, free of estate tax.

The Rights of a Surviving Spouse

In most common law states, the surviving spouse has a right to some portion of a deceased spouse's estate. Many states have rules requiring that at least a minimum share of the estate of the first spouse to die be transferred either outright or in a qualifying form to the surviving spouse. If the surviving spouse does not receive the minimum share, he or she would have a claim against the estate. The required percentage of the estate that is protected varies with each state. The net effect of these statutes is the limitation of the estate owner to transfer assets to others. This subject is discussed in greater detail in chapter 16.

Life Insurance

An excellent way to protect children from a prior marriage and still provide an economic benefit to a spouse is through life insurance. This can be structured favorably insofar as estate taxes are concerned by having a third party, such as an irrevocable trust, own and be the beneficiary of the insurance policy. Ownership of this kind will provide the surviving spouse with the benefits of the trust during lifetime and will pass on estate tax free after the trust terminates to the children of the insured spouse. A trust of this kind must contain a provision that the benefits of the trust will only be paid to the spouse if he or she is married to and living with the insured spouse at the time of death. If the parties are not married or are separated at such time, the trust can provide for the benefit to revert to the descendants of the insured spouse.

Charitable Bequests

If there are no descendants and the first spouse to die is charitably inclined and wishes to guarantee that the property will eventually pass to a particular hospital, museum, or university on the second spouse's death, the living trust or will of the first spouse can be drafted to take advantage of both the marital deduction and the charitable deduction. This would completely shield the assets from estate tax. There are basically two ways to accomplish this, detailed below.

Annuity Trust or Unitrust
The will or living trust can create either a charitable remainder annuity trust or a charitable remainder unitrust. In either case, the income

portion of the trust would be payable to the surviving spouse for his or her life. On the surviving spouse's death, the remainder must be paid to one or more "qualified charities" as defined in Section 501(c)(3) of the Code. The decedent's estate will be entitled to a marital deduction for the surviving spouse's income interest and a charitable deduction for the remainder interest.

There are problems with this approach, however. The complicated rules of this type of trust limit the amount of income that may be paid to the surviving spouse, and the rules governing charitable remainder trusts prohibit any invasions of principal (other than to satisfy the income requirement).

QTIP Trust with Charitable Beneficiary

A simpler way is if one or more "qualified" charities are named as the remainder beneficiaries of a QTIP trust. All of the trust income is payable to the surviving spouse, and the decedent's will or living trust can provide that the principal be invaded under certain conditions for the surviving spouse's benefit. The first spouse's estate receives a marital deduction for the full value of the QTIP. On the second spouse's death, the value of the trust is included in his or her taxable estate but is offset by a full charitable deduction.

Unified Credit Trust

If the first spouse has sufficient assets to mandate the establishment of a unified credit trust ($1,000,000 in property) in his or her living trust or will, there are a number of alternatives that may be considered. The unified credit amount can be left in trust for a surviving spouse for his or her life, and then pass free of estate taxes to the first spouse's children from a prior marriage (either outright, or in further trust, depending on the children's circumstance and ages). Another alternative is to have the income from the trust sprinkled or sprayed among the surviving spouse and the decedent's children, at the trustee's discretion. The final alternative is to have the unified credit amount pass directly to the children with little or no estate taxes being paid.

The unique issues that are raised by a subsequent marriage make it imperative that they be reviewed in advance. Waiting until after remarriage may be too late.

Premarital Agreements

A premarital agreement is often employed when the partners have been previously married. This type of agreement controls the distribution of assets in the event of death. It can also provide for financial and housing benefits in the event of a dissolution of the marriage. The use of premarital agreements should be considered whenever one of the parties is contemplating making a substantial gift to the other or where it is desirable to limit the statutory, common law, or community property rights of each party to the other's property or to limit or eliminate other claims of one against the other.

In some instances, the agreement does not focus on legal rights and duties, but rather, serves as a statement of the marital goals and relationship sought by the parties. This type of agreement may be incorporated into the more conventional type of premarital agreement.

In its common form, the premarital agreement involves a transfer, or the promise of a transfer, of property from a more affluent party to the other less affluent party. The promised transfer may be by living trust or will. If so, it does not preclude a larger gift than promised.

The agreement should really be considered as part of the estate plan of both parties and should be evaluated in terms of its legal estate, gift, and income tax consequences, the appropriate estate tax techniques, and general policy considerations. These considerations are discussed below.

Validity of Premarital Agreements

As a general rule, in order to be valid under state law, a premarital agreement involving property rights must be in writing, subscribed to by the parties, and acknowledged with the formalities required for the recording of a deed. In addition, it must be fairly arrived at and be fair and reasonable, both when entered into and at the time of any future trial involving the respective parties. Because of the difficulty in defining "fairness" and "reasonableness," as well as the uncertainty created by the requirement that the agreement be fair at some future date, a number of states now require instead that the agreement not be "unconscionable." Proving unconscionability is harder than proving unfairness. The Uniform Premarital Agreement Act adopts the standard of unconscionability.

Both parties must make a full and fair disclosure of all their income and property. If one or both fail or refuse to make the required disclosure, any agreement entered into may be open to later challenge by the injured party. Even when disclosure has not been made, it has often been held that the party attacking the agreement had sufficient knowledge of the defendant's assets through other means.

An agreement may be challenged based on a claim of fraud, duress, or taking advantage by putting financial pressure on a less advantaged spouse, but these claims are not easy to prove. However, the closer to the date of marriage that an agreement is signed, the more likely it is that a claim of duress or overreaching will be upheld.

There is no requirement that each party be represented by a separate attorney. However, when one attorney represents both parties, the courts will scrutinize the agreement more carefully, particularly if the agreement is one-sided or if there was a lack of disclosure. The education and business experience of a party waiving separate representation is also taken into account.

It is becoming more common to videotape the actual signing of the agreement. The opposing attorneys examine each party to establish that the person signing read and understood the agreement, had the opportunity to consult with his or her attorney, and signed voluntarily.

Postmarital Agreements

Even if the parties marry without having entered into a premarital agreement, many states permit spouses to alter their rights through a properly executed postmarital agreement. The bargaining power of the "richer" spouse in a second or subsequent marriage, after the marriage has been solemnized, is diminished in contrast to the bargaining power of the "poorer" spouse. For this reason, the more advantaged spouse should generally strive for a premarital agreement.

Postmarital agreements may be much more useful where: (1) neither spouse has been married before and the couple has been married (not necessarily happily) for some time; (2) no premarital agreement has been executed; and (3) the richer spouse controls nearly all of the marital assets. In these cases, both the "richer" and "poorer" spouses may have something to gain through a postmarital agreement. The richer spouse will be able to protect himself by reducing his or her estate's "exposure" in the event of death or divorce. The poorer spouse, for the first time during the marriage, will receive outright ownership of valuable assets without risking a divorce (so long as he or she waives state-law spousal rights). Though this might appear somewhat unattractive, a spouse who has control over very few assets might be willing to waive future assets in return for a sizeable sum of money or property which he or she could currently control or enjoy.

Another circumstance for a postmarital agreement is where one of the spouses believes that the premarital agreement may be defective and unenforceable (by reason, for example, of inadequate disclosure of the richer spouse's assets).

Still another circumstance where postmarital agreements make sense is where one spouse wishes to indicate that a particular asset of the marriage belongs to him or her, free from any interference by the other, either during the marriage or in the event of divorce. This is often done with interests in a family business. As compensation for giving up rights in the family business, the other spouse frequently will receive nonbusiness assets. These nonbusiness assets are usually less risky from an economic point of view but also less likely to produce income or gain.

It is imperative in this situation that each party be represented by separate counsel and that full disclosure of assets be made.

CHAPTER 18

Planning for Minors

$\mathcal{P}$lanning for minors (those under eighteen years of age) requires special estate planning. Since minor children cannot normally hold title to property, making gifts to, or for the benefit of a child, involves income, gift, and estate tax considerations.

This chapter details the different options that are available and the ramifications of each. Trusts that may be created to qualify for the permissible annual gift giving ($11,000) are described, as is whether to make a gift outright or place it in a trust.

If you have young children, you must be prepared in case a disaster should hit before they are capable of being legally and emotionally responsible for their affairs. A guardian might have to be appointed for their persons and property.

Guardians

In most states, a guardian of the person and property of a minor must be named in a will and cannot be designated in any other estate planning device, e.g., the living trust. The guardian selected by you must be approved by the court, which has the right to overrule your designation if it is in the best interests of the minor. An alternate guardian should be named in case the primary guardian does not serve.

Before designating a guardian, it is important to discuss your decision with the designated person to be sure he or she will serve if called upon.

In most states, minor children cannot own property outright. If you leave property outright to a minor child, the child will receive it when he or she is eighteen years old. However, you can designate a guardian to manage the property until the minor reaches eighteen years of age.

The guardian of the person, if financially responsible, can be designated to serve in the capacity of guardian of the property as well.

Trusts

You may also leave property to a child in a trust. If it is established in a living trust, the property avoids probate. If you leave property in a will, the property will go through probate before it is turned over to the trust.

Gifts to Children: Custodianship

Since minors cannot hold title to property, if you make a gift to a minor during your lifetime, it must be made pursuant to a state regulation. Many states employ the Uniform Gifts to Minors Act (UGMA), which permits you to give a gift to a minor by giving the gift to a custodian who holds title to the property for the benefit of the minor.

The UGMA covers gifts of money, securities, life insurance, and annuities. You can stipulate that the property is to be turned over to the minor at either age eighteen or twenty-one. In California (under the Uniform Transfer To Minors Act), it can be extended to age twenty-five. Some states also allow you to make gifts of realty, partnership interests, and tangible personal property in this fashion.

A custodian is given the power to invest, accumulate, or expend income or principal for the support, education, and benefit of the minor without regard to the parent's resources, obligation of support, or to the minor's other resources. Income from custodial property is taxed to the minor, but if used to discharge a parent's obligation of support, it will be taxed to the parent. In addition, the income tax effects are different for minors under and over the age of fourteen. (See "kiddie tax," discussed later in this chapter.)

A custodianship allows the minor access to funds at a relatively early age. If this is not your intention, you might prefer to set up a trust instead.

Estate Tax

Your minor child's custodial assets are included in his or her gross estate. They are not included in your estate unless you are the maker of the gift and also the custodian. If your estate is large enough to be liable for estate tax, and you wish to set up a custodial account for a child or a grandchild, you should not be the custodian. In the case of a grandchild, the parent of the minor child should be designated as the custodian. However, if your estate is not liable for estate tax (is under $650,000), it may be advantageous to name yourself as custodian if the account includes appreciated securities. If you should predecease the minor, this custodial property will then receive a step-up in basis upon your death, which will thereafter be advantageous for future income tax purposes.

Unearned Income of Minor Children (Kiddie Tax)

The net unearned income of a child under age fourteen is taxed at his or her parent's top marginal rate. The source of the income is irrelevant. Therefore, gifts of income-producing property to minor children may not result in any overall income tax savings for you. However, all income of children age fourteen or older is taxed at the standard tax rates.

Unearned income is anything that is not derived from personal services. It includes the following:

- Social Security or pension benefits to the extent they are includable in gross income
- Income from assets held in a Uniform Gift to Minors Act Custodianship
- Income from assets in a trust that is distributed to the child

Presently, the net unearned income for children under fourteen is the amount of the child's unearned income less the sum of:

1. $500; and
2. The greater of:
   a. $500 of the standard deduction, or
   b. The deductions allowed the child that are directly connected with the production of the child's unearned income

The standard deduction permitted for a child who is claimed by someone as a dependent is limited to the greater of $500 or the amount of the child's earned income. The net unearned income cannot exceed the child's total taxable income for the year. The $500 figure is adjusted annually for inflation, in increments of $50.

Because the unearned income of children age fourteen and over is taxed at the child's lower rate, you should make gifts to them which defer taxable income until the child reaches age fourteen. These are some ways of deferring unearned income through gifts:

- Growth stock which typically pays little in current dividends but is likely to increase in value over the years. The child can sell the stock after age fourteen and be taxed at the child's rate.
- U.S. government savings bonds (EE) with maturity dates after the child reaches age fourteen, unless the child already holds such bonds

and has elected to treat each year's accrual of interest as income. This election is irrevocable, even for newly purchased bonds. If no such election has occurred, the child may defer the interest on the bonds until age fourteen and then be taxed at his own rate.

- Since younger children will effectively be in the same tax bracket as their parents, investment strategies that make sense for you (e.g., municipal bonds) probably make equal sense for them.

There are still some tax advantages to transferring assets to children under age fourteen. The first $1,000 of income still gets preferential treatment, (all income received by the child of $1,000 or less is taxed at the child's standard rate), as does all of the child's income at age fourteen. Upper-income parents and grandparents can also save on estate taxes by making lifetime gifts to their children and grandchildren.

Gifts to Children: Trusts

Trusts may accumulate income for a minor and still qualify for the annual exclusion ($11,000) as long as all principal or income is paid to the minor by the age of twenty-one. Trusts paying all income to the minor and trusts with withdrawal power also qualify for exclusion.

If you are planning to make gifts to minor children, you may find the flexibility of a trust more suited to his or her purposes than the custodianship discussed in the previous section. Tax considerations, as usual, must be taken into account. Several alternate forms of trusts are discussed below.

Section 2503(c) Trust

The Code Section 2503(c) provides a vehicle for creating a trust for the benefit of a minor that qualifies for the annual gift tax exclusion ($11,000). This section provides that a gift to an individual under age twenty-one will not be treated as a gift of a future interest, (a gift from which the beneficiary will not have any present enjoyment and is thus not eligible for the gift tax annual [$11,000] exclusion), if the gift meets these requirements:

- The trustee has the power to expend the gift property and its income for the benefit of the minor before he or she reaches age twenty-one
- The minor has the right to receive the unexpended property and income at age twenty-one

- If the minor should die before age twenty-one, the principal and income of the trust must be paid to the minor's estate or to persons he or she chooses (by will or otherwise)

If you are concerned about potential estate tax liability, you should not name yourself as a trustee since the trust will be considered part of your estate if you die before the minor reaches the age of twenty-one years.

While a trust offers certain advantages over a custodianship in some situations, these differences narrow in states that have expanded the class of property includable under a custodianship. For most middle-income older people contemplating modest gifts to grandchildren, the custodianship is probably preferable.

Section 2503(b) Trust

The Internal Revenue Code provides another method, under Section 2503(b), for making a gift to a minor in trust which qualifies for the annual exclusion. This type of trust must be irrevocable and need only provide that all income be paid to the minor currently. The value of the gift is the value calculated under actuarial tables of the minor's right to the income of the trust during its term. For example, a gift in trust for life of the right to receive income from $10,000 to a child who is twelve at the time of the making of the gift is valued for gift tax purpose at 98.329 percent thereof, or the sum of $9,832.90.

If you are a grandparent setting up such a trust, you may not wish to pay the income directly to the minor, and, indeed, may have to pay it to a guardian in many states. Instead, the income can be made payable to the minor's parents to be expended for the minor's benefit, or the income could be paid to a custodial account for the minor.

Again, the expenses of setting up and administering this type of trust, as well as its advantages, should be compared with a custodianship.

Discretionary or "Crummey" Trust

An elderly grandparent may not find either of the preceding trusts to his or her liking. The Section 2503(c) trust requires distribution of the principal by age twenty-one and sometimes earlier. The Section 2503(b) trust requires distribution of income from the outset. A third alternative gives the trustee discretion to distribute or accumulate income and, in addition, to give the minor the power to withdraw the property transferred to the trust for a reasonable period of time after the gift is made. The minor's power to demand distribution of the property constitutes a present interest, and, therefore, gifts to the trust qualify for the annual gift tax exclusion ($11,000).

As the grantor, you are required to alert the beneficiary of his or her power of withdrawal and to allow a reasonable time for its exercise or waiver of the right of withdrawal. Thirty days' notice is considered reasonable. There is no need to appoint a legal guardian on behalf of the minor beneficiary, but the trust must not present any legal barrier to such an appointment.

To be sure that there is no potential gift tax liability to a minor beneficiary if the withdrawal power is in excess of $5,000, the trust must provide that the minor will eventually receive the property upon the termination of the trust at his or her stated age or that the minor can control its disposition by his or her will (by a power of appointment) if he or she should die before the trust's termination date.

The Crummey trust offers the person seeking to provide funds for young children the greatest flexibility by permitting discretionary use of income and delaying distribution of the principal of the trust beyond majority without forfeiting the annual gift tax exclusion.

The best way to establish a trust for a child which is to take effect after your death is in a living trust. If you wish, you can create a separate trust for each of your children. Your successor trustee will manage the trust and use the trust's property for the benefit of the child until he or she attains the age you designate is the termination date, at which time the trust property is turned over to the child.

❖

CHAPTER 19

Estate Planning for Families with Children Who Have Special Needs

*E*state planning for families that have a child with special needs must take into consideration a multitude of emotional, physical, and financial issues. This requires consideration not only of the child but of the family as a whole.

The only effective way to protect a special-needs beneficiary and ensure no loss of his or her government assistance is through the use of a trust fund. The type of trust fund and its important provisions are set forth in this chapter in detail. Included are sample trust provisions that should be contained in a trust of this kind for it to be legally and practically effective.

Each family must develop an estate plan that is tailored to the specific needs of all of its members, including the child with special needs. It is of particular importance to consult with professionals experienced in this unique kind of estate planning.

Who Is Going to Take Care of My Child?

The most important concern expressed by parents of a child with special needs is who will take care of their child when they are no longer here. Parents often find themselves asking questions such as, "What are my choices in designing a financial plan that can provide for my child in order to meet any possible future needs?" and "How can I establish a funding mechanism to pay for any needed services, and how can I be sure that these funds will be used for the benefit of my child without jeopardizing his or her entitlements to governmental benefits?"

If you die without a living trust or a will, your estate will be disposed of according to the laws of the state of your residence. If you have a spouse and children, the spouse will typically get a specific portion and the children the balance. If you have no spouse but only children, they will receive all of your property. When property passes to children in this manner, it is divided equally among them, whether or not they need it and whether or not they are competent and able to manage it. Thus, parents of a child with a disability are likely to wish for some different manner of distribution. These persons must have a living trust or a will.

Through their testamentary dispositions, parents can divide up their property however they think best, perhaps giving a larger share to the most needy child, which may be the one with a disability. There could be, however, several significant problems with this approach, such as the following:

- The disabled son or daughter may not have the capacity to manage property left to him or her outright.
- Property left outright to disabled persons will be counted as their assets and thus may make them ineligible for certain governmental benefits in which eligibility is based on need and a limitation of income and assets (SSI and Medicaid).
- With the additional assets counted as their own, disabled persons receiving governmental services may be subject to charges for care.

Thus, in many ways, leaving assets directly to a handicapped person who would otherwise be eligible for governmental benefits is very much like making a gift to the government.

What Are the Goals?

In the creation of every plan by a family, there are two overriding and paramount considerations:

- The assurance that, no matter what is formulated, the disabled person does not lose or become disqualified for applicable entitlement programs
- To the extent legally possible, the family assets, including the disabled persons share, are kept out of the reach of governmental authorities providing services to that person

Planning Early

Successful family planning in this regard must begin at the time the family becomes aware of the handicapping condition, whether it be at birth, at the commencement of an illness, at the occurrence of an accident, or at the final diagnosis of a disability.

Creating a Fund

The focal point in the planning for a handicapped person's needs is a fund. The form and structure of this fund must be in such a manner that it will not be considered a resource that would disqualify the handicapped person from receiving entitlement benefits.

Federal Entitlement Programs

The most important federal programs are those based upon the recipient's financial need. The two most significant are: (1) Supplemental Security Income (SSI), for aged, blind, or other persons with disabilities having limited income and resources, and (2) Medical Assistance, also known as Medicaid.

SSI and Medicaid Eligibility

Eligibility for SSI and Medicaid benefits rests not only upon the fact that the individual possesses some type of disability, but also upon the fact that the individual has limited income and resources. The vast majority of persons who qualify for SSI will automatically qualify for Medicaid. For a more detailed discussion of Medicaid, see chapter 23.

SSI Transfer of Assets

Federal legislation that became effective December 14, 1999 (the "Legislation") establishes a penalty period for applicants or recipients of SSI who transfer or give away their resources. The law provides that a thirty-six-month "look-back" period be applied starting with the date of the SSI application or the date of the transfer, whichever is later. Depending upon when and how much money is transferred, SSI eligibility may be withheld for as long as thirty-six months.

The law also provides, however, that if the transfer is made to a Supplemental Needs Trust, no penalty can be imposed; therefore, SSI eligibility would not be jeopardized. (This planning opportunity applies only to people under sixty-five years of age).

The Legislation imposes a period of ineligibility for SSI benefits on those who transfer resources on or before December 14, 1999, for less than "fair market value" during the thirty-six month "look-back" period immediately prior to the SSI application date or the date of the transfer, whichever is later. This ineligibility period applies both to individuals who transfer resources prior to applying for SSI and to those who transfer resources while they are receiving SSI. Although the period of ineligibility applies only to transfers made on or after December 14, 1999, the new system requires that individuals be asked if any resources have been transferred in the thirty-six month period prior to applying for SSI, even if part of that period is prior to December 14, 1999, because SSA must notify Medicaid of any transfers made so that the Medicaid transfer of assets rules can be applied.

Although the Legislation does not specifically address transfers of income, the new system clarifies that a transfer of income in the month of receipt, such as an inheritance, is considered a transfer of resources.

SSI Income

The social security regulations define income as anything a person receives, in cash or in-kind, that he or she can use to meet his or her needs for food, clothing, or shelter. There are two types of income: earned income and unearned income.

The regulations exclude certain items from their definition of income, one of which is the proceeds of a loan.

Loans

Since the proceeds of a loan are not considered income for SSI purposes, support to a disabled person should be made in the form of a loan, rather than on a gift basis (which is considered unearned income). By treating this assistance as a loan, the person will avoid reduction in his or her SSI benefits. It is advisable to sign a loan agreement that reflects the understanding that the value of the assistance must be repaid, although a clear and provable oral agreement will suffice. However, local legal requirements for creating an enforceable loan must be observed. For example, a disabled SSI recipient who may not have the legal capacity or ability to enter into a loan agreement may nevertheless be capable of receiving a loan, if state law holds that person liable or responsible for the reasonable value of necessities provided to him or her.

Any portion of borrowed funds that the borrower does not spend will be considered a countable resource or asset of the borrower, if he or she retains it into the month following the month of receipt. Therefore, in making advances to the disabled person under the terms of a loan agreement, caution should be exercised in not giving a larger amount than the person can spend before the end of the month. A loan should be made near the beginning of the month and the cash earmarked for certain monthly bills, which will also assure that no carryover balance develops.

Resources

Resources or assets are defined as cash or other liquid assets or any real or personal property that an individual owns and could convert to cash to be used for his or her support and maintenance.

An individual is eligible for SSI benefits in the year 2001 if his or her available resources do not exceed $2,000 ($3,000 for couples), plus a burial allowance of $1,500 per person, and all other eligibility requirements are met, which requirements include income limits for an individual living alone of $637 and for a couple, living by themselves, of $920. If an individual lives with others, the income limit is $573; for a couple it is $862. If an individual lives in the household of another, the income limit is $396.34; for a couple it is $596.67.

Pursuant to the 1996 law passed by New York State, all preneed funeral agreements established on or after January 1, 1997 by SSI applicants or recipients must be irrevocable. Under the provisions of the law, any amount can be put into an exempt, irrevocable, preneed funeral agreement, and none of the funds will be counted by Medicaid or SSI as resources or income. This prepayment must be deposited by the funeral director into a single irrevocable trust fund. The 1996 law removed the prior distinction between burial-space items, which could be prepaid in any amount, and non–burial-space items, which previously could be prepaid only up to $1,500. At any time prior to the actual services being rendered, the funeral director or the arrangements can be changed. Any funds remaining in the agreement after payment of all funeral expenses, however, must be paid the Department of Social Services. All exempt funeral arrangements created prior to January 1, 1997 continue to be tax exempt and do not have to be changed. It is important to note that resources of even $1 more than the threshold amount will result in the denial of benefits. Many times parents create an account for a child in the permissible amount, forgetting that very shortly, interest will accumulate and that the accumulation will render the individual ineligible. That $1 may result in the loss of three to four hundred dollars in benefits. If the individual is in a group home, even more may be lost in benefits.

Assets of the Handicapped Person

Due to the fact that qualification to obtain benefits under the entitlement programs is based upon the unavailability of income and resources, a person with special needs must, in effect, be disinherited, so as to be able to qualify.

These limitations create complexities in dealing with resources that are actually owned by a handicapped person. These assets must be disposed of prior to that person's application for benefits. These problems become further complicated if the person has a substitute or surrogate decision-maker such as a guardian.

Guardianship

Many parents fear that their child will be unable to make decisions regarding his or her personal affairs or will be unable to protect his or her own legal and civil rights without help. They, therefore, consider guardianship. Guardianship results in either a total or partial loss of rights and decision-making power for the handicapped individual. Therefore, families must seriously consider the disadvantages, as well as the advantages, before requesting the appointment of a guardian.

Guardianship is a most serious measure for safeguarding a disabled person's welfare and should be resorted to only when no less drastic option (such as informal guidance and advice, a special bank account, a trust, or a representative payee) will work. Guardians are appointed by a court, and state law prescribes the standards that must be satisfied before a guardian is appointed.

Guardianships may be total or limited. In a total ("plenary") guardianship, the ward may lose many legal rights, including the right to vote, to make contracts, to sign checks, and to choose whether and where to go to school. The ward also may lose the right to manage any property and assets. When a total guardian is appointed, the ward loses all of his or her decision-making authority, even though there may be decisions he or she is capable of making.

Limited Guardianship

A limited guardian has powers only in the areas specified by the court's guardianship order. In order to properly limit the guardian's role, the court first determines where the disabled person needs help and then empowers the guardian to make decisions for the ward in those areas. For example, in some limited guardianships, the guardian is given authority to make decisions regarding the ward's medical and educational needs, while the ward can still control the other areas of his or her life.

Unless the guardianship has been limited, the guardian will manage all of the person's personal and financial affairs. If the handicapped person is mildly or moderately disabled and capable of making some of his or her own decisions, guardianship may do more harm than good, as the loss of independence might undermine his or her efforts to manage his or her own life. However, if a person is severely or profoundly disabled, the loss of rights may be no loss at all, as he or she would not be able to exercise them anyway.

Third-Party Assets

In the family's development of a plan, assets that may pass to the disabled person upon the death of a third party must be traced and identified. These items can be in the nature of the following:

- Life insurance policies
- Pension benefits
- Bank accounts
- IRA accounts
- Stocks and bonds registered under the Gifts to Minors Act

Assets of this kind, like income and resources, have to be detoured and rerouted away from outright ownership and inheritance by a handicapped person.

Therefore, if a handicapped person is not to own resources or assets, gifts to such a person cannot be made whether by will or otherwise. If such a gift is made, the guardian of the ward could seek the authority of the court to remove the ward's share.

Renunciation of Inheritance

Can a special-needs person make a partial renunciation of an inheritance in order to retain medical eligibility? The answer used to be yes. Under OBRA 93 the answer is *no*. See chapter 23 for a more detailed explanation.

Moral Gifts

Many parents and many planners believe that a simple way to approach the problem of disinheritance is to make gifts, either outright or by inheritance, to the siblings of the handicapped child. Such a transfer would be accompanied by a written expression on the part of the parents as to the use and purpose of these funds for the benefit of the disabled person during his or her lifetime.

For a multiple of reasons, many of them obvious, this process should be carefully considered before going forward. For example:

- These funds would be subject to all claims by creditors of the person to whom the funds are given.
- They can be the subject of matrimonial claims by a spouse of such a person.
- They can become involved in the business reversals of such a person.
- Lastly, temptations, even by the strongest of persons, might cause these funds to be used for purposes other than those originally intended.

Trust Fund

The best available alternative to ensure that there is a "contingency fund" in existence to care for and assist the handicapped person during lifetime is to create a discretionary trust fund, whether created by will or an inter vivos irrevocable trust. The fund must be structured with the view toward insulating it against the rights of the authorities seeking reimbursement for services rendered to the disabled person under the existing entitlement programs.

The trust can be established providing the disabled child with a lifetime interest (life estate) in the trust income and principal. Upon the death of the beneficiary, the balance remaining in the trust fund should pass to the children of the disabled beneficiary, or, if there are none, to the beneficiary's siblings, or, if there are none, to other designated beneficiaries. During the term of a trust of this kind, the grantor can provide in the trust agreement for the benefits from it (income and principal) not used for the beneficiary with special needs to be sprinkled or sprayed to the siblings of the disabled beneficiary or to other family members.

Who Should Be the Trustee?

The trustee should, if possible, have an understanding of the handicapped person's needs and also sufficient financial expertise to invest and manage the trust's assets intelligently. If there is no one person known with both of these qualities, a trustee who is close to the family should be given the right to consult with and retain expert financial advisors. If a substantial amount of money is involved, an institution with expertise in trust management can be named to act as the "financial or corporate cotrustee" and a trusted friend or relative to act as "personal cotrustee."

A family member who would be paid a fee is a preferable selection. The payment of the fee reduces the grantor's reluctance to impose the role of "surrogate parent" on the person. The fee can also operate to strengthen the person's sense of responsibility.

However, these same close relatives may well be the eventual recipients of the principal of the trust upon its termination. Sometimes, this can lead to an apparent conflict of interest, and such a selection must be given careful consideration.

The Grantor's Intention

The trust should contain a provision with language reciting the intent of the grantor of the trust. Such a clause would state:

It is my intent that the beneficiary shall receive all government entitlements that the beneficiary would otherwise be entitled to but for distribution of income and principal from this trust. I recognize that in view of the vast costs involved in caring for a disabled person, distribution of income or principal to the beneficiary would be rapidly dissipated in the absence of the governmental benefits the beneficiary now receives or in the future would be entitled to. The trustees are strictly prohibited from distributing income and principal to the beneficiary if such distribution will serve to deny, discontinue, or reduce a government benefit which the beneficiary would otherwise receive. The income and principal shall thus only be used for those times of need of the beneficiary that will not be paid for by government entitlements. It is my intent that the beneficiary enjoy the maximum advantages of life and at the same time receive government entitlements.

A discretionary trust should clearly provide that the trustees are to use the assets to supplement and not to replace or supplant available government aid.

The Discretion of the Trustee

The basis upon which states rely when ordering a trustee to reimburse an agency or an institution for services provided deals with the scope of the trustee's discretion. The trust instrument, therefore, must provide that the trustees have absolute and uncontrolled discretion with regard to paying from the income or principal for the benefit of the beneficiary. Under a clause of this kind, a true discretionary trust is created, and the right of the beneficiary to receive any benefits does not exist. This protects both the undistributed trust income and the trust property from any third-party claims. Under this circumstance, an agency or institution would be unable to secure the aid of a court in compelling the trustee to reimburse it for services provided to the beneficiary, because the right of the beneficiary to these funds would not exist.

It is also difficult to predict over the beneficiary's lifetime (1) the cost of his or her care; (2) the amount of government aid he or she will receive; (3) what his or her state of health will be; and (4) the amount of the trust fund at the time of the demise of the grantor. Because the beneficiary's situation may change during his or her lifetime, it is additionally important that the trustees be able to provide for his or her changing needs. For these reasons, discretionary powers are more appropriate than imperative powers.

Escape Clause

In every trust instrument, a provision should be inserted which is called "an escape" or "fail-safe" clause. This clause would provide that the trust be made terminable, upon any attempt by any creditors (including authorities seeking reimbursement for services provided) to reach the trust fund. This would revoke the trust if such an event took place and would distribute the principal of the trust to the remainder beneficiaries. Such a clause would state:

> If at any time the trustees are directed by a court of competent jurisdiction to distribute the income or principal to the beneficiary such that the beneficiary would lose a government entitlement, this trust shall be void *ab initio* (from inception), and all remaining principal and accumulated income shall be distributed forthwith to the remainder beneficiaries.

Such a clause protects and preserves the principal in case the law should change after the creation of the trust.

Predeath Termination Clause

If a highly functioning disabled adult may overcome the disability later in life, a predeath termination clause should be considered. Likewise, a "failed work" test clause should be provided to retrigger the noninvasion clauses of the trust and retain the principal if the disability is not overcome. A sample predeath termination clause would be as follows:

> The trust shall terminate, at the discretion of the trustee, prior to the death of the beneficiary, if the beneficiary is substantially gainfully employed, for a continuous period of two years, and the treating physician certifies in writing, that the disability no longer limits the beneficiary from being substantially gainfully employed. At that time, 10 percent of the accumulated income and principal shall be distributed absolutely to the beneficiary. For each consecutive year of substantial gainful employment, an additional 10 percent of accumulated income and principal shall be distributed absolutely to the beneficiary. If there is a break in consecutive employment, the distribution test will be reinvoked. If there is no break in consecutive employment, in the last distribution year, the trust shall terminate with the distribution of all accumulated income and principal to the beneficiary, as the purposes of the trust will have been fulfilled.

Spendthrift Clause

The trust should also contain a provision preventing the beneficiary from pledging or encumbering the trust assets, thus preventing any creditor, including the state, from acquiring the assets in the trust. This is referred to as a spendthrift clause, and it is a valuable safeguard in the event that a beneficiary incurs significant debts.

Sprinkling Benefit Clause

The trust can provide the trustees with the ability to sprinkle or spray the benefits of the trust (income and principal) to other members of the family (siblings) or to organizations or persons providing services to the beneficiary. Such a clause would state:

> The grantor further authorizes the trustees, at their sole and absolute discretion, to pay or apply any income not so paid or applied to or for the benefit of a beneficiary, and/or members of his or her immediate family, to or for the benefit of the siblings of the beneficiary, per stirpes, for their support, maintenance, and care (and the children of the siblings if any sibling should not be living at such time); such payments or applications may be made in such amounts and proportions, without any obligations to make equal payments or applications, as the trustees shall, in their sole and absolute discretion determine, from time to time, to or for any facility, the beneficiary may be residing in and/or to any organization where the beneficiary may be a client or a participant in any program(s) sponsored by them, as the trustees shall determine, for the general uses of such facility and/or organization at such time or times, as shall be determined by the trustees, at their sole and absolute discretion. Any income not so paid over or applied as aforesaid shall be accumulated and added to the principal of the trust at least annually and thereafter held as a part thereof.

Housing Clause

With the current public policy toward deinstitutionalization, most disabled adults will not be institutionalized. Support groups across the country are working with government agencies to secure alternative housing for the disabled. Once this housing is established, the government entitlement programs will fund ongoing care through SSI or Medicaid. In the beginning, "start-up" monies may be needed, and trustees should be given the right to use trust funds for this purpose. Provisions related to this should be limited to "creating" housing and not "maintaining" housing, because SSI and Medicaid funds are not available for capital purchases of housing facilities.

To encourage nonprofit organizations or individuals to provide housing for the disabled adult child, the trust may include a special bequest to the provider of housing. Following is sample language for such a bequest:

> (_____ percent) to the organizations or persons who have provided appropriate housing for my disabled child in appreciation for those services. The total amount of this bequest or gift shall be equitably prorated by my trustee to such organizations or persons based on the number of years my disabled child was provided housing.

Irrevocable Inter Vivos Trust

Family members might consider establishing during their lifetimes an irrevocable inter vivos trust fund for a child with special needs. The fund could be set up with a modest or minimal sum. Upon the death of the grantor, additional assets could be added or poured over into the trust. A device of this sort can serve two purposes: (1) it can be established, tested, and fine-tuned while everyone is alive, and by the time of the grantor's death he or she will know that an ongoing functioning fund is in existence for a knowledgeable successor trustee; and (2) it can act as an existing fund to which legacies and gifts can be given by family members during their lifetimes and/or upon their deaths.

Supplemental Needs Trusts

The Supplemental Needs Trust discussed in this chapter is universally employed as a planning device for persons with disabilities in order to protect their government entitlements.

The states have protected these discretionary trusts from liability to the beneficiary's creditors and preserved eligibility for public assistance when the purpose of the trust has been found to provide the beneficiary with needs supplemental to those provided by governmental programs. Therefore, the trust instrument should state that its purpose is not to provide the primary care of the beneficiary, but rather for his or her supplemental needs and comfort. Examples of supplemental care needs might include grooming aids and other items relating to personal care; reasonable travel and related expenses to allow relatives and friends to visit the beneficiary and, if appropriate, allow the beneficiary to visit relatives and friends; reasonable expenses to assist the beneficiary in participating in recreational programs not otherwise provided where he or she resides; medical, dental, educational, therapeutic, and other professional services not paid for by private insurance or any governmental program; and expenses of a family member or friend to determine whether the needs of the beneficiary are being satisfied and, if necessary, to act as an advocate on his or her behalf. This last function may be very important if an appropriate person is available after the death of both parents. The advocate might visit the beneficiary at his or her residence to inspect living conditions; ensure that the beneficiary's educational, social, training, and medical programs are appropriate; evaluate additional needs; and assure that trust funds or governmental entitlements are properly expended for the beneficiary.

At the end of this chapter are illustrations of an inter vivos Supplemental Needs Trust suggested by the Supreme Court of Kings County, State of New York, as well as language for a testamentary Supplemental Needs Trust that would be set forth in a will.

Insurance

In connection with funding a trust, families whose assets are limited should consider life insurance. Whatever the need for insurance is in a normal family situation, the presence of a disabled member, who will need perpetual care, totally changes the equation.

Life insurance can create an instant estate to provide adequate security, if governmental care is not desired or if the disabled person is, or for any reason may become, ineligible for governmental care. For many, life insurance will be the single most effective way of assuring financial security for a dependent who needs a lifetime of care. After all, the government may someday reduce or do away with its funding, and only private funds would be available for a handicapped beneficiary.

Medicaid: OBRA 93

OBRA 93 recognizes the need to protect disabled persons during their lifetimes, even when they receive assets that would otherwise make them ineligible for Medicaid. The law protects proceeds received by a handicapped person from a successful lawsuit and provides for trusts to be created as follows:

- A trust containing the assets of an individual under age 65 who is disabled and which is established for the benefit of such individual by a parent, grandparent, legal guardian of the individual, or a court if the State will receive all amounts remaining in the trust upon the death of such individual up to an amount equal to the total medical assistance paid on behalf of the individual under a State plan under this title.

* * * *

- A trust containing the assets of an individual who is disabled that meets the following conditions:

    (i) The trust is established and managed by a nonprofit association. (Various not-for-profit organizations have established *"master trusts"* for this purpose.)

    (ii) A separate account is maintained for each beneficiary of the trust, but, for purposes of investment and management of funds, the trust pools these accounts.

    (iii) Accounts in the trusts are established solely for the benefit of individuals who are disabled, by the parent, grandparent, or legal guardian of such individuals, by such individuals, or by a court.

    (iv) To the extent that amounts remaining in the beneficiary's account upon the death of the beneficiary are not retained by the trust, the trust pays to the State from such remaining amounts in the account an amount equal to the total amount of medical assistance paid on behalf of the beneficiary under the State plan under this title.

These two sections present unusual planning opportunities for disabled persons who meet the defined criteria. Under these sections, it is permissible to fund these described trusts with "assets of a disabled individual." There is no limitation as to how those assets are acquired by the disabled person. Therefore, assets could be received from a settlement or a judgment from litigation, or an inheritance or assets acquired by the individual through earnings or investment prior to disability.

Pursuant to these provisions, upon the death of the disabled person, the trust funds will be applied to repay the state for its Medicaid outlay and any excess assets would pass to family members.

Trust Agreement

This TRUST AGREEMENT made this _____ day of _____, _____ (DATE), between (NAME), as Guardian of the property of (NAME) as "Grantor," and (NAME) as "Trustee" is established pursuant to an Order of the Supreme Court of the state of New York, (CNTY) County. The "Grantor" (NAME) currently resides at (ADDRESS). The "Trustee" (NAME) currently resides at (ADDRESS).

1.0   Trust Name: The Trust shall be known as the (NAME). The purpose of the Trust is that the Trust's assets be used to supplement, not supplant, impair or diminish, any benefits or assistance of any Federal, State, County, City, or other governmental entity for which the Beneficiary may otherwise be eligible or which the Beneficiary may be receiving. The Trust is intended to conform with New York State EPTL 7-1.12.

1.2   Declaration of Irrevocability: The Trust shall be irrevocable and may not at any time be altered, amended, or revoked without Court approval.

1.3   EPTL 7-1.6: EPTL 7-1.6 or any successor statute, or any similar statute of any jurisdiction, shall not be applied by any court having jurisdiction of an inter vivos or testamentary trust to compel against the Trustees' discretion, the payment or application of the trust principal to or for the benefit of (BENEFICIARY), or any beneficiary for any reason whatsoever.

2.0   Administration of Trust During Lifetime of Beneficiary: The property shall be held in trust for the Beneficiary, and the Trustee shall collect income and, after deducting all charges and expenses attributed thereto, shall apply for the benefit of the Beneficiary, so much of the income and principal (even to the extent of the whole) as the Trustee deems advisable in his sole and absolute discretion subject to the limitations set forth below. The Trustee shall add the balance of net income not paid or applied to the principal of the Trust.

2.1   Consistent with the Trust's purpose, before expending any amounts from the net income and/or principal of this Trust, the Trustee shall consider the availability of all benefits from government or private assistance programs for which the Beneficiary may be eligible. The Trustee, where appropriate and to the extent possible, shall endeavor to maximize the collection and facilitate the distribution of these benefits for the benefit of the Beneficiary.

2.2   None of the income or principal of this Trust shall be applied in such a manner as to supplant, impair, or diminish any governmental benefits or assistance for which the Beneficiary may be eligible or which the Beneficiary may be receiving.

2.3   The Beneficiary does not have the power to assign, encumber, direct, distribute, or authorize distributions from this Trust.

2.4   Notwithstanding the above provisions, the Trust may make distributions to meet the Beneficiary's need for food, clothing, shelter, health care, or other personal needs, even if those distributions will impair or diminish the Beneficiary's receipt or eligibility for government benefits or assistance or if the Trustee determines that the distributions will better meet the Beneficiary's needs, and that it is in the Beneficiary's best interests, notwithstanding the consequent effect on the Beneficiary's eligibility for, or receipt of, benefits.

2.5   However, if the mere existence of this authority to make distributions will result in a reduction or loss of the Beneficiary's entitlement program benefits, regardless of whether the Trustee actually exercises this discretion, the preceding paragraph (2.4) shall be null and void and the Trustee's authority to make these distributions shall terminate and the Trustee's authority to make distributions shall be limited to purchasing supplemental goods and services in a manner that will not adversely affect the Beneficiary's government benefits.

2.6   Additions to Income and Principal: With the Trustee's consent, any person may, at any time, from time to time, by Court order, assignment, gift, transfer, deed, or will, provide income or add to the principal of the Trust created herein, and any property so added shall be held, administered, and distributed under the terms of this Trust. The Trustee shall execute documents necessary to accept additional contributions to the Trust and shall designate the additions on an amended Schedule A of this Trust.

3.0   Disposition of Trust on Death of Beneficiary: The Trust shall terminate upon the death of (BENEFICIARY) and the Trustee shall distribute any principal and accumulated interest that then remains in the Trust as follows:

3.1   The New York State Department of Social Services, or other appropriate Medicaid entity within New York State, shall be reimbursed for the total Medical Assistance provided to (BENEFICIARY) during his lifetime, as consistent with Federal and State Law. If (BENEFICIARY) received Medicaid in more than one State, then the amount distributed to each State shall be based on each State's proportionate share of the total amount of Medicaid benefits paid by all States on the behalf of the Beneficiary.

3.2   All remaining principal and accumulated income shall be paid to the legal representative of the Estate of the Beneficiary.

4.0   Trustee: (NAME) is appointed Trustee of this Trust. If for any reason, (TRUSTEE) is unable to or unwilling to serve as Trustee, then (NAME) shall serve as Successor Trustee, subject to the approval of the Supreme Court, (CNTY) County.

4.1   Consent of the Trustee: A Trustee shall file with the Clerk of the Court (CNTY) County, a "Consent to Act" as Trustee, Oath and Designation, duly acknowledged.

4.2   Bond: The Trustee shall be required to execute and file a bond and comply with all applicable law, as determined by the Supreme Court (CNTY) County.

4.3   Resignation: A Trustee may resign by giving written notice, a signed and acknowledged instrument, delivered to (i) the Supreme Court (CNTY) County; (ii) the Guardian of the Beneficiary, if any; and (iii) the Beneficiary. The Trustee's resignation is subject to the approval of the Supreme Court (CNTY) County.

4.4   Discharge and Final Accounting of Trustee: No Trustee shall be discharged and released from office and bond, except upon filing a Final Accounting in the form and manner required by Section 81.33 of the Mental Hygiene Law and obtaining judicial approval of same.

4.5   Annual Accounting: The Trustee shall file during the month of May in the Office of the Clerk of the County (CNTY), an annual report in the form and manner required by Section 81.32 of the Mental Hygiene Law.

4.6   Continuing Jurisdiction: The Court shall have continuing jurisdiction over the performance of the duties of the Trustee; the interpretation, administration, and operation of this Trust; the appointment of a successor Trustee; and all other related matters.

4.7   Powers of Trustee: In addition to any powers that may be conferred upon the Trustee under the law of the state of New York in effect during the life of this Trust, the Trustee shall have all those discretionary powers mentioned in EPTL 11-1.1 et seq., or any successor statute or statutes governing the discretion of a Trustee, so as to confer upon the Trustee the broadest possible powers available for the management of the Trust assets. In the event that the Trustee wishes to exercise powers beyond the express and implied powers of EPTL Article 11, the Trustee shall seek and obtain judicial approval.

4.8   Appointment of a Successor Trustee: Appointment of a successor Trustee not named in this Trust shall be upon application of the Court.

4.9   Compensation of Trustee: A Trustee shall be entitled to such compensation as may be allowable under the laws of the state of New York. In addition, the Trustee shall be entitled to be reimbursed for reasonable expenses incurred by the Trustee in the administration of this Trust.

5.0   Miscellaneous Provisions: [to be used as needed]

5.1   Governing Law: This Trust Agreement shall be interpreted and the administration of the Trust shall be governed by the laws of the state of New York; provided, however, that Federal law shall govern any matter alluded to herein which shall relate to or involve government entitlements such as SSI, Medicaid, and/or other Federal benefit programs.

5.2   Notifications to Social Services District: The Trustee shall provide the required notification to the Social Services District in accordance with the requirements of section 360-4.5 of Title 18 of the Official Regulations of the State Department of Social Services, and any other applicable statutes or regulations, as they may be amended. These regulations currently require notification of the creation or funding of the trust; notification of the death of the beneficiary; and, in the case of trusts exceeding $100,000, notification in advance of transactions that substantially deplete the trust principal (as defined in that section).

5.3   Savings Clause: If it is determined that any provision hereof shall in any way violate any applicable law, such determination shall not impair the validity of the remaining provisions of the Trust.

5.4   Usage: In construing this Trust, feminine or neuter pronouns shall be substituted for those of the masculine form and vice versa, and the plural for the singular and vice versa in any case in which the context may require.

5.5   Headings: Any headings or captions in the Trust are for reference only, and shall not expand, limit, change, or affect the meaning of any provision of the Trust.

5.6   Binding Effect: This Trust shall be binding upon the estate, executors, administrators, and assigns of the Grantor and any individual Trustee, and upon any Successor Trustee.

IN WITNESS WHEREOF, the undersigned have executed this Agreement as of the date and year first above written.

DATED: GRANTOR:

_____

(NAME) as Guardian of the Property of (NAME)

DATED: TRUSTEE:

_____

(NAME) (TRUSTEE)

STATE OF NEW YORK   )
) ss.:
COUNTY OF NEW YORK   )

On the _____ day of _____, in the year 200__, before me, the undersigned, personally appeared _____, personally known to me or proved to me on the basis of satisfactory evidence to be the individual(s) whose name(s) is/are subscribed to the within instrument and acknowledged to me that he/she/they executed the same in his/her/their capacity, and that by his/her/their signature(s) on the instrument, the individual(s), or the person(s) upon behalf of which the individual(s) acted, executed the instrument.

_____

NOTARY PUBLIC

STATE OF NEW YORK   )
) ss.:
COUNTY OF NEW YORK   )

On the _____ day of _____, in the year 200__, before me, the undersigned, personally appeared _____, personally known to me or proved to me on the basis of satisfactory evidence to be the individual(s) whose name(s) is/are subscribed to the within instrument and acknowledged to me that he/she/they executed the same in his/her/their capacity, and that by his/her/their signature(s) on the instrument, the individual(s), or the person(s) upon behalf of which the individual(s) acted, executed the instrument.

_____

NOTARY PUBLIC

SCHEDULE "A" To Supplemental Needs Trust

Schedule of Assets

Suggested Language for Last Will and Testament

[ARTICLE #]:   I give and bequeath (the sum of $_____ or ____ percent) of my estate to my Trustee hereinafter named as a Supplemental Needs Trust for the benefit of (name of beneficiary). My Trustee shall hold, manage, and reinvest the same bequest and shall have the sole and absolute discretion to expend or not expend principal and/or income for the benefit of said beneficiary, subject to the following purposes, terms and conditions:

A. My Trustee shall hold, manage, invest, and reinvest these funds and collect the rents, interest, dividends, and other incomes therefrom. My Trustee, in consultation with the lifetime guardian of said beneficiary, shall pay the income and/or principal from this trust fund after proper charges and expenses to the guardian of the person or property of said beneficiary, or directly to a service or property provider for the benefit of said beneficiary, as requested by [his/her] guardian. My Trustee is authorized to pay from the income and corpus of this trust any sums that may be needed or useful in enhancing the lifestyle of said beneficiary, or for any costs or expenses [he/she] deems of extraordinary or compelling necessity. Any distribution from this Trust shall be at the sole discretion of the Trustee and not subject to court review.

B. Payments by my Trustee for the benefit of the person or property of said beneficiary shall be made subject to the following uses and conditions:

1 (a) It is the testator's intent to create a Supplemental Needs Trust that conforms to the provisions of section 7-1.12 of the New York Estates, Powers, and Trusts law. The testator intends that the trust assets be used to supplement, not supplant, impair, or diminish, any benefits or assistance of any Federal, State, County, City or other governmental entity for which the beneficiary may otherwise be eligible or which the beneficiary may be receiving. Consistent with that intent, it is the testator's desire that before expending any amounts from the net income and/or principal of this trust, the Trustee consider the availability of all benefits from government or private assistance programs for which the beneficiary may be eligible and that, where appropriate and to the extent possible, the Trustee endeavor to maximize the collection of such benefits and to facilitate the distribution of such benefits for the benefit of the beneficiary.

1 (b) None of the income or principal of this trust shall be applied in such a manner as to supplant, impair, or diminish benefits or assistance of any Federal,

State, County, City or other governmental entity for which the beneficiary may otherwise be eligible or which the beneficiary may be receiving.

2 (a) Neither income nor the principal in the hands of my Trustee, before the interest and/or principal is actually paid or delivered to the guardian of or for the benefit of said beneficiary, shall be subject to voluntary or involuntary anticipation, encumbrance, alienation, or assignment, either in whole or in part, nor shall such interest be subject to any judicial creditors or claimant of said beneficiary.

2 (b) The beneficiary does not have the power to assign, encumber, direct, distribute, or authorize distributions from this trust.

3. Certain needs of said beneficiary may be provided for by my Trustee from the income and/or principal, including additional food, clothing, or health services not provided; stereos, tape recorders, VCRs, television sets, or other electronic items; vacations; trips; and birthday and holiday gifts, or similar tangible items, if they are not otherwise provided by governmental financial assistance and benefits or by the provider of services.

4 (a) Notwithstanding the provisions herein, the Trustee may make distributions to meet said beneficiary's need for food, clothing, shelter, or health care even if such distributions may result in an impairment or diminution of said beneficiary, receipt or eligibility for government benefits for assistance but only if the Trustee determines that (i) said beneficiary's needs will be better met if such distribution is made, and (ii) it is said beneficiary's best interests to suffer the consequent effect, if any, on said beneficiary's eligibility for or receipt of government benefits or assistance.

4 (b) However, if the mere existence of the Trustee's authority to make distributions pursuant to this subparagraph shall result in the beneficiary's loss of government benefits or assistance, regardless of whether such authority is actually exercised, this subparagraph shall be null and void and the Trustee's authority to make such distributions shall cease and shall be limited as provided in paragraphs two and three above, without exception.

5 In making any distribution to or for the benefit of said beneficiary, the Trustee should consider what benefits said beneficiary may be entitled to from any governmental agency, including but not limited to Social Security Administration benefits, Veterans Administration benefits, Medicaid (including medical assistance and day-treatment program assistance), and Supplemental Security Income benefits. I request that my Trustee assist said beneficiary in collecting, expending, and accounting separately for all such governmental assistance benefits but not commingle them with the trust fund.

6. This trust shall terminate upon the death of said beneficiary. Upon the termination of this trust, my Trustee is directed to pay such portion of the burial

costs and expenses including the cost of a burial lot and a marker of said beneficiary, not covered by insurance or otherwise from [his/her] property other than the income and principal of this trust and to pay over and distribute the remaining principal and any accrued and accumulated income as follows: (Insert provisions for distribution of the remaining assets in the trust.)

Sample Language to Dispose of Remaining Assets in the Trust

(A) If not otherwise provided for, a sum to cover burial expenses, including plot and grave marker.

(B) The balance of the principal and remaining income of the trust shall be paid in equal shares to my other children then surviving and to the issue of my deceased children, per stirpes and not per capita.

CHAPTER 20

Persons with the Risk of Acquired Immune Deficiency Syndrome (AIDS)

*T*here are a multitude of factors that must be taken into consideration with regard to the special interests of persons with AIDS. These include the mental state of the individual, the special relationship that partners have, and the nature of their relationships with their families.

Safeguarding the estate from potential challenges (will contests) from other family members has to be a primary goal. The living trust can be the foundation for an effective plan and will serve to dissuade potential claims.

The Need to Plan Is a Must

The AIDS virus attacks the immune system. Therefore, the individual becomes vulnerable to a host of other potential diseases, such different forms of cancer, pneumonia, and diseases that invade the nervous system and eventually cause brain damage. Approximately two-thirds of AIDS victims develop dementia, which is an impairment of the intellectual function of the mind in the areas of language, emotions, and judgment. However, these problems taken individually do not mean that a person afflicted with this disease lacks testamentary capacity (the ability to create a legal will). Testamentary capacity is a legal standard. It is incumbent upon every attorney to determine if his or her client is capable of making a will. Most of the persons who contract this disease are relatively young (approximately only 10 percent are over sixty years of age).

The ever-increasing number of persons afflicted by this disease calls for a special focus on estate planning in this segment of our population. In this category, one of the main goals is to protect against successful

213

challenges. Homosexual males are the principal victims of AIDS. Drug users and some heterosexual individuals are victimized as well, but under normal conditions they will not require a special focus on their estate plans beyond their providing for incapacity. The need for special planning arises out of the relationships that homosexuals have with their companions. A 1990 U.S. Census survey of the nation's 91 million households shows that 2.6 million are unmarried heterosexual couples, and 1.6 million are couples of the same sex. In the vast majority of situations the laws of this country do not afford these people any rights at all except on an isolated basis. Therefore, unmarried couples have a greater need to address estate planning than married couples. For a married couple, in most instances, laws of the state take over when no planning has been done.

In the main, our states have no laws that authorize a marriage between homosexuals. The courts of some states have permitted the legal adoption of one homosexual by another. Some state courts have refused adoption to take place where it is discovered that there exists a homosexual relationship. The rationale is that if the court granted an adoption, the person seeking the adoption could be subject to criminal liability for abuse or incest of the adoptee. Adoption legally granted would provide the adopted person with the status of a child with respect to inheritance rights. In certain communities housing is subject to rent control and only family members may succeed to the benefits of the original tenant. In 1989, New York State's highest court held that a long-lasting relationship between homosexuals living together in a rent-controlled apartment satisfied the family succession requirement of the law. In the same year, the City of New York extended city-employee insurance coverage to homosexual companions. In San Francisco, laws provide for the registration of homosexual couples, giving those registered insurance and other benefits that they would not otherwise be entitled to. In Austin, Texas, a recent policy permitted health insurance benefits to be extended to domestic partners. This is further indication that estate planning for unmarried couples is quite different than for married couples.

Legal and Liability Considerations

The requirements and concerns in this kind of estate planning include, but also go far beyond, the status of the relationship between the individual and his or her family—whether it be good, caring, or strained. There are also potential liability questions that have to be considered. It has been reported that the estate of Rock Hudson was held accountable for large damages for failure to disclose to his companion that he suffered from AIDS. This may lead to the legal responsibility of disclosure not only to long-term partners but to short-term relationships as well.

Financial Concerns

Due to the prospect of extremely large medical costs throughout all phases of the disease, including hospital and custodial care costs, and the loss of earnings that will accompany the disabling effects of the disease, the following should be considered:

Cash value life insurance acquired while the person is insurable can later be withdrawn to fund these costs. Policies that have recently emerged offering living benefits should be investigated. Health care providers can be designated as beneficiaries of the insurance policies to pay for the costs of care while the person was alive.

Retirement plans can be invaded to generate cash flow. A person should consider the use of these vehicles to the extent allowed, and should create these funds as well and take advantage of the tax benefits. Medicare covers those aged sixty-five and older and is not available to the vast majority of this population.

The availability of Medicaid is dependent on financial need. Benefits and eligibility requirements vary from state to state. As set forth elsewhere in this book, there are minimum levels of financial assets one can own before qualifying. This program is for the indigent. However, one can qualify after impoverishing oneself once the appropriate penalty period has transpired.

Advanced Directives

Many victims of AIDS accept their terminal prognosis and express a desire to limit medical treatment. As such, living wills and health care proxies are extremely important to permit their wishes to be carried out and to have no extraordinary procedures prolong their lives (see chapter 21). In addition, much emotion and pain will be avoided if the question of the disposition of the remains of the person are addressed during his or her lifetime. In most states, the directions of a person as to his or her funeral and burial arrangements will generally be strictly followed. A durable power of attorney should be in place in anticipation of the time when a victim of AIDS will not be able to manage his or her affairs.

Wills

If disinheritance of a family is the main theme of the will, it must be properly drafted and executed to achieve this result. If a homosexual is legally married, the rights of a surviving spouse have to be addressed so that he or she will not take action against the will. This can be dealt with in advance by a waiver.

Challenges

The main challenge to a will is focused on the failure of proper execution. Therefore, all of the formal requirements of the state in which it is made should be observed and documented. The second most frequent challenge is that the estate owner was unduly influenced to make out a will that resulted in a distribution in favor of the person doing the influencing. Given the fact of the many biases that are rampant in this country, the estate owner has to anticipate that the rationale employed by a court will be on traditional social standards and attitudes as opposed to what is becoming socially acceptable today.

An attorney should prepare and supervise the execution of the will. The execution should be memorialized in a memorandum. If the testator is hospitalized or is known to be ill, and because the disease in many instances brings on dementia and depression, a physician might be present and attest to the competency of the testator in a signed statement. If at all possible, the physician should be one who has known the testator over a period of time and has some experience with AIDS. Witnesses to the will should not be related to the testator, and they should at the same time execute an affidavit attesting to proper signing of the will in accordance with the laws of the state in which it was signed. A film or video could be made of the execution of the will.

A challenge may be brought on the grounds of undue influence on the part of the companion of the testator. In other words, the question that could be raised is: Is that the will of the testator or is it the will of someone else? It must always be established that the will is the voluntary independent expression of the person. If the attorney was selected by the testator, so much the better, but if the beneficiary/companion recommended the attorney, care must be taken to establish and show the lawyer/client relationship that exists is with the person whose will is executed and not the beneficiary. The beneficiary should not participate in conferences with the attorney. Meetings should take place at the attorney's office with office associates as participants and witnesses, and whatever can be done should be done to document that the will was the independent act of the person who created it. The establishment of a bequest to a possible challenger with a disinheritance clause if that person challenges the will is an effective will provision and an effective technique to discourage a will contest.

Trusts

The use of a living trust is an important consideration. It is more difficult to upset a trust than a will.

AIDS victims, in making dispositions of their property, usually have two main testamentary objectives: (1) the provision of security for the victim's companion for a period of time (life or a term of years); and (2) after this period, to provide benefits for remainder persons (relatives or charity). An irrevocable trust for a term of years or life of the companion, followed by a gift to other beneficiaries, can serve this purpose. The nature of the relationship of the parties will determine the term of the benefits.

If an irrevocable trust is created, gift taxes based on the full value of the property at the time the trust is created will be due, but they may be offset or reduced by the unified credit. If the beneficiary is an AIDS victim, his or her interest may be short-lived, and by the same token, the vesting of the trust property in the remaining beneficiaries will be sooner than might otherwise be expected.

Life Insurance

Life insurance may be important for several reasons. It is a way of providing benefits to the victim's companion without costs and probate.

There may be a question of insurability if the insured person dies within the contestable period. As with a will, a challenge could be made on grounds that the beneficiary designation was made under undue influence, having been made at a time when the insured was mentally impaired as a result of his or her disease. The timing of the making of the beneficiary designation is therefore important.

Certain kinds of group term insurance offered under company plans or by professional groups may be obtained without evidence of insurability. This kind of life insurance can accomplish the desired goal.

Private Annuity

A private annuity arrangement between the AIDS victim and an individual chosen to be the beneficiary may be especially appropriate from a transfer tax standpoint because of the person's presumed short life expectancy.

Joint Purchase of Property

A joint purchase of property by the AIDS victim and beneficiary may be extremely significant. The property is purchased from a third party with the AIDS victim acquiring a life income interest and the other party a remainder interest. Each party pays out of his or her own funds the full value of his or her interest actually determined. The transfer tax benefit lies in the victim's shorter actual life expectancy as against the life expectancy assigned by Internal Revenue Service tables for the purpose of determining the value of the life and remainder interests.

Lifetime Gifts

If the AIDS victim holds or is about to acquire property or funds in his or her own name, he or she might want to consider placing it in joint ownership with his or her companion. The gift would be subject to gift tax and the full value of the property would then pass to the survivor at death. Probate would be avoided, and the gift would be voidable only if the challenger were able to prove fraud on the part of the companion.

Lifetime gifts under the umbrella of the $11,000 annual gift exclusion and the unified credit are other options open to the AIDS victim. Both the creation of a joint tenancy and an outright gift of property under the annual exclusion ($11,000) can serve to save estate taxes.

Standard Guardianship

The AIDS situation stresses the requirement of the designation of a guardian for a child of a parent who has a terminal or incapacitating disease. To settle this problem, the state of New York in 1992 enacted legislation which permits an individual who is dying, incapacitated, or is at risk becoming so, to petition the court for a standby guardian. The authority of the guardian covers both the activities of the relative of the incapacitated person (a child) during his or her lifetime (the incapacitated person) and after his or her death. The state of Florida has also enacted comparable standby guardian legislation.

This kind of law affords comfort to a single parent who, anticipating this kind of debilitating situation, can witness the designation of a guardian during his or her lifetime.

The basic formats and devices that are involved in estate planning for persons with AIDS are, in most instances, similar to planning for any other person. Special needs in estate planning arise because laws that are not applicable to same-sex partners create a difference between their legal rights and those of the rest of the people in this country.

For the professional who reads this chapter, remember that "an ounce of prevention is worth a pound of cure." The anticipation of a "contest" starts with the first visit to your office and must be anticipated from that moment on.

❖

CHAPTER 21

Surrogate Planning for the Senior Citizen

*T*he graying of America means that many more people are facing the issues of aging. It is anticipated that by the year 2000, 35 million people (approximately 13 percent of the total population) will be over the age of sixty-five. In approximately thirty-six years, this group will make up over 20 percent of the national census. It is, therefore, important to consider nonfinancial aspects of estate planning.

The process of estate planning encompasses more than mortem and postmortem decisions. A complete estate plan will include the preparation of surrogate instruments or advance directives. These lifetime tools provide advanced planning in the event of your losing the capacity to make decisions. This is all the more important in today's society as a result of the medical advances which are allowing many of us to outlive our mental capabilities.

Competent adults have the right to make decisions regarding their own health care, including the right to refuse life-sustaining treatment. This right is based upon the common law right to give or withhold consent, based upon the Fourteenth Amendment's right to liberty. Advance directives such as health care proxies or living wills afford these rights to a person who does not have the capacity to make such decisions, by designating a surrogate or an agent to make medical and health care decisions for them.

If you become incapacitated and cannot make health care or financial decisions, another person will have to make these decisions for you. Therefore, you have a few choices. If you do nothing, the people closest to you will have to seek legal help by petitioning the court for the appointment of a guardian or conservator. This type of proceeding, because of the costs and time delay, should be avoided if at all possible.

The second choice is to create the advance directives while you are healthy and select those who will act for you when you cannot act for yourself. If nothing else, the cost savings, in comparison to the court costs, is enough of an impetus for you to act when you are able.

Health Care Decisions

Living trusts, like health care proxies, are types of advance directives. The rationale behind giving a third party the right to make your health care decisions is that when you are mentally incapacitated, you are entitled to the same rights you had when you were competent. These rights include the right to refuse medical care services. No one can be required to undergo any particular surgical procedure or be forced to take a medication. This is true, as well, as far as life-sustaining measures are concerned. A person who has capacity can refuse all life-sustaining procedures. Our courts have upheld an individual's right to refuse food and hydration.

Most of our states have created, by statute, a special durable power of attorney for health care decisions. A few states have created a general durable power of attorney that permits you to authorize your agent to make your health care decisions in the event that your mental capacity deteriorates.

Property Management

If you no longer have the mental capacity to act in a competent manner, the management of your property is at risk. The techniques that will insure the orderly management of your assets center around the durable power of attorney, joint tenancy, and the living trust.

Most of the problems created by powers of attorney that lack appropriate powers can be circumvented by the creation of a living trust. In addition, even though the states generally recognize each others' laws, on powers of attorney, there are differences. In Florida, only blood relatives can serve as an attorney-in-fact. Certain states do not permit springing powers. In Georgia, a power of attorney automatically survives incapacity unless provided otherwise, whereas in most states it is not durable unless specifically set forth in the instrument.

To avoid the costly problem of guardianship and court intervention, there is no better method to deal with the orderly management of your entire affairs than the living trust. The assets are in place and no marshaling is necessary. Your trustees can act from the moment of your incapacity and the trust will continue in existence until after your death and be used to distribute the assets thereafter. This is quite different from a power of attorney which automatically terminates upon your death.

Because of potential tax liabilities (gift and income), joint tenancy should only be implemented between nonspouse cotenants and between spouses for small bank accounts. With the durable power of attorney and living trust, there is no transfer of assets and no such exposure to transfer and income tax liabilities.

The Family Limited Partnership ("FLP") is also a useful planning device. By retitling assets out of your name, both the living trust and Family Limited Partnership avoid the necessity of probate and the need for a guardian. Both of these techniques provide a vehicle for succession planning. Assets such as real estate and securities and even life insurance may be placed into the FLP. A person's residence should not be transferred to an FLP because of the potential loss of the availability of income tax benefits, such as deductions of interest and real estate tax and the sheltering of gains through the available exemption. One method of avoiding loss of those benefits is to transfer the residence to the FLP subject to a retained life estate with the reservation of a special power of appointment. In such a case the income tax benefits would be applicable and the heirs of the estate owner would receive an asset with a stepped-up basis, and it would be includable in the estate for estate tax purposes.

Advance Directives

The vast majority of deaths in this country occur in institutions. This creates the distinct possibility of being kept alive by artificial means when there is no hope of survival except by those methods. Most people prefer to die with dignity rather than subject themselves and their families to this process. By the use of advance directives, you can set the stage for a time when you cannot act yourself, as to the use of life-support systems.

The alternatives are as follows:
- Do or say nothing (This will require the use of life-support systems to keep you alive as long as possible)
- Clearly direct that artificial means should not be employed to prolong life
- Create a durable power of attorney or health care proxy and designate to an agent the authority to make such decisions
- You can set up thresholds for discontinuing artificial life support in your living will or health care proxy

What Is a Living Will?

A living will is not a will in the sense that we understand that term. It is nothing more than an instrument that expresses your intentions regarding the use of life-support systems if you are terminally ill and there is no hope for recovery.

State laws vary and the document may have other powers. A living will is directed to medical decisions. Under it you do not designate anyone to make decisions; you simply express your wishes if certain circumstances were to exist. The application of the living will is narrowed to the use of life-support systems. As states have developed durable powers of attorney or health care proxies, the use of living wills has been reduced, as these documents allow you to express your wishes and designate someone to be sure they are carried out.

Most people, to be certain that their wishes are understood and carried out, will create both a living will and a health care proxy. In such cases, the living will serves as a guide and supplement to the agent under the proxy instrument.

Many states have adopted statutes to honor the living will. The state of New York has not done so, but recognizes the contents of them by case law. Living wills have been accepted by courts of various states in dealing with health care matters for an incompetent individual.

Where Should a Living Will Be Kept?

A living will should be kept separate from the health care proxy but accessible to friends and family. Friends and family members who are likely to stay in touch with the patient, despite his or her incapacity, are desirable custodians for a living will, in addition to the appointed health care agents.

A related question is how to keep living wills current. Periodic review is desirable because values and feelings about what constitutes an acceptable existence may change over time. Maintaining living wills among tax files or other routinely handled documents helps to keep them visible for annual review and revision as desired. If you travel extensively you might want to take a copy with you.

Health Care Proxies

A health care proxy is a document that provides for all health care aspects, not just life-sustaining measures. Many states have adopted health care proxy or surrogate decision-making statutes. These documents permit an agent to make a broad range of health care decisions for a person. The living will and the health care proxy are not incompatible documents. Depending upon state law, the provisions of a living will outlining life-prolonging measures can be incorporated into a health care proxy.

In New York, a properly appointed health care agent can be authorized to make any or all health care decisions for a particular person by the use of a simple document known as a health care proxy. It can be exercised without any need for clear and convincing evidence of the person's wishes, a notable change in New York law.

A health care proxy is a type of advance directive. Advance directives are oral or written directions concerning the health care desired once a person has lost the capacity to make decisions.

The New York State statute mandates that the following four elements be in the proxy document:

1. Names of principal and agent
2. Statement of intent that the agent is to have authority to make health care decisions on behalf of the principal
3. Signature and date by the principal or another acting on the principal's behalf
4. Two witnesses who observe the execution and sign below the statement that "the principal appeared to execute the proxy willingly and free from duress"

The statute provides a form that has been adopted and distributed by the State Department of Health. It also permits the use of customized documents, as long as they include the above elements.

Capacity Presumed

Almost any adult can execute a health care proxy, because the capacity to do so is legally presumed.

In New York, an agent's authority can take effect only during periods of the principal's temporary or permanent decisional incapacity. Unlike some other states, New York does not allow for a person to authorize the agent to act at a time when he or she has decision-making capacity.

The New York statute permits you to limit the agent's authority by including health treatment instructions. Such instructions might limit the agent's authority in decisions involving surgery or might specify the agent's powers regarding the use of artificial nutrition and hydration.

If you want to grant an agent unlimited discretion concerning, for example, artificial feeding, you need only indicate that the agent "knows my wishes concerning artificial nutrition and hydration."

At a minimum, copies of health care proxies should be distributed to the named agent, substitute agent, and personal physician. It is preferable to distribute them also to family members and friends. If others are likely to be involved in treatment, such as a local hospital or treating specialists, copies should be delivered to them for inclusion in your medical records. A note taped to your driver's license or wallet card can be used to indicate the existence, name, and telephone number of the health care agent.

Agent decision-making procedures are wholly inconsistent with both the underlying doctrine of self-determination and agency principals. If your wishes are "reasonably known," the agent must make decisions consistent with your wishes. If your wishes are "not reasonably known and cannot with reasonable diligence be ascertained," with one exception, an agent must make treatment decisions consistent with your best interests.

The exception to the use of the "best interests" test applies to decisions about artificial nutrition and hydration. If your wishes are not reasonably known or ascertainable, the agent may not decide on your behalf about the use of this kind of treatment. The "best interests" test may not be applied in this situation.

Because an agent makes a treatment decision, the agent is entitled to receive sufficient medical information to give an informed consent.

Powers of Attorney

A power of attorney is a document that deals with financial affairs. It is a relatively short and uncomplicated instrument. It can be used to protect your property during a period of incapacity without the need of court intervention. The power of attorney is simply a document wherein another person (the "attorney-in-fact") is authorized to act in place and on behalf of the person (the "principal") with regard to the property of the principal. An alternate agent can be designated as well. All of the states have adopted the "durable" power of attorney, which makes the power of attorney survive your incapacity and can continue after such an event. A power of attorney can be created for a singular purpose with the agent authorized to act in a limited fashion, such as purchasing or selling real property. Many people are hesitant to confer the management of their affairs to another and therefore provide that the authority to act may only be effective when incapacity is confirmed by their physician. Many states, however, do not have such "springing event" statutes.

Many states do not permit gifts to be made on your behalf unless such authority is expressly stated in the power of attorney. The ability of the agent to transfer assets of a mentally disabled principal is significant for estate planning purposes. This right can continue the principal's program of lifetime giving and maximize the use of the unified credit and the annual exclusion during the period of incapacity. Under such a right, charitable gift giving programs can continue as well.

A power of attorney can be revoked at any time prior to your incapacity. The nature of the creation of a power of attorney does not require the transfer of title to any assets for it to take effect. There are no filing or recording requirements. Usually spouses or partners are given the authority to act for each other. When there is no spouse, children are normally designated, and if there are none, then usually a trusted friend or professional is designated as the agent.

Coordination with the Living Trust

As has been discussed in detail in chapter 8, the power of attorney and the living trust are documents that require coordination.

Even if you use a durable power of attorney, property in your living trust remains subject to your trustee, not your attorney-in-fact. However, a properly prepared durable power of attorney will serve you in many other areas, such as the ability of your agent to make gifts to you, file your income tax returns, commence litigation on your behalf, create trusts for you and your beneficiaries, and a whole list of other important financial and estate planning measures and procedures.

CHAPTER 22

Retirement Benefits

*T*he Internal Revenue Service has ruled that taxpayers may pass money in individual retirement accounts, stretching out the income tax liabilities for many, many years. By doing so, an estate can be maximized through the tax deferred growth of this property. Unfortunately, most financial advisors do not understand the applicable rules, and as a result, are improperly advising their clients.

This chapter sets forth the ABCs on how these rules work and how you can best take advantage of them. You can even set up a trust to serve as a beneficiary of your retirement plan and thereby create both estate and income tax shelters. In addition, this chapter explains the latest new proposed regulations on Required Minimum Distributions, which were issued by the Internal Revenue Service at the beginning of 2001.

In a subsequent marriage, a trust can be used not only to provide benefits for a surviving spouse but also to protect the principal for children of a different marriage. These trusts must be irrevocable, yet many estate planners make the error of recommending a revocable living trust to be the beneficiary thereof.

Taxes Involved

Tax-deferred retirement accounts like IRA, Keogh, and 401(k) plans are governed by three possible tax consequences and various distribution rules. Estate tax can be assessed unless an exemption or marital deduction is available. Income taxes are due as benefits are withdrawn from the plan. If an estate is subject to estate tax, any income taxes due at that time can be reduced by certain credits for estate tax paid. The Taxpayer Relief Act of 1997 eliminated the 15 percent excise tax on inter vivos "excess distributions" from retirement plans and repealed the excise tax on "excess accumulations" upon the death of a plan participant.

Estate Plans for Retirement Assets

Retirement assets are actually illiquid at death. This means that since income taxes have to be paid when they are withdrawn, they are really not—in dollars—what they seem to be. In order to pay estate and excise taxes, which are usually triggered when the second spouse dies, distributions must be made from the retirement plan or IRA, which will be subject to income tax at such time (an asset of this kind is called "income in respect of a decedent"). After taking into account the deduction for any estate taxes paid, the effective income tax bracket is 15–20 percent. This 15–20 percent loss factor is analogous to the loss that occurs when real estate or business interests must be liquidated to pay estate taxes, hence the concept "illiquid retirement plan assets." For retirement plans of $1 million or more, the total loss factor (estate, income, and excise taxes) can be 70–80 percent.

A simple and cost-effective way to plan for the loss is to purchase a life insurance policy on the husband or wife or both ("second-to-die"). There are three ways to fund the insurance premium: (1) a portion of the annual retirement distributions is gifted to an irrevocable trust that owns the policy; (2) a single life policy is owned by a subtrust in the qualified plan; or (3) a single life or second-to-die policy is owned by a profit sharing plan.

Decisions

Payments from a qualified retirement plan or IRA must commence in the year the participant reaches seventy and a half years of age (by April 1 of the following year). This is your required beginning date (the "RBD"). The Small Business Job Production Act of 1996 defers required distributions until retirement for those who continue to work. However, this rule does not apply to IRAs nor to owners of 5 percent or more of a business.

Therefore, at age seventy and a half, certain decisions have to be made that combine both estate and tax planning:

- How much money should be withdrawn each year?
- Who should be named as a beneficiary for any funds left in an account after the account holder's demise? It is important to note that you can now change your beneficiary at any time.

Distributions can be taken in one of the following ways: (1) a lump sum distribution (the entire distribution would be subject to income taxes); (2) in periodic installments over a specified number of years; or (3) in periodic installments over a specified number of years based upon the table that provides for same.

Estate Tax Consequences

The value of any undistributed retirement benefits will be included in the participant's estate for estate tax purposes. If a surviving spouse is designated as the beneficiary of the proceeds, there will be no estate taxes because of the unlimited marital deduction. This applies whether the surviving spouse receives a lump sum distribution or an annuity.

Income Tax Consequences

Retirement benefits are subject to income taxes when distributed. If someone receives a lump sum distribution as a result of the participant's death, the overall tax consequences will be substantial.

For example, if your child receives a lump sum distribution as a result of your death, the proceeds from the plan are deemed income in respect of decedent (IRD). This means that the entire benefits will be included in your estate for estate tax purposes and that your child will have to report the distribution on his or her income tax return—however, receiving a credit on this return for a portion of the estate tax paid on this asset.

Spousal Rollover

If a surviving spouse receives a lump sum distribution as a result of the participant's death, the proceeds may be rolled over into the surviving spouse's IRA account. This is known as a "spousal rollover." Only the spouse of a participant has this option. Once rolled over, the funds are subject to IRA rules (they cannot be withdrawn without penalty until age fifty-nine and a half), but the surviving spouse need not take any distributions until age seventy and a half. Income taxes, therefore, will be deferred until the funds are actually withdrawn. After the death of the account holder, the surviving spouse must by December 31 of the year following the owner's death elect the rollover and choose new beneficiaries.

Noncitizen Spouse

A revenue ruling sets forth how a surviving spouse who is not a U.S. citizen can take advantage of the Individual Retirement Account (IRA) spousal rollover rules while securing the estate tax marital deduction for the IRA proceeds of which she is the designated beneficiary.

In this situation, the decedent died owning three IRAs that were the community property of the decedent and his spouse under applicable state law. The surviving spouse, a non–U.S. citizen, was the primary beneficiary of each of the IRAs, and after the decedent's death, could withdraw the entire balance of any of them at any time.

Bequests to non–U.S. citizens are not eligible for the federal estate tax marital deduction unless they are in the form of a "qualified domestic trust" (QDOT). In order to qualify the IRA proceeds for the federal estate tax marital deduction and to take advantage of their rollover provisions available to surviving spouses who are designated beneficiaries of IRA proceeds, the surviving spouse established a QDOT.

The QDOT agreement provided that the trustee was to comply with any applicable rules relating to qualification of the trust estate as a QDOT for purposes of marital deduction (such as the requirement that the QDOT have a U.S. trustee) and as an IRA. The surviving spouse proposed to roll over the decedent's community property one-half interest in his IRAs to this trusteed QDOT within sixty days of receipt. The Service ruled that the decedent's community property interest in the IRAs could be rolled over to the QDOT. The surviving spouse therefore would not be subject to income tax on the amounts rolled over, and such amounts would qualify for the federal estate tax marital deduction.

Apparently, because the IRA proceeds passed outright to the surviving spouse under the terms of the decedent's will and the surviving spouse herself set up the QDOT after the decedent's death, the QDOT did not have to be in a form which would otherwise qualify for the estate tax marital deduction under the code.

A QTIP Trust as a Beneficiary

Another possibility is to designate a QTIP trust as beneficiary. In order to do this, (1) the QTIP trust must be irrevocable (if the participant has reached age seventy and a half); (2) the trust must be valid under applicable state law; (3) the trust must clearly identify the spouse as beneficiary; and (4) the trust instrument must have been delivered to the plan administrator, trustee, or IRA custodian. The qualified plan or IRA must distribute all of the income to the QTIP trust unless the minimum distribution amount is higher, and all of the income earned by the plan or IRA and by the QTIP trust must be distributed to the spouse.

Similar to the situation in which the spouse is the direct beneficiary, an estate tax deferral is available via the marital deduction. The life expectancy of the surviving spouse is the measuring life for the withdrawals from the qualified plan or IRA. Since many state laws do not consider distributions from qualified plans or IRAs to be trust income, the QTIP trust must define income for purposes of the distributions as including such items. Because the spouse may need more than the minimum amount or the income from the qualified plan or IRA, the trustee of the QTIP trust must have the right to withdraw more than the income if necessary.

A surviving spouse could compel a trustee of a QTIP trust to make unproductive assets productive. The spouse could be given the right to invade the corpus of the trust, in lieu of income distributions, if the principal of the trust is unproductive. No one other than the surviving spouse can receive distributions of income or principal from either the IRA or the trust during the surviving spouse's lifetime.

This type of device is an important element in estate planning for a subsequent marriage. It permits income to be provided to a spouse and preserve the principal for the children of a prior marriage.

A problem exists with many 401(k) and IRA retirement account plans in that they fail to satisfy the requirements of the Code. If the trust requirements are not met, the rules require estate taxes to be paid on all retirement money. Generally, company 401(k) plans and IRA retirement accounts do not have the necessary distribution structure and required QTIP options.

If a QTIP or credit shelter trust is designated as a beneficiary, some planning flexibility is lost. Specially, the spouse cannot roll over the amount into his or her own IRA and start a new measuring period based on the spouse's life expectancy. Any balance payable after the spouse's death will be paid to the beneficiary over the balance of the spouse's life expectancy.

If a QTIP trust is designated as beneficiary and the spouse survives, the spouse is not entitled to defer payment of the excise tax. Accordingly, the excise tax must be paid at the death of the participant or IRA holder. A tax clause in the living trust or will should identify the source of the excise tax payment to guard against the payment having to come from the qualified plan or IRA assets. The estate plan should recognize that the excise tax is a deduction to the estate. Some assets should probably be included in the estate to permit the utilization of the deduction.

A Credit Shelter Trust as a Beneficiary

A unified credit shelter trust is another possible beneficiary. Such a trust must meet the same four requirements described above for a QTIP trust. In addition, the qualified plan or IRA must distribute the minimum distribution amount, which would be measured by the life expectancy of the spouse if the spouse is the oldest eligible beneficiary. The distributions must be made by the plan or IRA to the credit shelter trust, but the trust can be an accumulation trust or one that has so-called sprinkling provisions. The trustees should be allowed to withdraw more than the minimum amount in any year, thus permitting access to the funds should the need exist, providing protection against possible adverse tax law changes, and allowing withdrawal if the qualified plan is terminated. In this case, deferral of the estate tax comes by way of the unified credit.

Charity as a Beneficiary

If a charity is to receive assets from an estate, the designation of the charity as beneficiary of the qualified plan or IRA will eliminate both the estate and income tax. Proper planning requires that a tax clause be included in the will identifying the source of payment of the excise tax amount if it is not to be paid from the qualified plan or IRA.

Living Trust

On December 30, 1997, the Department of Treasury issued a proposed modification to the proposed regulations, which would allow a revocable inter vivos trust or testamentary trust to be the beneficiary of a retirement account if the requirements of the regulations are met.

Roth IRA

Besides a regular IRA account, a second option for contributing to an IRA—the Roth IRA—was established under The Taxpayer Relief act of 1997. Contributions to this IRA will be nondeductible, but distributions will not be includable in income if certain conditions are met: The distribution must be made after the first five years of establishing a Roth IRA and either after the individual reaches fifty-nine and a half years of age, because of death or disability, or for first-time-home-buyer expenses. A Roth IRA contribution can be made at any age but is phased out for single taxpayers with AGIs between $95,000–$110,000 and for joint filers with AGIs between $150,000–$160,000.

In addition, amounts invested in existing IRAs can be converted to a Roth IRA for taxpayers with an AGI of less than $100,000 with some tax cost. Amounts converted that would have been includable in income had they been withdrawn are currently taxed. If the conversion was made prior to January 1, 1999, this amount can be included in income over four years. Married persons filing separately cannot take advantage of the conversion provision.

The New Proposed Regulation for Required Minimum Distributions

On January 11, 2001, the Internal Revenue Service issued proposed regulations that establish new guidelines for determining required minimum distributions from IRAs and other certain qualified plans. The new regulations represent a major modification of the former regulations that were proposed in 1987 and never finalized. The brand-new proposed regulations restate and replace the 1987 proposed regulation, although many of the concepts and rules set out in the 1987 proposed regulations are contained in the revised proposed regulations.

A public hearing on the proposed regulations was scheduled to be held on June 1, 2001, and the Internal Revenue Service anticipates that the regulations will become final for calendar years beginning on or after January 1, 2002.

Effective Dates

IRA owners can use the proposed regulations or the existing ones to determine required minimum distributions for 2001. The Service has issued further guidance to make clear that the new tables are for distributions that may be made by April 1, 2001 (applicable to IRA owners attaining age seventy and a half in 2000). This applies whether or not the IRA agreement is amended to incorporate the new regulations. Qualified plan participants, however, cannot use the new regulations until the plan documents are amended to incorporate them.

Revised Rules for Lifetime Distributions

The most important change under the new proposed regulations focuses on the calculations of the required minimum distributions from a qualified plan or IRA during the IRA owner's or plan participant's lifetime.

Distributions under the Prior Proposed Regulations

Under the prior proposed regulations, the determination of the Required Minimum Distribution was based upon the life expectancy of the IRA holder and the designated beneficiary. At the designation of the IRA holder, the minimum distribution could be determined on the joint life expectancies of the participant and the beneficiary, the recalculated joint life expectancies of the participant and the beneficiary (only if the beneficiary was the spouse of the participant), the life expectancy (either on a fixed term or recalculated) of the holder, or a combination of the foregoing. In determining life expectancies, a beneficiary who was not the spouse of the holder was treated as being no more than ten years younger than the holder. This was designated as the Minimum Distribution Incidental Benefit rule (MDIB).

Upon determining the method for computing the Minimum Distribution, one could not change it by selecting a different beneficiary or another method for how the calculation was to be made. A person could increase the Minimum Distribution by designating a beneficiary who was older than the prior beneficiary, but the holder could not extend the deferral period by designating a beneficiary who was younger than the prior beneficiary.

Distributions During Lifetime

The new proposed regulations provide a table, referred to as the "Uniform Table," under which a uniform distribution period can be determined. This table is based upon the joint life expectancies of the IRA holder and a person ten years younger than the holder. The table is the same that was used under the former proposed regulations when a nonspouse beneficiary was named who was more than ten years younger than the owner (the MDIB Table). The table recalculates life expectancies each year.

The table is available to any holder without regard to the identity of the beneficiary, or no beneficiary if none has been named. This means that a single holder of an IRA who designates a nonperson (a charitable organization) as a beneficiary can have the deferrals heretofore available only to a holder who had designated a younger person as a beneficiary. The age of the holder is the only ingredient necessary for input into the Table. The Uniform Table is presented at the end of this chapter.

There is one exception to the use of the table, which is where the sole named beneficiary is the holder's spouse who is more than ten years younger than the owner. In such a situation, the actual joint life expectancies of the owner and the spouse must be used and recalculated. The latter would create smaller minimum distributions than under the table.

The proposed new regulations alter the date on which the named beneficiary is to be determined. Under the prior proposed regulations, the determination was made at the death of the holder. Under the new proposed regulations, this determination shall be made on the last day of the calendar year following the year of the holder's death.

The new rule does not permit the appointment of a designated beneficiary after the holder's death. The new proposed rule would, however, afford the named beneficiary or beneficiaries the opportunity to recast who would receive the benefits for purposes of the required minimum distributions and the manner in which they would be received. A disclaimer by a beneficiary would make such adjustments.

Death of the Holder before Required Beginning Date

Once the designated beneficiary has been clarified, the new rules are not substantially different from the prior regulations. If a single person is the named beneficiary, that person is required to commence receiving distributions under the five-year rule or over his or her life expectancy. Under the five-year rule, the entire IRA must be distributed by the end of the fifth year following the holder's death.

If there is more than one (1) named beneficiary, the distributions will then be based on the life expectancy of the oldest beneficiary.

Death after the Required Beginning Date

The new rules for determining distributions if the holder dies after his or her required beginning date are almost the same as the regulations or distributions where death is before the required beginning date. The difference is that the holder's distribution for the year of death must be distributed by the end of the calendar year of his or her death, and the five-year rule does not apply.

Spouse Named as the Only Beneficiary

Where the spouse is named as the only beneficiary of an IRA, the required minimum distributions are different. In most situations when the spouse is the only beneficiary, the most advantageous plan is for him or her to roll over the IRA into his or her own IRA or elect to treat the inherited IRA as his or her own. The benefit of the spousal rollover is to obtain smaller distributions on the life of the spouse under the table, with the right to designate the beneficiary thereof.

If the holder has not reached his or her required beginning date at the death of the owner, a spouse has the options of doing the following:

- Electing the five-year rule.
- Wait until whichever date is later, either the end of the year in which the owner would have reached his or her required beginning date or until December 31st of the year following the year of the holder's death. At the later of the two dates, the spouse must then commence to receive distributions over his or her expectancy. The rules permit a spouse to recalculate his or her life expectancy each year rather than requiring the use of a fixed, certain term.

Other Important Provisions
- Subsequent Beneficiary

The regulations provide that a named beneficiary, after the holder's death, can name a subsequent beneficiary in the event of death of the named beneficiary. However, the required distribution period is the life expectancy of the original named beneficiary.

- Trust as Designated Beneficiary

The rules regarding a trust as a designated beneficiary remain mostly the same:
- The trust must be valid under state law.
- The beneficiaries of the trust must be identifiable.
- The trust must be irrevocable, or will be at the plan owner's demise.
- Trust documentation must be provided to the administrator of the plan.

Observations

The proposed new regulations greatly simplify the minimum distribution rules and permit postdeath planning. However, the naming of beneficiaries remains significant in order to allow maximum deferrals and the distribution of the plan in accordance with the plan owner's wishes.

Caveats
- The Internal Revenue Code requires that you start drawing from your IRA (and paying tax on the distributions) the year that you reach seventy and a half. Usually, the payments must be made by the end of each year (December 31), but in the first year you are entitled to a three-month grace period.
- You can change the beneficiary of your IRA at any time.
- IRAs and certain other retirement plans can be used in your estate plan to take full advantage of your estate tax exemption and that of your spouse by the funding of a qualified marital deduction trust (QTIP) so as to defer the estate taxes or of a credit shelter trust that will permit you to control the ultimate disposition of the principal of the trust.
- If you intend to make any charitable gifts, use your IRA. Not only will you receive an estate tax deduction, no income taxes will be required to be paid by the charity when it receives the gift.
- A taxpayer who inherits an IRA must pay taxes on the gift. For example, federal and New York income and estate taxes on retirement fund property could exceed 85 percent. At your death, the

aggregate of the taxes can effectively wipe out your plan. This can be totally avoided by the implementation of charitable planning. Plans such as IRAs, 401(k)s, 403(b)s, and defined contribution plans can be used for charitable gifts. To save taxes all you have to do is change the allocation of your assets among your beneficiaries.

• Your profit-sharing plan can be used to purchase life insurance. As a general rule, if whole life insurance is purchased, the cumulative premium cannot be more than 50 percent of the cumulative employee's contribution attributed to the participant's account. If term insurance is purchased, the amount that can be used cannot exceed half the foregoing amount. The purchase of life insurance with profit-sharing-plan contributions can only be accomplished if the plan permits it. If the life insurance in the plan is owned in a manner so that the participant has no "incidents of ownership," the proceeds of the life insurance should not be included in the participant's estate for tax purposes. If the life insurance proceeds are part of a trust that is set up to exclude it properly from a spouse's estate, the proceeds will escape taxation in two estates.

Uniform Table

AGE OF THE OWNER	DISTRIBUTION PERIOD
70	26.2
71	25.3
72	24.4
73	23.5
74	22.7
75	21.8
76	20.9
77	20.1
78	19.2
79	18.4
80	17.6
81	16.8
82	16.0
83	15.3
84	14.5
85	13.8
86	13.1
87	12.4
88	11.8

AGE OF THE OWNER	DISTRIBUTION PERIOD
89	11.1
90	10.5
91	9.9
92	9.4
93	8.8
94	8.3
95	7.8
96	7.3
97	6.9
98	6.5
99	6.1
100	5.7
101	5.3
102	5.0
103	4.7
104	4.4
105	4.1
106	3.8
107	3.6
108	3.3
109	3.1
110	2.8
111	2.6
112	2.4
113	2.2
114	2.0
115 and older	1.8

❖

CHAPTER 23

Medicare and Medicaid

$\mathcal{W}$ hat are Medicaid and Medicare? Who is entitled to the benefits of these programs?

The thought of being impoverished as a result of long-term care haunts people. Asset preservation strategies are important to individuals who want to protect their estates from financial decimation. Medicaid is the only government program that offers an alternative to the disastrous financial results that can come from long-term nursing home care. This chapter discusses these available entitlements and what the requirements are for eligibility.

Medicaid is a program for needy persons and is jointly funded and administered by the federal government and the states. All of the states participate in this program. The federal government contributes about half the costs. Each state administers its program and can set its own standards. Medicare on the other hand is totally under the federal system and is for the population who are aged or for persons with disabilities.

The Omnibus Reconciliation Act of 1993 (OBRA 93) changed many of the rules relating to Medicaid. In this chapter you will find out how to create a trust, and thereafter, transfer your assets into it and qualify for Medicaid benefits.

Overview

Medicare is a government health insurance program for the aged and people with disabilities. The Medicare system does not make provisions for sheltering a family from the catastrophic costs of nursing home care. It is not a long-term care plan and does not begin to cover all of one's health care needs.

For example, it does not cover prescription drugs, vision, hearing, dental care, custodial care, and private duty nursing. Despite Medicare's limitations, it is the foundation for all other health insurance. It is virtually impossible for senior citizens to obtain any health insurance without Medicare coverage.

Medicare is divided into two parts. Part A, Hospital Insurance (HI), covers hospital, skilled nursing facility, home health, and hospice services. Part B, Supplemental Medical Insurance (SMI), covers physician services, durable medical equipment, ambulance services, therapy service, and laboratory tests.

Medicare enrollment is automatic for all persons—regardless of income—who are: (1) sixty-five or older and eligible for social security or railroad retirement benefits; (2) have been receiving social security disability income for at least twenty-four months; or (3) have end-stage renal disease (ESRD). However, a person who does not meet these eligibility requirements but who is sixty-five or older and a U. S. citizen or a legal alien residing in the United States for at least five years may elect to enroll in Parts A and B or Part B alone.

Medicaid

The only available source to defray home or nursing home care expenses is the Medicaid system. Because individuals can qualify by meeting the minimum threshold requirements, people will plan their estates to achieve these levels. By transferring their assets and subsequently meeting the qualifications standards, the assets are preserved for the next generation.

Medicaid is a joint federal-state program of medical assistance for needy persons who are aged, blind, or disabled or who qualify for cash benefits under the Aid to Families with Dependent Children (AFDC) program. Each state operates its Medicaid programs according to general standards set by Congress but administers them by a state agency, with the costs of administration split roughly fifty-fifty between the state and the federal government.

Besides being an American citizen or a permanent resident alien, an applicant for Medicaid must show that he or she is: (1) aged, blind, disabled, or the parent of a minor child; and (2) financially needy according to program criteria. Persons age sixty-five and older meet the first standard. Those who qualify for Supplemental Security Income (SSI) benefits in many states satisfy the criteria for both SSI and Medicaid. (See chapter 19 for a detailed discussion on SSI benefits.)

Financial Need

Financial need is established when an individual's (or couple's) income and resources fall below Medicaid ceilings. For 2001, the monthly income limit for an eligible individual was $645, or $920 for an eligible married couple. The resource or asset limit level, effective January 1, 2001, is $3,750 for a single person and $5,400 for a couple, plus a burial fund of $1,500 per person or any amount in an irrevocable preneed funeral arrangement. Aged, blind, or disabled persons whose incomes and resources are above these limits may nevertheless qualify for Medicaid if their net income and resources, after their medical bills are paid, fall below these limits.

What counts as income for Medicaid purposes is different from the definition of income used by the Internal Revenue Service for income tax purposes. For Medicaid, it means anything that a person receives in cash or in-kind that can be used to meet the person's needs for food, clothing, or shelter is considered income.

An applicant with resources in excess of the permissible limit is required to spend them down, give them away, or sell them until the balance is within the allowable limits.

Financial Responsibility of Spouses for One Another

Medicaid considers the income and resources of each spouse to be available to the other (a process called "deeming") when the spouses live together in the community and one applies for Medicaid.

If spouses separate but neither is institutionalized and one of them applies for Medicaid, deeming ends at the close of the month in which they separate. Deeming continues for six months, however, if both of the separated spouses apply for Medicaid.

When one spouse is institutionalized and the other remains in the community, the "community spouse" is permitted to retain or acquire a minimum monthly maintenance needs (income) allowance of up to $2,103 (New York, 2000) from the institutionalized spouse. A community spouse can also retain up to $84,120 (2000) in nonexcluded resources without affecting the institutionalized spouse's Medicaid eligibility. Any excess income in the community spouse's name is considered not available to pay for the institutionalized spouse's care.

New York couples with substantial unearned income (for example, interest and dividends) who anticipate that one spouse is likely to enter a nursing home and apply for Medicaid might be advised to transfer this income to the community spouse's name. If this income exceeds the community's spouse's allowance of $2,019, that spouse will be allowed to keep the excess, subject only to the voluntary contribution option. The same result could be obtained by purchasing an annuity in the community spouse's name.

Uncooperative Community Spouses

New York State rescinded its previous policy of denying the monthly income allowance to a community spouse who refused to use excess resources for the care of the institutionalized spouse.

The state will, however, deny Medicaid to an institutionalized spouse where the community spouse does not reveal income and resource information, unless the denial causes "undue hardship." The state, however, has never denied Medicaid to a spouse because the other spouse refuses to contribute to the costs of care of the applicant spouse.

Exempt Transfers

Certain assets or resources are exempt from the coverage of the transfer rules and therefore their transfer for less than fair market value is not penalized. The term "resources" has the same meaning here as it does under the SSI program, except for the person's home. Thus all resources that are exempt for SSI purposes are also exempt from the transfer penalties. Therefore, the total value of an exempt resource (e.g., a car or a life insurance policy) can be transferred without penalty.

The law does not penalize the transfer of a home during the thirty-six month look-back period if the residence is transferred for the sole benefit of the institutionalized person's spouse, or to a blind or disabled child, or to any of the following:

- A dependent child
- A sibling with an equity interest who had resided in the home for one year prior to the applicant's admission to a medical institution or nursing facility
- The son or daughter of the individual who had lived in the home for two years prior to the institutionalization and who had cared for the individual
    In addition, no transfer of any asset is penalized to the extent that:
- The asset was transferred to the community spouse or a blind or disabled child.
- A satisfactory showing is made to the state that the individual intended to dispose of the asset either at fair market value or for other valuable consideration, or the asset was transferred exclusively for a purpose other than to qualify for medical assistance.
- The state determines that denial of eligibility would cause an undue hardship.

Some important aspects of the rules are listed below:

- Transfers of assets in order to qualify for SSI benefits are not penalized, regardless of how close they occur to the date of SSI eligibility.
- Many states do not consider the resources of the community spouse to be available to the institutionalized spouse after the month in which the institutionalized spouse establishes eligibility for Medicaid. As such, a transfer of assets by the community spouse after this time will not affect the institutionalized spouse's benefits. A person could, therefore, transfer an exempt asset, such as a residence, to the ownership of the community spouse (an exempt transfer), and once Medicaid eligibility is established, the community spouse would be free to transfer the exempt asset without penalty.
- Transfers of assets in order to qualify for Medicaid also are not penalized, regardless of when they occur, provided the eligible person receives only home- or community-based Medicaid services and only those Medicaid services that are not equivalent to the level of care provided in a nursing facility.

Specific Techniques for "Spending Down"

What is the optimal amount of nonexempt assets that should be transferred to permit an individual to qualify for Medicaid after a penalty period?

The Fifty-Fifty Strategy

Many advocates urge a fifty-fifty strategy. This method is implemented by an individual transferring half of his or her nonexempt resources to a nonspouse and retaining the other half to pay for nursing home costs during the penalty period created by the transfer.

Using the Medical Expense Deduction

An alternative to the fifty-fifty strategy is for the person who is about to enter a nursing home to transfer all of his or her assets to a favored family member living in the community. The community person is then expected to spend approximately half of the transferred amount to pay for the institutionalized person's care. This payment is a medical expense deduction for the community person, while at the same time it is treated as a spend-down payment for the institutionalized person and thereby shortens the penalty period. The unspent half of the transferred assets remains with the community person, as in the fifty-fifty strategy, while the penalty period is roughly the same for the institutionalized person.

The chief advantage is the income tax savings for the community person through the medical expense deduction.

Disclaimers and Forced Shares

Can an institutionalized spouse disclaim an inheritance without jeopardizing Medicaid eligibility? The issue can arise either after the person is receiving Medicaid, making the inheritance an available resource, or prior to application for Medicaid, making the renunciation a transfer of assets (if the testator died within thirty-six months of the person's applying for Medicaid).

The decisions regarding this issue are few and split. North Dakota holds that the disclaimer is not a transfer of assets. However, New York and Connecticut courts have ruled to the contrary. New York has reached a similar result in a case involving a surviving spouse who failed to exercise her statutory right of election against the will of her deceased husband.

Lifetime Uses of a Personal Residence

If the transferor retains only a lifetime right to the use and occupancy of a residence, rather than a life estate, some states do not count this interest as an asset for Medicaid purposes, even though it is still part of the transferor's estate. A clause should be placed in a gift deed of the personal residence retaining the right to the use and occupancy of the property.

It has also been reported that many jurisdictions are treating the life estate, for Medicaid purposes, as an available resource for the transferor while institutionalized. In these situations, the state assumes that the premises can be rented, and therefore, it imputes the fair market rental value of the home and thus requires contribution to the costs of care.

To avoid this result, one of two strategies can be adopted:
- Argue that the home must be kept vacant for the possible return of the person to live there.
- At the time of the original transfer, limit the life estate to the use and occupancy of the person, thereby preventing its rental to others.

Effective October 22, 1993, the New York State Department of Social Services changed the treatment of the home of a Medicaid applicant or recipient who leaves the home to enter a nursing home. As a result, in this state, Medicaid will no longer include the homes of institutionalized Medicaid applicants or recipients as a countable resource if they clearly express their intent to return home at a future date. The "intent to return home" need only be a written statement from the individual (or authorized representative) expressing the intent to eventually return home.

Upon the death of a nursing home resident, Medicaid will be entitled to reimbursement from the estate of that person for any services provided, including recovery against any home which the Medicaid recipient owns individually at the time of his or her death.

OBRA 93 confirmed that for Medicaid purposes the disclaimer of an inheritance is considered a disqualifying transfer.

Transfer of Assets

According to OBRA 93, a person who enters a nursing home and is receiving Medicaid or applies for it after admission may be denied eligibility if he or she (or the person's spouse) has transferred any nonexempt asset for less than fair market value during the thirty-six month period (known as the "look-back" period) prior to qualifying for Medicaid while institutionalized. The look-back period is sixty months for payments made from a revocable living trust other than to or for the benefit of the Medicaid recipient or spouse. This sixty-month period also applies to the transfer to any irrevocable trust of assets which cannot be paid under any circumstances to the individual or spouse and to a prohibition on the payment of income from an irrevocable trust to the individual or spouse.

On August 21, 1996, the Kennedy-Kassebaum Health Insurance Portability and Accountability Act of 1996 (the "Act") was signed by the President. The legislation, which became effective January 1, 1997, imposes criminal penalties for acts involving Medicare or Medicaid. Section 217 of the Act criminalizes certain transfers of assets made for the purpose of qualifying for Medicaid benefits to pay for nursing home care. This legislation imposed liability on anyone who "knowingly and willfully" disposed of assets if such disposition resulted in a period of ineligibility. The legislation was viewed as imposing liability on the person who transferred the assets and possibly on an advisor who counseled such a transfer.

The Balanced Budget Act of 1997, signed into law on August 5, 1997, amended paragraph (6) of section 217 so that it now provides that whoever:

> (6) for a fee knowingly and willfully counsels and assists an individual to dispose of assets (including by any transfer-in trust) in order for the individual to become eligible for medical assistance under a State plan under Title XIX, if disposing of the assets results in the imposition of a period of ineligibility for such assistance under section 1917c ... shall

i) in the case of such a statement, representation, concealment, failure, conversion by any person in connection with the furnishing (by that person) of items or services for which payment is or may be made under the program, be guilty of a felony and upon conviction thereof fined not more than $25,000 or imprisoned for not more than five years or both; or

ii) in the case of such a statement, representation, concealment, failure, conversion, or provision of counsel or assistance by any other person be guilty of a misdemeanor and upon conviction thereof fined not more than $10,000 or imprisoned for not more than one year, or both.

Thus the latest amendments to 217(6) have removed the liability of the person actually transferring the assets and impose liability on anyone who willfully counsels and assists the person in disposing of the assets.

This amendment apparently is directed toward elder law attorneys and others who are consulted about Medicaid planning in order to prevent them from advising their clients accordingly.

The question that is posed by the new law is: When is a period of ineligibility "imposed." Is it upon transferring an asset that renders one ineligible for Medicaid or only if the transferor applies for Medicaid during a period of ineligibility and is denied eligibility as a result of the transfer?

When an individual applies for Medicaid for nursing home care, the state Medicaid Agency looks back at transfers of assets made in the prior thirty-six months, or sixty months for transfers to or from certain trusts. If a transfer of assets is made during this look-back period by either an applicant or his or her spouse and the transfer does not fall within any stated exemption, then a period of ineligibility for Medicaid from the beginning of the month following the transfer is imposed. The "period of ineligibility," also known as the "transfer penalty period" is calculated by dividing the dollar amount of the transfer by the average monthly cost of nursing home care in the state or community. Under the present provision of 217(6), it is the imposition of this ineligibility period that results in criminal penalties.

One interpretation of the word "imposition" is that if a person who has previously transferred assets waits out what is called the "look-back period" and then files an application subsequent to the expiration of a look-back period, such a filing of an application at that point could not possibly involve the imposition of a period of ineligibility for benefits under the Medicaid program.

The effect and enforceability of this new law, including the constitutionality of a law that constitutes a restraint on free speech, is being carefully analyzed. All individuals and agencies that provide Medicaid counseling should advise their clients accordingly.

Inter Vivos Trusts

Under OBRA 93, certain inter vivos trusts are considered to be the assets of the Medicaid applicant. These are trusts created by the applicant, his or her spouse, and a court or administrative body acting with legal authority in place of, on behalf of, at the direction of, or upon the request of either spouse. This rule applies regardless of the purposes for which the trust was established, whether the trustees have or exercise any discretion under the trust, any restriction of when or whether distributions can be made from the trust, or any restrictions on the use of distributions from the trust.

Exempt Trusts

Certain inter vivos trusts, under OBRA 93, however, are not considered assets of the Medicaid applicant, including: (1) a trust for the benefit of a disabled person under age sixty-five, provided the state will receive from the trust at the beneficiary's death reimbursement for Medicaid services provided to that person; and (2) a pooled-asset trust for a disabled person (not limited to persons under sixty-five) managed by a nonprofit association that meets certain standards and from which the state may recoup Medicaid assistance at the beneficiary's death. Therefore, property of a disabled person received through a lawsuit can now be protected for that person's benefit during his or her lifetime.

Living Trusts

Transfers of assets by an applicant or the spouse to a revocable living trust do not trigger a period of ineligibility because the assets are still considered to be available to the grantor, but the use of the trust funds for any other purpose than for the spouses' benefit is considered a transfer. Assets transferred to an irrevocable trust that could be paid to or used for the benefit of either spouse are also considered a countable resource, and any actual payments to them are income, while the balance of the trust assets are subject to the transfer rules.

"Income Only" Medicaid Rules Clarified

OBRA 93 sets forth rules governing "income only" trusts, which are irrevocable trusts that reserve to the grantor income on the principal of the trust for life, but do not allow the grantor any access to the principal of the trust during his or her lifetime.

If a person establishes an irrevocable trust guaranteeing the income of the trust to himself or herself for life but excludes the distribution of the trust corpus to himself or herself, the corpus of the trust will not be considered an available resource to the individual after the applicable transfer-of-assets waiting period (sixty months).

While the look-back period differs for transfers of assets in trust and outright transfers, a transfer of approximately $200,000 into a trust would result in a waiting period of approximately three years in the city of New York. Therefore, the waiting period can be limited for transferred assets to three years even if a trust is used by transferring $200,000 to a trust and simultaneously transferring additional amounts outright because, no matter how much is transferred outright, the individual would simply wait out the three-year look-back period for outright transfers. More assets could be transferred into trust by planning ahead and waiting out the longer period.

If the trust permits the grantor the right to appoint the remainder of the trust (after his or her death) to a limited class of people, then no gift tax is payable at the time the trust is created.

An individual who places his or her residence in an "income only" trust and retains a testamentary "limited power of appointment" will also preserve the income tax benefit from capital gains upon the sale of the property permitted under the Internal Revenue Code. This benefit would not be available if the property were given away.

When such a trust is created and the individual enters a nursing home, the state will receive the income from the trust, which is an indirect incentive or a way for the state to fund these costs.

Tort Settlements

Disabled persons whose disabilities were caused by a third party may be able to obtain a substantial settlement or judgment. If the settlement or award is used to fund a Supplemental Needs Trust (SNT), it will not disqualify the recipient from qualifying for Medicaid.

The Omnibus Budget Reconciliation Act of 1993 (P.L. 103-66, OBRA '93) exempted assets placed in SNTs from Medicaid eligibility determinations. Thus, an SNT funded with the assets of a disabled individual under sixty-five years of age is not treated as an available resource for purposes of Medicaid qualification, and the transfer of the disabled person's assets to the trust is not considered a disqualifying gift. Upon the death of the beneficiary, however, remaining trust principal must be used to reimburse the state for medical assistance paid on the beneficiary's behalf. If the disabled person is over age 65, the assets may be placed in a "pooled" trust established by a not-for-profit organization, but the usual transfer of asset penalty rules will apply. However, the New York Courts have determined that the sum to satisfy the lien can be derived only from that portion of the recovery "that it intended to compensate each plaintiff for past medical expenses" and instructs the courts below to allocate the portion of the settlement for medical expenses. Thus, the portion allocated to pain and suffering and economic loss can still be earmarked for the SNTs.

Strategies

It is only uncompensated transfers that generate a penalty for Medicaid-planning purposes, while transfers for valid consideration may be freely made without penalty. An annuity transaction is a transfer for valid consideration that can result in the transferor's immediate eligibility for Medicaid without really surrendering the transferred asset.

An annuity is a fixed annual payment for the duration of a person's (the annuitant's) lifetime. The usual annuity contract involves a transfer of funds in return for specified annual payments based on the annuitant's reasonable life expectancy.

The trend in using annuities for Medicaid planning has been to purchase commercial annuities (e.g., through an insurance company). Private annuities are recognized when assets other than cash are involved. This is because insurance companies will not accept any other assets, such as a home or other real estate, closely held business interests, or even appreciated securities. For these assets, and even for cash, the private annuity, in many instances, is becoming a much more attractive option.

Typically, the private annuity will be between members of a family, but this is not a requirement. As with a commercial annuity, it can be for the life of the purchaser or for the joint lives of the purchaser and another (such as husband and wife), or any other form that an annuity may customarily take. The typical private annuity, however, will not have a term certain, so that payments will cease on the annuitant's death and the contract performance will be completed; therefore, no part of the transferred property is included in the annuitant's estate for estate tax purposes.

For Medicaid purposes, the transfer of property in return for a private annuity is treated identically to the purchase of a commercial annuity. That is, the projected value of payments must be actuarially sound based on the annuitant's life expectancy and the applicable interest rates.

If the annuitant's state of health is such that, according to the diagnosis of a physician, there is a greater than 50/50 chance he or she will die within a twelve-month period, then the tables may not be used and the transaction would not qualify.

Federal Recovery Against Annuities

The intervention by a federal agency in January of 2000, covering estate recovery against the beneficiary of an annuity, jeopardizes the use of annuities as an estate planning technique.

Recovery by a state of Medicaid expenditures against the beneficiary of an annuity, which goes to a beneficiary on the death of the policyholder and the purchase of which is not a transfer of assets for less than market value as long as the term of the annuity does not exceed the life expectancy of the annuitant, may be possible.

In a letter from HCFA Regional IX to the California Department of Health Services, HCFA determined that a state has a right to seek recovery of Medicaid expenditures for an annuity policyholder, from the surviving beneficiary of the annuity, up to the value of the remainder interest in the annuity. Under the federal Medicaid statute, states must try to recover from an estate for permanently institutionalized persons and have the option to recover for any other Medicaid services for individuals age fifty-five and over.

The scope of the estate recovery includes any property within an individual's estate as defined for probate purposes and may include such assets conveyed to a survivor, heir, or assign of the deceased individual through joint-tenancy, tenancy in-common, survivorship, life estate, living trust, or other arrangement.

HCFA indicated that annuities are private arrangements that pass ownership outside of probate. However, a state could determine that under Medicaid law, annuities could be treated like trusts, life estate, or joint tenancies.

HCFA indicates that recovery against annuities could not begin until the calendar quarter ninety days after an amendment to its State

Medicaid Manual. In addition, the state's own Medicaid plan would have to be amended to include annuities in its definition of an estate.

Caveats

- If you apply for Medicaid, you cannot give away the annual exclusion ($10,000) without incurring a Medicaid penalty. Don't confuse the Medicaid transfer of assets rule with the tax-free gift tax exclusion.
- Medicaid provides long-term benefits to persons sixty-five or over or disabled persons who qualify under the financial requirement rules. In certain situations even a high income will not bar the obtaining of Medicaid.
- Medicaid is available in all states.
- Medicaid does not pay cash benefits to its recipients.
- Limitations.

Providers of healthcare throughout the country are not required to be members of the Medicaid programs. This means that in certain areas it may be difficult to find a medical specialist who will accept Medicaid. If your physician refuses to accept Medicaid payments (because of the lower reimbursement than other providers and because of the amount of paperwork), you will be required to find a new personal physician.

Medicaid cannot afford to provide you with the amount of in-house services (nurses, care-givers, attendants) you may require or wish for. Only your money can purchase these options. This may mean a dissipation of your property, but the quality of your life should be paramount.

The future of the Medicaid system is uncertain. Currently, across the nation and in Washington, D.C., it is one of the topics that is the subject of serious debate regarding both paring down and in certain instances eliminating the governments participation and funding.

A trust created under your living trust or will to take effect after your death, for the benefit of your surviving spouse, or a handicapped child, in the form of a discretionary special needs trust, which prevents the principal from being considered a resource or asset for Medicaid purposes and which applies the income from the trust at the discretion of the trustee, will not only permit the person to qualify for Medicaid but will preserve the principal of the trust for the next generation!

The format for such a trust (set forth in living trust) for the benefit of a surviving spouse could be in the following form:

Trust for Surviving Spouse That Preserves Medicaid Eligibility

(1) To hold, invest, and reinvest the same, to collect and receive the income, and after paying all expenses incidental to the management of the trust, pay to my spouse, or apply for the benefit of my spouse, _____ during his/her lifetime so much of the income and principal as the Trustees, in their absolute discretion, determine to be advisable for his/her support, comfort and maintenance and for his/her final funeral expenses upon his/her death.

(2) In the event that my spouse should enter a medical institution, the Trustees shall apply the principal and income of the trust for his/her comfort but not for his/her food, clothing or shelter.

(3) In making such payments and expenditures, the Trustees shall take into account any funds or assistance the Trustees know to be available to my spouse from governmental and private sources.

(4) The interest of my spouse in the income or principal of this trust shall be free from the control or interference of any of his/her creditors or of any government agency providing aid or benefits to him/her and shall not be subject to attachment or susceptible of any anticipation or alienation.

(5) In making such payments and expenditures, the Trustees need not consider the effect such distributions may have upon the interests of the remainder of the trust.

(6) The Trustees shall consult regularly with my children to ascertain my spouse's needs and desires and may follow his/her recommendations in making payments and expenditures in my spouses behalf.

(7) Upon my spouse's death or in the event that the terms and conditions of this trust are challenged in court by any governmental agency, the trust shall terminate and the corpus of the trust, together with any accumulated income thereon, shall be paid absolutely to my children in equal shares, per stirpes.

Medicaid Seeks Recovery from All Refusing Spouses

Since a recent court decision, described below, New York City and some other countries are seeking recovery from all refusing spouses of the cost of care provided to their Medicaid recipient spouses. Recovery is being sought whether the sick spouse is in a nursing home and the community spouse is refusing to contribute income or resources in excess of the community spouse allowances or the sick spouse is receiving community services or home care and the well spouse is refusing to contribute income or resources. Previously, Medicaid waited until the death of the second spouse to seek recovery from that spouse's estate for the cost of care furnished to the Medicaid-eligible spouse. Now, New York City Medicaid and some other counties are sending letters to all refusing spouses requesting that they reimburse Medicaid for the cost of their sick spouse's medical care. If no response is sent to this letter, Medicaid files a lawsuit for payment of an outstanding debt in the amount paid by Medicaid for the care of the sick spouse. These lawsuits are based upon a 1998 case brought by New York City Medicaid against a community spouse who refused to contribute his resources in excess of the community spouse resource allowance to the care of his sick spouse on nursing home *(Medicaid Commissioner of the DSS of the City of New York* v. *Benjamin Spellman)*. Both the original court and the Appellate Division of the First Department ruled that Medicaid could seek reimbursement from refusing spouses during their lifetimes without waiting to seek recovery from their estates after death.

CHAPTER 24

The Protection of Assets

$\mathcal{T}$he explosion of litigation in this country has been caused by many factors: the growth of the legal profession, the contingent fee system, the expansion of theories of legal liability, and the large awards returned by juries including the granting of punitive damages. These changes have given rise to the need for asset protection devices.

With proper planning, assets can be forever insulated and protected against claims of third parties.

Offshore Trusts

For expatriates and the citizens of many countries, one of the principal benefits of offshore trusts is low taxes. Since assets are held offshore and are not part of an individual's estate, they can often appreciate free of domestic taxes. For the same reasons, offshore trusts are also frequently exempted from inheritance taxes.

Under U.S. law, however, offshore trusts owned by citizens of this country, whether expatriate or resident, are subject to the same taxes as any other assets.

What does make offshore trusts attractive is the protection they provide from legal challenges. For example, in common law countries, spouses can successfully contest the terms of wills if they can convince juries that they have been inadequately provided for. However, according to Nicholas Landor, a trust administrator at Hill Samuel in London: "Trusts established in offshore centers have never been challenged successfully on such grounds because legal precedents make it clear that the wishes of a trust's creator are primary to all other concerns."

No matter how controversial or complicated the terms of an inheritance may be, they are just about inviolable to claims by a third party when property is held in an offshore trust. In the United States today, it is risky for professionals to own all of their assets outright. Malpractice awards are substantial and in many instances cannot be covered by insurance. But, if a professional transfers assets to an offshore trust, they can be protected. The offshore trust strategy would also be useful for a businessman contemplating substantial personal guarantees or becoming involved in an unsure business venture.

The key to successful offshore asset protection is a clear no-liability condition at the time the trust is created. All offshore jurisdictions have rules against financial fraud, the deliberate avoidance of creditors, or other attempts to avoid legitimate financial claims. If there are no questions about solvency or debt at the time the trust is established, then these jurisdictions consider trusts as separate entities that are free from all future claims on the assets held by the trust.

Certain offshore centers such as the Cayman Islands, the Bahamas, and the Cook Islands have taken steps to further strengthen the protection of these trusts. To clarify questions about the timing of claims made against a trust, these countries have passed statutes of limitations beyond which legal challenges to the trust cannot be made. In the Cook Islands, for example, challenges to the trust must occur during the first three years of the life of the trust. In the Bahamas, lawsuits must be brought within the first two years. And in the Cayman Islands, challenges are only valid within the trust's first six years of existence.

An offshore trust brings with it the further advantage that it removes litigation out of local courts. The foreign jurisdiction will normally not enforce a foreign court's decision without relitigating it.

Certain foreign jurisdictions do not recognize the judgments of American courts. As such, and in order to make a claim on the assets in the trust, a new case has to be brought in the foreign court based upon the local law. The claim has to be victorious, and then a fraudulent conveyance proceeding has to be brought against the trust. This would require the claimant bringing to the foreign jurisdiction witnesses, exhibits, and all other evidence required to sustain the claim. This of course assumes that the foreign court will accept jurisdiction over the matter in the first place. This entire process tends to discourage third parties from proceeding in such a fashion. Also, most of the jurisdictions that permit the creation of the asset protection trusts do not permit contingency fee arrangements. As such, local attorneys are required to represent a claimant and have to be compensated accordingly.

Generally, in foreign jurisdictions, transfers of assets may be open to challenge under two sets of legal rules, one being known as fraudulent conveyance rules. The second set of rules deals with bankruptcy law. Once an offshore trust is created, its assets can be moved anywhere. The advantage of having an existing offshore trust is that if someone files a claim against your personal assets, the trust is not subject to the fraudulent conveyance restrictions. In fact, the trustees are obligated to take whatever action is necessary to preserve trust assets, including moving the assets anywhere in the world. Today, transactions with foreign countries are no more complicated than conducting business in another state.

Although title to the asset is held overseas, it is not necessary for the owner to part with control of the transferred property. The property may be protected by transferring it to a domestic limited partnership. The owner can receive a 99 percent interest in the property as a limited partner and a 1 percent interest as a general partner. The owner can then transfer his or her 99 percent limited partnership interest to a foreign trust. As the general partner, control of 100 percent interest of the assets is effective while owning only a 1 percent interest. Although the owner has parted with ownership of 99 percent of the interest in the assets, the foreign trustees do not directly control the assets; rather, they hold a passive interest in the limited partnership and the property will remain in the United States.

In the event creditors pressure the owner and question the structure of the trust and partnership in a U.S. Court, the assets held at the limited partnership level may be transferred offshore to a foreign entity, which will substitute for the domestic limited partnership, over which the owner exercises a similar level of control.

Domestic Protection

Most of the states in this country have laws designed to protect creditors that invalidate asset transfers made at certain times or made with the intent to defraud creditors, such as when someone who has liabilities, contingent or otherwise, transfers property for less than its full value.

Planning to protect one's property can also have significant estate planning advantages. Protection devices can include trust gifts, life insurance, qualified retirement plans, and marital property division.

Recently, the U.S. Supreme Court ruled on the question as to whether state law permitting access by creditors to pension plan assets of a bankrupt individual could be preempted by federal law. The court decided favorably for plan participants by protecting funds set aside in Keogh and qualified plans. In addition, today most states now protect all IRAs from the claims of creditors in the event of bankruptcy.

In many states, property held jointly by married couples is not subject to seizure by creditors unless both spouses are obligated and then only by particular creditors. Furthermore, in most states if a deed to real property is in the name of husband and wife, a tenancy by the entirety is presumed to be created. In such a case, if the debtor-spouse dies first, the other spouse will own the property free and clear. If the nondebtor spouse should die first, creditors could then proceed against the property to satisfy debts of the surviving spouse. When creditors face these type of situations, they will often attempt to settle claims as opposed to waiting for the death of a spouse.

Many states have homestead exemptions which protect a certain amount of the equity in a residence from creditors. In most instances, the only requirement to obtain such protection is simply filing a form requesting it. In the states of Florida, Kansas, Minnesota, South Carolina, and Texas, the dollar amount of homestead protection is not limited. At the end of this chapter is a schedule of the homestead exemptions available in the various states.

Properly prepared trusts can also protect assets from creditors. As previously discussed in chapter 14, integrating a life insurance policy with an irrevocable trust can protect the policy owned by the trust and, under the proper circumstances, will shelter it from estate taxation.

Outright gifts to family members can be a form of asset protection if made at the appropriate time. This, however, may not be possible if recipients are minors or persons who are unable to manage investments. In such situations, trusts can be created wherein control is retained and the donor can even be the trustee and retain full control over the management and distribution of the property.

The Alaska Trust

Effective January 1, 1997, the state of Alaska established itself as an important situs for the creation and administration of irrevocable trusts for both protection against creditors and estate planning purposes. The Alaska statute provides that so long as the creator of a trust has not retained the rights to revoke the trust, the trust will be valid against creditors unless the assets transferred to the trust are intended to delay or defraud the creditors or unless the transfer was made at a time when the creator was in default by thirty days or more in making child support payments.

The Alaska statute also provides that an Alaska trust may continue in perpetuity. Under the new law, four requirements must be met for the laws of Alaska to govern the administration of the trust:

- One of the trustees must be a "qualified person," meaning that one of the trustees must be a trust company with its principal place of business in Alaska, a bank with trust powers with its principal place of business in Alaska, or an individual resident of Alaska
- At least some part of the trust assets must be deposited in Alaska, either in a checking account, time deposit, certificate of deposit, brokerage account, trust company fiduciary account, or other similar account located in Alaska
- The Alaskan trustee's duties must include both the obligation to maintain trust records and the obligation to prepare or arrange for the preparation of the trust's income tax returns, although neither of these duties must be exclusive to the Alaskan trustee
- Part of the trust's administration must occur in Alaska, including physical maintenance of the trust's records in Alaska

Prior to the passage of the Alaska Trust Act, there was no domestic jurisdiction wherein a grantor could "retain" the discretionary right to trust income or principal and yet have the transfer considered a completed gift for federal transfer tax purposes, and therefore not have the property included in the grantor's estate. In most jurisdictions, trust doctrine provides that where a person creates a trust for his or her own benefit, a trust for support, or a discretionary trust, his or her creditors can reach the maximum amount which the trustee under the terms of the trust could pay to him or her or apply for his or her benefit.

Alaska now provides creditor protection to a qualifying trust notwithstanding the grantor's right to receive discretionary distributions, and thereby avoids the necessity of making substantial inter vivos gifts in order to reduce the amount of one's taxable estate.

Domestic Family Limited Partnerships

Domestic family limited partnerships have become a popular technique for protecting accumulated wealth, as well as for estate tax planning (see chapter 25). As useful as they are, there are disadvantages for potential asset protection purposes:

- The partnership entity continues to be subject to the local system of law
- Free access to the partnership assets will be prevented if a creditor obtains a court order to attach and freeze the partnership assets
- The potential ability of a creditor to establish that the purpose of the creation of the partnership was for reasons other than estate planning

Another strategy to protect assets is the limited liability company (LLC). For a detailed discussion of this entity, see chapter 25.

Trusts

Domestic trust law generally restricts the nature and extent of benefit and/or control that a creator of a trust can retain. Our laws generally provide that if you do not place the assets of the trust out of your reach (irrevocable trust), the trust property will not be placed out of the reach of a creditor.

If you create a trust at a time when there is absolutely no fraudulent conveyance issue, it could be attacked years after its creation if you have retained any benefit or control from or over the property placed in the trust.

An asset protection trust integrated with an overall estate plan can accomplish everything a typical inter vivos living trust can accomplish, including avoidance of probate, confidentiality, asset administration in the event of the creator's disability, continuity upon the creator's death, and estate tax planning.

Homestead Exemptions

STATE	EXEMPTION ($)	STATE	EXEMPTION ($)
Alabama	5,000	Maine	12,500
Alaska	27,000	Maryland	None
Arizona	100,000	Massachusetts	$100,000
Arkansas	2,500	Michigan	3,000
California	Limited	Minnesota	No limit
Colorado	30,000	Mississippi	75,000
Connecticut	None	Missouri	8,000
Delaware	None	Montana	40,000
District of Columbia	None	Nebraska	10,000
Florida	No limit	Nevada	95,000
Georgia	5,000	New Hampshire	30,000
Hawaii	30,000	New Jersey	Yes
Idaho	50 over the mortgage	New Mexico	20,000
Illinois	7,500	New York	2,000
Indiana	7,500	North Carolina	Yes (Value is set by statute)
Iowa	Unlimited (but does not apply to debts dated preownership)	North Dakota	80,000
Kansas	No limitation	Ohio	None
Kentucky	5,000	Oklahoma	5,000
Louisiana	15,000	Oregon	15,000

STATE	EXEMPTION ($)	STATE	EXEMPTION ($)
Pennsylvania	None	Virgin Islands	30,000
Rhode Island	None	Virginia	5,000
Tennessee	5,000	Washington	30,000
Texas	No limit-acreage limit	West Virginia	5,000
Utah	8,000	Wisconsin	40,000
Vermont	30,000	Wyoming	10,000

❖

CHAPTER 25

Family Limited Partnerships and the Limited Liability Company

For wealthy families, the family limited partnership can be the cornerstone of their estate plan. The ability to do business in partnership form and limit your liability can be very significant. This chapter discusses in great detail limited liability companies, what they are and their benefits.

There are at least eighteen states that have laws permitting the creation of limited liability companies (LLC). The purpose of this kind of entity is the avoidance of unlimited liability on the part of the general partners in a general partnership. Under general partnership law, general partners are liable for all of the obligations of the partnership, to the extent that the partnership assets are not sufficient to satisfy the same. In a limited liability company, none of the members of the company have any personal responsibility for the obligations of the company. In a professional limited liability company, each member is liable for his own misconduct, and it is only the property of the negligent party and his supervisor that is available to a damaged third party.

In a general partnership, the injured third party can look to the personal property of all of the partners to the extent that the partnership assets are not sufficient to satisfy his or her claim.

Overview of the Family Limited Partnership (FLP)

Currently, one of the most exciting topics in the field of estate planning is the use of the Family Limited Partnership for the purposes of wealth transfer.

Under such a plan, an individual contributes property to a limited partnership, in exchange for general and limited partnership interests.

Thereafter, gifts of limited partnership interests are made to family members or trusts for their benefit, with the individual donor retaining the general partnership interest.

In a limited partnership, the general partner is the individual who has the exclusive management and control over the partnership assets. This includes the determination of the timing and the amount of distributions to all of the partners as well as the compensation to the general partner for services rendered to the partnership.

Even though the general partner has retained control over the assets of the partnership, the gifts of the partnership interests will not be included in his or her estate. The values of the transferred limited partnership interests for gift tax purposes, due to lack of marketability and minority discounts, will be less than the value of the same partnership assets.

The discounts represent a recognition by the government that a minority interest in a business is not readily saleable and that the owner of a minority interest has no control over the property owned. Depending upon certain factors, the amount of the discount may vary between 10 percent and upwards of 50 percent. In addition to the use of the $1,000,000 exemption in making gifts of these interests ($2,000,000 if the gifts are split between spouses), the Family Limited Partnership can be used to take advantage of the generation-skipping transfer tax exemption ($1,100,000 in 2002).

Assets that are subject to a large discount could therefore be transferred, not only avoiding gift taxes, but generation-skipping transfer taxes as well, which are taxed at the rate of 55 percent of the value of the gift.

Until the Internal Revenue Service issued a ruling in 1993 permitting these discounts, it had maintained that if members of a family owned all of the entity, the family controlled it, and any gift or sale of a minority interest was not entitled to be discounted in value for gift tax or sale purposes.

A byproduct of the Family Limited Partnership is a lower tax bracket for the limited partners through income shifting. Another advantage of the Family Limited Partnership is that creditors of the limited partners cannot touch the assets of the limited partnership.

What Is It?

The term "family" implies that the partnership is owned by family members. A limited partnership has both "general partners" (who run the partnership) and "limited partners" (who as passive investors, have no vote nor any voice in the management). General partners have unlimited personal liability for partnership obligations, while limited partners have no liability beyond their capital contributions.

The partnership ownership can be divided among the general and limited partners in any way the partners designate. In a Family Limited Partnership, the interest of the general partner is usually 1 percent and the balance of the interests is owned by the limited partners. Since the general partner has the only vote on partnership business decisions, it makes no difference how small that interest is for voting and, therefore, control purposes.

In a Family Limited Partnership, both general and limited partners share income, loss, tax attributes, and cash flow based upon their ownership percentage interest in the partnership.

How It Works

The general partner transfers property to the partnership in exchange for the ownership of the entire limited partnership interests. He or she thereafter will eventually, on an annual basis, transfer limited partnership percentage interests of the limited partnership to members of his or her family by taking advantage of the annual exclusion ($10,000). This process may go on for years, depending upon the value of the assets, the number of beneficiaries, and the amount he or she wants to transfer.

The Advantages

There are many tax and nontax benefits to the Family Limited Partnerships. They include:

- Reduced asset values for transfer tax purposes through valuation discounts
- General partner's ability to make substantial gifts and also maintain control of the assets
- Sheltering of gifts from the creditors of the recipients of the gifted interests
- Continuing control of income from transferred assets, since distributions from the partnership must be authorized by the general partner
- A means to segregate partnership assets as separate assets and not marital assets
- Gifts of limited partnership interests will qualify for the annual gift exclusion since they are present interest gifts
- Reduced probate costs with respect to real estate located in other states

- The advantage of enjoying tax, management, and operational flexibility that may not be available in other formats

What Assets Should Be Funded in the Partnership

The most advantageous would be those that are most likely to appreciate in value. Real estate interests, marketable securities, and cash can be transferred to the partnership. The reason that the gift of a limited partnership interest is discounted for transfer tax purposes is due to the fact that the recipient receives a minority interest, which is nonvoting, and as such cannot exercise any control over the investment nor realistically can he or she sell it in the open market. In addition, the partnership agreement usually places restrictions upon the limited partner's transfer of his or her partnership interest without first offering the interest to a group usually consisting of close family members.

If the senior members of a family do not wish to have the next generation own their interests in the family limited partnership outright, an irrevocable trust can be formed. Their partnership interests can be gifted to it. A parent could even serve as the sole trustee without having any beneficial interest in the trust, and the powers of the trustee could be limited to an ascertainable standard, which means that the income from the principal in an FLP would be applied on a discretionary basis, for the health, maintenance, and welfare of the beneficiary.

For those who have significant assets, Family Limited Partnerships may be the best answer to reducing transfer taxes. The ruling by the Internal Revenue Service that minority interest discounts for closely held business interests can be claimed, even when related family members own the entire entity, has opened the door to wide use of this very significant strategy.

Asset Protection Trusts and Family Limited Partnerships

The best of both worlds can be accomplished when Asset Protection Trusts (APT) and Family Limited Partnerships (FLP) are combined. The combination can be achieved merely by one or more gifts to the trust of a limited partner's interest. Control over the partnership assets can be maintained by the general partner. If a general partner of a Family Limited Partnership is facing potential creditors, choices may be available that might otherwise not exist. These could include having an offshore trustee remove the domestic trustee of an APT and cause the liquidation of the FLP. In this instance, the assets of the partnership would be distributed to the APT based on its ownership share. Thereafter, and in the exercise of the trustee's legal responsibility to preserve the assets in the interests of the beneficiaries, the foreign trustee could place the distributed assets out of the jurisdiction of the general partner's residence, which then places the battle over those assets in the foreign court.

Limited Liability Companies (LLC)

The LLC is really a hybrid partnership-corporate entity. It has the flow-through income tax characteristics of a partnership and the limited liability qualities of a corporation. It has been described as a limited partnership with no general partner and an S corporation without partnership restrictions.

The background for this form of organization comes from the desire and need for a business structure that is taxed as a partnership, yet protects its owners from unlimited liability. The general and limited partnerships offer the desired flow-through tax treatment, but the general partner (or partners) in each instance have unlimited personal liability for partnership debts. This corporation form limits the liability of its owners but does not offer the flow-through tax treatment of the partnership. The S corporation comes closest to the desired objectives, but the S corporation is less flexible than the partnership and is subject to certain restrictions that render it impractical in many situations.

The first limited liability company statute was enacted in Wyoming in 1977. Today, about forty states have approved this form of entity, including the states of New York and New Jersey.

LLC Basics

The LLC is an unincorporated entity with two or more members formed under state law. The LLC is formed by filing articles of organization with the appropriate state agency. Those articles of organization state the name of the entity, the date of creation, the names of the managers, if any, and the nature of the business. These articles of organization are similar to the certificate of limited partnership for a limited partnership.

Structurally, then, the LLC has the look of a partnership. The LLC does not issue stock certificates; the interests of the members are described in a document known as the operating agreement, a document that looks and works much like a partnership agreement. The operating agreement describes the interest of each member in LLC profits, liabilities, and capital.

Owners of the LLC are referred to as members. All the members will be responsible for the management of the LLC unless the operating agreement specifies one or more managers to manage its affairs. The manager need not be a member of the LLC and there is no restriction with respect to who can be a manager. Therefore, members can consist of corporations, partnerships, nonresident aliens, trusts, or any other legal entity in addition to individuals. Members should consider entering into agreements with each other, similar to buy/sell or shareholder agreements providing, among other things, for the management of the business and the division of its profits and losses.

The obvious advantage of the LLC over the partnership is the absence of personal liability of any of the principals. In the general partnership, all the partners have personal unlimited liability for the debts of the partnership. Even the limited partnership must have at least one general partner and that general partner is personally liable for the debts of the limited partnership. In the LLC, none of the members, whether they are managers or not, are personally liable for the LLC debts. In fact, the members of an LLC can participate in the management of the LLC without exposing themselves to personal and unlimited liability. In contrast, if a limited partner takes on management responsibilities, he or she also takes on the personal liability of a general partner.

Estate Planning Considerations

The members of the LLC face all the estate planning problems and challenges encountered by other owners of closely held businesses. While there has not been a great deal of experience with LLCs, the issues with respect to the valuation of the interest of a member should be identical to those of the partner in a partnership and a stockholder in a corporation.

For estate planning purposes, the LLC has advantages over an S corporation with regard to certain step-up in basis provisions, and because an LLC is subject to partnership tax provisions, it is not subject to what is commonly called the "Anti-Byrum" Amendment. This amendment is very technical and covers what happens when a donor transfers an interest in property consisting of shares of stock of a corporation, and retains certain rights over the property. In a 1995 case, the following took place.

On May 1, 1995, Jack Green owned 250 shares of stock in Greenco, his family's closely held business. The 250 shares represented 25 percent of the outstanding stock of Greenco and had a fair market value of $2,500,000. Jack's brothers Harold, Mike, and Bob each owned a 25 percent interest in Greenco. Greenco's value had been increasing rapidly, and Jack wanted to transfer some of his shares to his son, Roy, so that the appreciation on these shares would avoid taxation in Jack's gross estate. At the same time, however, Jack did not feel Roy was ready to have a voice in corporate decisions and wanted to keep the right to vote the shares he transfers.

On May 2, 1995, Jack transferred one hundred shares to Roy, but retained the right to vote these shares for the rest of his life. When Jack dies in 2005, the family members still have the same respective ownership interests in Greenco. Assume that at the time of Jack's death, the 10 percent interest held by Roy has increased in value to $2,000,000.

On these facts, the full $2,000,000 value of the stock in which Jack retained the voting rights would be included in his gross estate under Code Sec 2036(b). Although Jack owned only 15 percent of the Greenco stock directly during the last three years of his life, the 85 percent owned by Roy, Harold, Mike, and Bob are attributed to him under Code Sec. 318, and he is deemed to own 100 percent of the Greenco stock at the time of his death.

The problem illustrated in this example might not have been encountered if Greenco had been an LLC instead of an S corporation. Code Sec. 2036(b) applies to stock in corporations and not to ownership interests in a partnership. Because LLCs are subject to the partnership tax provisions and not the corporate tax provision of the Code, the "Anti-Byrum" Amendment would presumably not be applicable to them.

Recent Governmental Developments

Revenue Ruling 93.12, which permitted the use of cutting-edge estate planning devices, has caused the Internal Revenue Service in recent times to go public in the areas of discount planning. The government wants to block abuses that are taking place and stop the sham transactions that are being created. These are occurring in circumstances where discounts are being taken for 50 percent to 80 percent on portfolios consisting only of readily marketable securities in false family limited partnerships or where the sole function of the creation of the FLP and the taking of the discount on transfers is to reduce the estate tax.

There is presently no stated Internal Revenue Service position with respect to the acceptable range of discounts, nor is there any specific standard being employed by the government to stop the taxpayer from overreaching.

Some examples of the egregious situations that have been reported are detailed below:

The Service recast the transfer of FLP units as a sham in a marketable securities partnership formed two days prior to the death of a ninety-two year old, where transfer was made by a power of attorney holder, and disallowed a claimed 50 percent discount.

In another case, a physician was advised that he could establish an FLP and transfer all his real estate to the partnership (with himself as a 1 percent general partner and trusts for the benefit of his three children owning 99 percent limited partnership interests), when at the same time he was negotiating a settlement of substantial income tax liability with the Internal Revenue Service pertaining to other matters. The doctor was denied a discharge of his indebtedness to the government and the transfer to the FLP of his real estate, at a time when the government was pursuing collection, constituted a willful attempt to evade or defeat the taxes he sought to be discharged.

In another case, the FLP was formed two days before the decedent's death when the decedent was terminally ill and had been removed form life support. The Internal Revenue Service took the position that the valuation discounts should be disallowed. One theory was that the formation of the partnership and the transfer of the partnership's interests should be treated as a single testamentary transaction and therefore the partnership should be disregarded for purposes of estate tax valuation under the sham transaction doctrine.

In another case, the Internal Revenue Service held that the value of transferred property is included in a decedent's gross estate if there is an express or implied understanding at the time of transfer that the transferor will retain the economic benefits of the property. In this situation, the decedent created three family limited partnerships and transferred interests in them to her children. A partnership bank account was created for each partnership, but partnership income was not deposited into this account. Instead, in violation of the partnership agreements, it was deposited into the decedent's personal checking account and commingled with her other assets. Thus, the decedent was managing the assets exactly as she had before the transfer. This fact, combined with the acknowledgment by the children that formation of the partnership was merely a way to allow the decedent to assign interests in partnership assets, indicated that there had been an implied understanding that the decedent would retain the enjoyment of the property for her life.

The FLP is certainly a valid and significant device in the estate planning process. In addition to the preservation of wealth and reduction of estate, gift, and generation-skipping taxes, it offers an asset protection feature. This technique and other value reduction devices should be used under proper circumstances. "Deathbed" eve filings for bankruptcy transfers are cases of misuse and improper situations. For future planning, a solid foundation needs to be constructed to insure that the vehicle is viable.

Family Limited Partnerships (FLPs) Update

The government's campaign against the FLP has not been successful in the Courts. In January 2000, a federal district judge in San Antonio, Texas ruled in the Matter of E. Church Estate that the decedent's holdings could be valued at less than half of the fair market value for estate tax purposes. There were three other cases in the same year that rejected the challenges of the government to the FLP discounts and sustained the taxpayer's valuation discounts.

In addition to meeting the technical requirements in the formation of an FLP, the following should exist:

- The partners should follow all the procedures required by state law and the partnership agreement in all actions they take with respect to the partnership.
- The general partner should retain only those rights and powers normally associated with a general partnership interest under state law, and no extraordinary powers.
- The partnership should hold only business or investment assets (or both) and not hold assets for the personal uses of the general partner.
- The general partner should report all partnership actions to the limited partners, and the limited partners should act to assure that the general partners do not exercise broader authorities over the partnership affairs than those granted under state law and the partnership agreement.

The points in the following list should be considered in planning and administering an FLP:

- The partnership should be formed first and interests transferred at a later date.
- A professional, independent appraiser should be used to value the underlying partnership assets (with the exception of liquid assets, i.e., cash and marketable securities).
- The FLP should be created when the donor is healthy. Before his death in 1992, Sam Walton wrote a biography wherein he explained how his family beat estate taxes. In 1953, he put his business into an FLP and gave shares—at very low values—to his children. Today each of the Walton children is worth $17 billion.
- In the partnership agreement, make reference to the nontax purposes for its formation, such as:
- Asset projection
- Bringing assets together for common management

- Permitting the donees to observe the donor's management philosophies
- Limiting the transfer of assets outside of the family
- Reducing probate costs
- Making it easier to make gifts of various assets in a group of assets
- For the state of jurisdiction of the partnership, choose a state with favorable partnership laws, such as Delaware (it does not automatically allow a limited partner to withdraw from the partnership).
- The partnership agreement should deny a limited partner the right to withdraw.
- The partnership term should be of a long duration.
- The general partner can be a corporation.
- The partnership agreement should provide for the annual distribution of the net income.
- The transfer of partnership interests should be subject to restrictions.
- A donor should not give shares of voting stock in a closely held corporation to an FLP in which the donor is the general partner.
- Do not use the partnership funds for personal use.
- Do not put your residence into a partnership. If you do, you must pay rent (the partnership is supposed to be set up for business purposes).
- Try to put a mixture of assets into the partnership.
- Do not mix an offshore trust with a partnership.
- Do not set up the partnership on your deathbed.
- Be careful in mixing charity and partnerships.

CHAPTER 26

Estate Planning for the Business Owner

$\mathcal{I}$f you have an interest in a business, you have to take into consideration a variety of factors that will affect this interest during your lifetime and at the time of your death.

This chapter outlines what must be contemplated. This includes whether such an interest will be sold when you die, who will succeed to the management after your death should you place this interest in trust to be managed by your trustees, how will it be valued, and how the taxes will be paid.

In this chapter, you will learn about important strategies that should be considered during your lifetime, such as the buy/sell agreement, the use of life insurance, and avoiding probating your business interests.

Today, as a result of a recent revenue ruling (1993), minority business interests can be gifted away or sold at a discounted value for gift tax purposes. These very important methods are discussed, as well as the significance of structuring your estate in order for it to qualify for an estate tax payment deferral (which can be up to fourteen-plus years).

If you own an interest in a business, no matter the form of ownership—sole, partnership, or corporate—you must have an estate plan. It is important to make provisions for the succession of management and future ownership. It has been said that many closely held businesses fail to survive past the first generation due to lack of proper planning. If a business is to be sold or liquidated, arrangements for these events have to be considered. If there is to be a continuity, a decision has to be made on the method of transfer to the survivors, whether outright or in trust. The assets of a business should be sheltered from estate taxes to the extent possible, and probate should be avoided to insure a prompt continuity at the least amount of expense.

Usually, it is not advantageous to discontinue a business immediately upon the death of the sole owner, unless it is a single-person business. Some flexibility should be afforded to the survivors to continue its operation until it can be liquidated or sold by them on the most favorable terms. This can be done by ensuring that there are key employees in place who will agree to continue to operate the business for a period of time on an agreed compensatory basis, usually for something more than just a salary—for example, a participation in the profits.

If there is more than one owner inheriting the business, and there may be a conflict on whether to keep, sell, or liquidate the business, having in place an estate business plan will help to deal with an issue of this kind. The beneficiaries of an interest in a business who continue as owners usually do not have any input into the management of the affairs of the business. This is usually left in the hands of the other surviving owners. As such, the beneficiaries have to rely on the controlling owners for a return on their investment.

Following are three concerns all family business owners must address as they plan their estates:

- Who will take over the business if I die?

  Owners often fail to develop a management succession plan. It is essential to the survival of the business that successor management, whether from the family or otherwise, be available to take over the stewardship.

- Who should inherit my business?

  This may not be an asset that should be split equally among children. For those active in the business, inheriting it may be critical to their future motivation. To those not involved in the business, the interest may not be seen as valuable. Perhaps the entire family feels entitled to equal shares in the business. This issue has to be resolved to avoid discord and possible disaster later on.

- How will the Internal Revenue Service value the business?

  Because family-owned businesses are not publicly traded, it is usually impossible to know the real value of the business. The final value placed on the business for estate tax purposes is often determined only after a long and tedious battle with the Internal Revenue Service. It is critical that the owner plan ahead and make sure there is enough liquidity in his or her estate to pay estate taxes, in addition to providing support for heirs.

Estate Tax Breaks for Family Businesses

With the potential severity of estate taxes, Congress recognized that family businesses might have to be sold just to pay the bill. To help lessen the tax burden, Congress provided two types of relief for business owners.

Section 303 Redemptions

The company can buy back shares of stock from an estate without the risk of the distribution being treated as a dividend for income tax purposes. Such a distribution must, in general, not exceed the estate taxes, funeral, and administration expenses of the estate. To qualify, however, the value of the business interest included in the estate must exceed 35 percent of the value of the adjusted gross estate.

If the redemption qualifies under Section 303, there will be no negative income tax consequences to the distribution, and cash from the corporation can be made available to pay expenses. This is an excellent way to pay estate taxes.

Section 6166 Estate Tax Deferral

Normally, estate taxes are due within nine months of death. However, if a closely held business interest exceeds 35 percent of the adjusted gross estate, the estate may qualify for a deferral of tax payments. Under this provision, no payment other than interest need be made until four years after the normal due date for taxes owed on the value of the business. Annual interest payments must begin within nine months of death.

The tax on the closely held business interest then can be paid over ten equal annual installments. Thus, a portion of the tax can be deferred for as long as fourteen-plus years from the original due date. While interest will be charged on the deferred payments, the interest rate is only 4 percent of the tax related to the first $1,100,000 of the closely held business interest. Interest allocable to the value of the business that exceeds the first $1,100,000 is charged at current market rates.

In order to qualify for this type of treatment, the business is usually closely held and the value of the business interest included in the estate must equal at least 35 percent of the adjusted gross estate.

Example: Assume 50 percent of the estate is composed of a family business interest and that the total estate tax liability is $1 million. Half of the liability, the tax allocable to nonbusiness interests, will be due at the normal due date of the return (nine months after death). The other $500,000 of liability may be paid in ten installments, starting five years and nine months after the estate owner's death and ending fourteen years and nine months thereafter.

Real Estate

Real estate that is used for a business can be valued in a different way than other assets. For estate tax purposes, it can be valued at its "present use" rather than the "highest use" yield, so that farm property can be valued as its use as a farm rather than a potential location for a commercial development (shopping center, etc.). In order for this rule to apply, the following conditions must exist:

- The value of the family business must equal 50 percent of the gross estate.
- The value of the real estate of the business must be at least 25 percent of the overall estate.
- The decedent or a member of his or her family must have used the real estate for the business during five of the preceding eight years.
- There also exist certain restrictions on the sale or mortgage of the property for a period of up to fifteen years after the receipt of the tax considerations.

Using Life Insurance

Instead of paying the tax in installments, heirs can use life insurance proceeds to pay estate taxes. There are several advantages to this method. Insurance provides an immediate source of guaranteed liquidity and avoids a forced sale of business or other estate assets.

The estate must have cash to pay interest on the deferred tax installments. This amount can be quite substantial, particularly if the liability is paid over the full deferral period. An additional "hidden" obligation is keeping the estate open during the deferral period. By paying the tax with insurance proceeds, the legal administrator avoids any additional administration costs. Provided that ownership is structured properly, it is possible to have the proceeds available to pay taxes, yet not have them taxed at the estate owner's death (see chapter 14).

Gifting the Family Business

The key to reducing estate taxes is to limit the amount of appreciation in the estate. As an example, assume that a business is worth $500,000 today but is likely to be worth $1 million in three years. By giving away the business stock today, the future appreciation of $500,000 will be kept out of the estate owner's taxable estate.

There may be no better gift than an interest in the family business, which may be the fastest appreciating asset owned.

Minority Discount

Those who plan to make a gift of an interest in a family business should be aware of a recent ruling by the Internal Revenue Service that makes it possible to transfer a larger share of a family business without paying tax because a minority stake in the business can be valued at a discount.

The Internal Revenue Service revenue ruling said that a gift to a family member can be made at a "minority discount." The discount is a recognition that a minority interest, which is an interest that has either no vote or is less than a controlling (usually 51 percent) interest, in a piece of real estate or other property may be worth less than face value because it cannot easily be sold and the owner may have little control over the whole property.

Although the Internal Revenue Service has long recognized minority discounts, it had excluded family businesses, reasoning that when the entire business was held by family members, the family controlled it and there was, in effect, no minority. A number of court decisions over the years, however, found in favor of the discounts for family members, and the Internal Revenue Service reversed itself in February 1994.

This ruling means the Internal Revenue Service has recognized that family members, too, have their fights and their disagreements and that just because people are related does not mean they have the same idea about running a business. Here is how the ruling might help save on estate taxes, which can be substantial, when transferring shares in a family business. Each taxpayer is entitled to give $11,000 a year to any number of people without paying gift taxes. A couple can give $22,000 to each of their children, or others. By making use of the minority discount, then, an individual or couple can transfer a larger percentage of the business without the involvement of transfer taxes.

Although the Internal Revenue Service did not authorize a particular percentage discount in its ruling, most people feel that 30 percent is pretty safe for tax planning purposes.

Furthermore, a couple need not be the sole owners to take advantage of the minority discount. The Revenue ruling stated that the discount would be permitted, "whether the donor held 100 percent or some lesser percentage of the shares of stock immediately before the gift."

The minority discount has applications beyond the $11,000 annual gift provision. Anytime a business is broken into pieces, the discount may apply. Consider the example provided by the Internal Revenue Service: One person owns all the shares of stock in a corporation. He or she transfers 20 percent to each of his five children. Even though the family still has 100 percent of the company, the value of the shares can be discounted.

Advantage of the discount can be taken through a sale of property as well as through the gift technique. Let us say a person plans to use the minority discount to sell some commercial property. The property is valued at $400,000 and generates $40,000 a year in income. The person plans to sell it to his or her four children for a total of $280,000.

The children will pay a parent a purchase price of $280,000, with interest, over twenty years, so he or she will receive income from the property. Because the property was sold for less than its market value, incurring a capital loss, the parent will get the return of principal tax-free, although he or she must pay income tax on the interest. If the parent still owned the building, he or she would have to pay tax on the income in any event. The estate owner in this situation would sell the shares separately to the four children, each receiving a one-quarter interest and paying $70,000 for his or her respective share.

Part of any gift giving program should include the family entering into a buy/sell agreement (see below). Such an agreement could prevent a spouse of a child from owning the shares of the family business. In addition, and at the time of the gift giving to the children, shares could be given to the grandchildren in trust. The trust, with its income, could purchase life insurance on the life of the parent of the grandchild and if the parent should predecease the grandparent, the trust could purchase the shares of stock of a predeceased child of the estate owner.

Estate Freeze

A flexible strategy for the business owner was reinstated in late 1990 when Congress retroactively repealed the "estate freeze" legislation that had become law in 1987. Prior to the enactment of this law, it was common for business owners to recapitalize their business, retain a preferred stock interest, and give all of the common stock interest to their beneficiaries. This way, they remained in control of their company and "froze" the value of their stock for estate tax purposes. All future appreciation affected only the common shares, not the owner's preferred stock.

Congress recognized the estate tax loophole and created Section 2036(c) in an attempt to prevent future estate freezes. The section was under constant attack since its creation and was finally repealed retroactively in 1990. In its place, Congress passed legislation that once again permits the use of estate freezes, but only if certain requirements are met.

Gifting family business interests can be a very effective estate tax saving strategy. Caution has to be taken because of some of the problems involved. The value of the gift can have both gift and estate tax ramifications. The Internal Revenue Service may challenge the value placed on the gift and try to increase it substantially.

The Buy/Sell Agreement

When a business has multiple owners, whether it be a partnership or corporation, its owner must create a plan that is consistent with the owner's business plan.

A powerful tool to help keep control of the future of a business is the buy/sell agreement. This is a contractual agreement between the shareholders and their corporation, between a shareholder and other shareholders of a corporation, or among partners in a partnership. Without such an agreement, chaos can arise among the business owners. In such an event, the law of the state where the business is located will be applied. This can produce disastrous results. For example, the law of most states provides that, upon the death of a partner, the partnership must be dissolved, unless an agreement among the partners provides to the contrary.

If a sole proprietor wants his or her business to continue after death, a designee, if possible, should be named to continue the business for the benefit of the survivors. The agreement controls what happens to a business interest in the event of a specific event, such as the disability or death of a shareholder. For example, the agreement might provide that, at the death of the partner or shareholder, or upon a permanent disability, his or her interest is bought back by the business entirely. As an alternative, the agreement might provide that the other individual owners purchase the partners interest or that the business is to be sold or liquidated.

A well-drafted buy/sell agreement can solve several estate planning problems for the closely held business owner:

- It can provide a ready market for the interest in the event the owner's estate wants to sell upon death.
- It can set a price for the shares. In the right circumstances, it can also fix the value for estate tax purposes.
- It can provide for a stable continuance of the business by avoiding unnecessary disagreements caused by an unwanted new owner.
- The valuation of the decedent's interest in the business has valuable meanings to the beneficiaries. In the first instance, it sets a standard for either the purchase of it by the surviving owners or a sale to third parties if the agreement among the owners permits such a transaction. The value is required to be known for estate

tax purposes even if the estate is not subject to estate tax. Even though the government is not bound to accept a value set by partners, it can view it as a basis if the valuation method is reasonable.

These methods for determining value are usually set forth in the agreement of the owners, which agreement could provide, *inter alia:*

- The establishment of a flat dollar amount for the disabled or deceased owner's interest.
- Setting up an appraisal method to value the business.
- Agreeing on the method to establish a book value of the business.
- Providing a capitalization of net earnings method to determine the value of the business.
- In most instances, providing that if the disabled or deceased owner's interest is not purchased by the remaining owners, the business is to be liquidated and the net proceeds distributed to the owners, including the disabled owner and the estate of a deceased owner.

Life Insurance and the Buy/Sell Agreement

Life insurance may serve a major role in funding a buy/sell agreement because it provides the ready cash to finance a transaction in the event of death of a shareholder. Proceeds may be received free of income and estate taxes. The proceeds are paid to the deceased shareholder's estate, and the executor then assigns the stock to the remaining shareholders or corporation.

However, watch out for a tax trap that may exist in buy/sell agreements. For example, assume a corporation funds a buy/sell agreement by buying $1 million worth of life insurance for each shareholder. The life insurance proceeds paid to the corporation are free from regular income tax but subject to the alternative minimum tax (AMT), a flat tax designed to ensure that corporations pay their fair market share of taxes. Under the AMT rules, 75 percent of the insurance proceeds, or $750,000, is taxed at a 20 percent rate, yielding a tax bill of $150,000. As a result, the company actually holds only $850,000 worth of life insurance net of taxes, not the $1 million policy face value.

To avoid this potential problem, the insurance policies should be owned individually rather than through the corporation. In this instance, each owner owns a life insurance policy on the other, subject to the terms of the buy-out agreement among them. For individuals who conduct their business as S corporations, the AMT is not an issue, because the insurance proceeds flow through directly to the individual shareholder's income tax returns.

Probate Avoidance

In most instances, in order to keep a business free of outside involvement, the probate process should be avoided. Subjecting a business to probate, in many jurisdictions, places the management of the business in the hands of the court during the probate administration. This can be avoided by the use of the living trust, which for most tax and administrative reasons is usually the best choice.

The owner of the sole proprietorship should likewise consider selecting a living trust as the best way to avoid probate. If a business is owned by more than one individual, whether it be in partnership, corporate form, or joint venture form, the living trust is certainly the best probate avoidance device. Each business agreement among the owners would provide for the ability of each owner to transfer his or her interest to a living trust. Each of the owners would therefore incorporate into his or her living trust provisions that are consistent with the business plan, for example, rights of the surviving owner to purchase the interest of a deceased owner.

Unless lifetime planning has taken place providing for an orderly continuity of affairs, the business owner and especially the owner of a sole proprietorship runs the risk of his survivors encountering a potential decimation of this asset because of the problems that might arise.

The Job Protection Act of 1996

The Job Protection Act of 1996 (the "Act") expanded the type of trust that is eligible to own shares of stock in a Subchapter S corporation.

Under prior law, only a certain type of trust such as a Qualified Subchapter S Trust (a "QSST") could be a shareholder in an S corporation. A QSST is a trust that under its terms: (1) permits only one current income; (2) the principal of the trust can only be distributed to that beneficiary; (3) the income of the trust must be distributed to the beneficiary.

These requirements prevented a QSST from sprinkling or spraying its benefit among more than one beneficiary or accumulating the income.

The Act expanded the type of trust allowed to own shares of stock in an S Corporation to include the "electing small business trust" (an "ESBT"). To qualify as an ESBT, all beneficiaries of the trust must be either individuals or certain charitable organizations and all interests in the trust must have been acquired by it either by gift or bequest. Each beneficiary of the trust will be counted as a shareholder, the number of which was increased by the Act to seventy-five from thirty-five. The Trust can have multiple beneficiaries, and its benefits can be distributed among its beneficiaries, or its income can be accumulated. The remainder beneficiaries can be different from the income beneficiaries, i.e., income to spouse for life with remainder to children.

A downside to the use of this trust is that the income which is received by the trust from the S corporation will not be taxed to the beneficiary but to the trust at its maximum individual rate. Income received by the trust from sources other than the S corporation is subject to the normal rules of trust taxation.

Chapter 9 contains a detailed explanation of the new provisions of the Code permitting an estate to exclude qualified family-owned business interests from the gross estate. The extent of the exclusion plus the amount of the estate exempted by the unified credit cannot exceed $1.3 million. As the applicable exclusion amount increases from $1,100,000, the values of qualified family-owned business interests that may be excluded decreases. The exclusion is only available for estates of persons dying after 1997 and effective December 31, 2003 is repealed.

Significant Recent Trends

What follows is a discussion of significant recent trends.

Blockage discount

Blockage discounts represent the adverse effect upon fair market value arising from the additional competition that real properties create if offered concurrently on the market. If a portfolio of properties is sufficiently large within an applicable market so that a concurrent offering of the properties would reduce the value, then a blockage discount for residential apartment property within a prescribed neighborhood of a major city is applicable.

Capital Gains Tax Liabilities

A taxpayer can reduce the fair market value of a gift of an interest in a corporation to take into account potential capital gains tax liabilities that may be incurred if the corporation were liquidated or distributed or its assets were sold, even in the absence of any plans for a liquidation, sale, or distribution.

❖

CHAPTER 27

Estate Planning for the Surviving Spouse

*E*state planning for the surviving spouse can involve a number of issues, including appropriate election in the first estate, the proper use of the marital deduction, disclaimers, and income tax planning. This chapter discusses a few of these considerations.

The Marital Deduction

As a general rule, property that qualifies for the marital deduction in the estate of the first spouse will be includable, for estate tax purposes, in the estate of the surviving spouse. The postponing or deferral of the estate tax in the first estate, combined with the use of the deceased spouse's exemption or unified credit amount, in a credit shelter trust, creates a larger financial base for the surviving spouse, since this should mean that there is no federal estate tax due in the first estate.

Asset Allocation

The failure of ensuring that each spouse owns a sufficient amount of property to apply the available exemptions and credits could result in a greater estate tax after both are deceased. As a general rule, it is proper planning to be sure that each spouse has sufficient assets in his or her name to use the unified credit and GST exemptions. Since there is no gift tax between spouses, this can be accomplished by inter vivos transfers from the wealthier spouse, whether outright or in trust. In large estates, and in order to avoid the maximum percent federal bracket, it may not be correct to use the unlimited marital deduction. For example, a person who leaves an estate worth $7.5 million entirely to his or her surviving spouse would place the estate in a maximum percent federal bracket. In such a situation, it may make good planning to pay a portion or all of the estate tax in the first estate or, in the alternative, it would have been proper planning for a portion of the survivor's property to have been transferred to the spouse who died first.

Disclaimers by the Surviving Spouse

A qualified disclaimer made by the surviving spouse is treated as if such interest had never been transferred to him or her. A disclaimer may be desirable in the following circumstances:

General Disclaimers

If the estate of the surviving spouse is large, so that the acceptance of a bequest would result in increasing the estate tax payable on death, in excess of what could be saved by accepting the bequest and thereby reducing the estate taxes of the estate of the first to die, then a disclaimer should be considered. The loss of the use of money used to pay the higher estate taxes in the estate of the first to die must be considered in such a situation.

Disclaimer by Surviving Spouse to Save the Unified Credit

In the situation where the entire estate provides for an unlimited marital deduction, the decedent's unified credit would be wasted. However, the waste can be avoided by having the surviving spouse make an appropriate disclaimer of a fractional part of the amount passing to him or her under the unlimited marital deduction bequest. The amount disclaimed would fall into the nonmarital trust and ultimately would pass to the remainder beneficiaries.

Disclaimer of Unified Credit Amount

A surviving spouse may disclaim his or her life interest in a unified credit trust. By doing so, the unified credit bequest will pass to the decedent's alternate beneficiaries (usually the children of the decedent and the disclaiming spouse). If only the unified credit amount is disclaimed by the surviving spouse, no added tax will be due, unless, under state inheritance tax laws, nonspousal beneficiaries are given lower exemptions or are subject to higher rates of tax than spousal beneficiaries. No federal estate tax will be due by reason of a shift in ownership of a unified credit legacy. Disclaimers of a unified credit trust interest by the surviving spouse can be useful if the surviving spouse decides that sufficient assets exist so as to provide his or her lifetime support.

Disclaimer of Pension Benefits and IRAs

The Internal Revenue Service has ruled that a disclaimer of benefits under a qualified employee retirement plan is allowable and is not treated as an alienation of plan benefits.

In a Letter Ruling, a surviving spouse transferred her one-half interest in the decedent's IRA, which was community property, to an IRA in her own name with her children as beneficiaries. She then disclaimed the maximum amount of her interest in the decedent's one-half interest that would incur no estate tax and transferred the undisclaimed portion of the decedent's one-half interest to her own IRA by a direct trustee-to-trustee transfer. The disclaimed portion of the decedent's interest in the IRA was ruled not to be includable in the surviving spouse's estate.

In another Letter Ruling, disclaimers were used successfully to permit a surviving spouse to roll over IRAs originally payable to the decedent's estate. Under the decedent's will, the IRAs passed to a residuary qualified terminable interest property (QTIP) trust. The spouse, the decedent's children, and the minor and unborn issue of the decedent—through their guardian ad litem—executed qualified disclaimers of a pecuniary amount of the residuary estate equal to the value of the IRAs and, in the case of the children and the minor and unborn issue, all their interest in any property passing under state intestacy law. The personal representative then funded this amount passing to the spouse with the IRAs. The government ruled that the IRAs passed directly from the decedent to the surviving spouse and qualified for the marital deduction.

Disclaimer of Community Property

A surviving spouse can make a "qualified disclaimer" of a decedent's rights in community property, regardless of the fact that she may have retitled certain of the community assets to her own name. So long as the survivor did not draw any funds or income from the accounts listed on the disclaimer (and made the disclaimer within nine months of the decedent's death), the act of retitling the assets did not constitute acceptance of the decedent's share of the community property interest or its benefits.

Disclaimer in Favor of the Surviving Spouse

A person other than the surviving spouse may make a disclaimer that results in the property disclaimed passing to the surviving spouse. In such a case, the disclaimed interest is treated as passing directly from the decedent to the surviving spouse and would increase the marital deduction. The increased marital deduction, in turn, would reduce the decedent's estate taxes, while possibly increasing the taxes of the survivor's estate.

Such a disclaimer might be effected, for example, where bequests to children exceed the exemption equivalent of unified credit. The children could disclaim that portion of their bequests that would eliminate or reduce the estate tax as much as possible. Children might do this for a variety of reasons, including concern for the spouse's needs. But they may also do so with the reasonable hope that gifts in the amount of their disclaimed bequests will later be forthcoming, in installments if need be, to minimize or eliminate gift taxes. Also, depending on a variety of circumstances, they may benefit by the estate tax savings.

Disclaimer of Marital Property

The Internal Revenue Service has increased the use of disclaimers by surviving spouses that allow joint marital property to be disclaimed. Code Section 2518 allows disclaimers of one-half the property held as joint tenants if the surviving spouse disclaims within nine months after the death of the joint tenant, regardless of when the joint tenancy was created.

Use of Disclaimer to Create a Marital Deduction Trust (QTIP)

The Tax Court of the United States has ruled, in a memorandum decision, that an estate was permitted to elect QTIP treatment for a trust that by its strict terms permitted the accumulation of income. *The Lasiter Est. v. Comr.* case involved the estate of Henry Lassiter, a Georgia resident, who left a 1970 will that provided that the decedent's residuary estate was to be divided into two trusts: (1) a general power of appointment marital trust, the funding of which was limited to a pre-1982 marital deduction; and (2) a residuary trust, which provided for income and principal to be distributed among the decedent's wife and descendants. Specifically, the trustee of the residuary trust was to pay "such part of the income and/or principal . . . as it [deemed] necessary to provide for the support in reasonable comfort" of the decedent's wife, as well as "to provide for the support and education of [the decedent's] children and the descendants of any deceased child. . . ." In addition, the decedent's wife was given an inter vivos and a testamentary limited power of appointment over the residuary trust principal.

Through a series of disclaimers, the family sought to convert the residuary trust into a QTIP marital trust and thereby avoid having to limit the marital deduction to one-half of the decedent's adjusted gross estate. Therefore, the children and the court-appointed guardian for the decedent's minor child, et al., claimed their respective interests in the residuary trust during their mother's lifetime, including any rights as possible beneficiaries under the decedent's wife's inter vivos power of appointment. The decedent's wife, who was also the decedent's personal representative and trustee, also executed a disclaimer in which she disclaimed her inter vivos power of appointment over the trust as well as any various fiduciary powers.

On the federal estate tax return, the estate took the position that all of the probate assets passed to the residuary trust, for which the personal representative elected QTIP treatment. Determining that the decedent's wife did not have a qualifying income interest in the residuary trust, the Internal Revenue Service disallowed the full marital deduction with respect to the residuary trust and limited the marital deduction to one-half of the decedent's adjusted gross estate.

The court held for the estate, allowing the marital deduction for amounts passing to both trusts. The court stated that the disclaimers would all be effective under state law and that they were qualified. The court held that the guardian ad litem had the power to disclaim on behalf of the minor et al., in light of the very substantial tax savings that would inure to the benefit of those persons on whose behalf the disclaimers were made. The disclaimers, therefore, eliminated the interests of the children et al. during the wife's lifetime and the rights of the trustee to distribute trust funds for their support and education. This left the wife as the only beneficiary who could receive distributions from the residuary trust during her lifetime. The Tax Court then noted that this left the wife and her estate as the only beneficiaries of the residuary trust during her lifetime.

Estate Tax versus Gift Tax

The method by which the gift tax is actually computed has a direct bearing on the advisability of making intra-family gifts since it may cost less *total* transfer tax to give away an amount of property than to leave it to someone at one's demise. The gift tax is computed on the amount of the transfer to the recipient. The estate tax is computed on the amount of the property held by the estate owner on the date of death, including that portion of the estate tax that will be used to pay the tax and, thus, not received by the beneficiaries. Therefore, one of the differences between subjecting property to estate tax as opposed to gift tax is that the federal estate tax system is inclusive and the gift tax system is exclusive. It may be better for a family, for the surviving spouse, having inherited property, free of taxation and fleshed up in basis, to give such property to descendants, thereby subjecting it to lower gift taxes.

As previously discussed in chapter 25, there are several vehicles, such as a Family Limited Partnership (FLP) or a Limited Liability Company (LLC), that can be used for gift-giving purposes while the donor retains control of the investment as a general partner and reduces the value of the gift by way of a discount. Grits, Grats, and Gruts are available as well for inter vivos transfers.

One offsetting consideration in making lifetime gifts instead of testamentary transfers is that the donor pays a gift tax now to save estate taxes later. Thus, the lower tax on large lifetime transfers over large testamentary transfers must be weighed against the lost use of the money, also taking into account (1) income tax savings from income shifting and (2) estate tax savings from removing the future appreciation and the gift taxes paid from the donor's gross. If the donor dies within three years of having made the gift, however, the gift taxes are included in the donor's gross estate, and the computational advantages of the lifetime transfer are lost.

Remainder Interests

Under the Code, the remainder interest in a QTIP Trust will be taxable in the surviving spouse's estate. In a recent case, the surviving spouse purchased the remainder interest from the remainder beneficiaries, causing a merger of the two properties' interests (income and remainder) and, as a result, extinguishing the trust. The Internal Revenue Service has not ruled that the amount paid in the acquisition of the remainder interest was a gift since the surviving spouse "in effect" already owned the property in the trust.

Conclusion

The surviving spouse has to contemplate the use of other estate tax–saving devices, such as charitable transactions and the use of the gift-giving exclusion and exemption, all of which are discussed in detail in this book. Lifetime gifts provide not only a method of avoiding probate and eliminating administration costs but also help protect the assets of the estate. They can produce savings and afford benefits for the entire family in the following ways:

- If the gift is made more than three years before the donor's death, any gift taxes paid will not be included in the donor's estate.
- If the gift is to a family member in a lower income tax bracket, there will be a reduction of family income taxes.
- The income earned on the gifted property, after taxes, will be excluded from the donor's gross estate.

- Death taxes will be reduced.
- The annual exclusion and exemption gifts can remove assets from the donor's estate without federal and state transfer tax

There should be no hesitation in the surviving spouse to implement an estate plan that has as a goal the conservation of the estate and the protection of wealth that has taken a lifetime to accumulate.

CHAPTER 28

The Cutting Edge: Value Reduction Strategy in Discount Planning

$\mathscr{A}$n estate faced with a large federal estate tax calls for highly aggressive estate planning. The following are a few of the "hottest topics" created in estate planning today.

The Family Limited Partnership: Various Techniques

A Family Limited Partnership (FLP) can be used to transfer property interests all within one (1) family unit, but at significant discounts from what otherwise would be fair market value. The thrust of the FLP is to make lifetime transfers of property at significant reductions in the tax otherwise payable on the transfer of property at death. The use of the FLP requires a substantial inter vivos taxable gifting program. The latter calls for a deep concern about saving taxes for the beneficiaries and a willingness to make significant gifts during the estate owner's lifetime.

Technique. The family member contributes property (real estate, cash, marketable securities) to the FLP in return for an ownership interest in the capital and profits of the partnership.

The partnership interests are broken down into general partnership (GP) interests and limited partnership (LP) interests. The GP assumes management responsibility and personal liability for partnership obligations not satisfied by the FLP's assets. The personal liability of the LP is limited to their investment.

Typically, the family member receives a 1 percent GP interest and a 99 percent LP interest. Gifts are then made of LP interests to children and grandchildren (in Trust).

The transfer (gift) tax value of the LP interests are substantially less than the underlying asset value. The reduction in value or discount is a result of lack of a ready market and the LP's inability to make decisions regarding the management of the FLP, to demand distributions, and to force a liquidation of or withdrawal from the partnership. The leverage of valuation discounts can be further enhanced by selling LP interests to a Defective Grantor Trust.

Sale to a Defective Grantor Trust

Technique. This plan calls for an installment sale of property (LP interests) to an irrevocable trust (grantor) in exchange for a balloon promissory note. Prior thereto, a trust is created that will be treated as owned by the grantor for income tax purposes but not for transfer (gift and estate) tax purposes.

In order to avoid characterization of the transaction as merely a gift with a retained interest, it is generally suggested that the trust be "seeded" with an initial gift of assets equal to at least 10 percent of the value of the property ultimately to be purchased from the grantor.

The grantor then sells property to the trust in exchange for a promissory note usually calling for payments of interest-only during the term of the note with a "balloon" payment at the end. The purchase price may be significantly discounted, depending on the nature of the property.

Certain types of property will tend to maximize the estate-freezing potential of this technique. The sale of an interest in a family limited partnership (FLP) will allow for substantial discounts for minority interests and/or lack of marketability while enabling the grantor to maintain effective control of the business. Potential for posttransfer appreciation will also enhance the estate freeze, as will the ability to funnel income into the trust.

Generally, the note would call for annual interest payments by the trustee to the grantor. However, the interest can be accrued. Payments may be made from the "seed" money (or additional gifts made by the grantor to the trust) or investment earnings thereon or from income generated by the purchased property or, if necessary, by return of some portion of the property in kind to the grantor.

Upon maturity of the note, principal is repaid to the grantor (or his or her estate or heirs) in cash or in kind. Repayment in the event of death may be facilitated by life insurance on the grantor's life, owned by the trust. Use of life insurance also reduces the need to sell low-basis assets and may provide the trustee with cash to acquire other assets from the estate.

One of the other advantages of the grantor trust is that all trust income would be taxable to the grantor, not the trust, which results in additional tax-free gifts being made to the trust's beneficiaries. By paying the tax, the grantor is reducing his or her taxable estate by the amount of the tax paid plus the appreciation thereon.

FLP: Estate Discount

Technique. An FLP is formed by the estate owner. The general partner would be a Sub S Corporation formed by the estate owner. The estate owner would sell to his or her children controlling voting shares of the Corporation, and the Corporation would thereafter, as a general partner, manage the limited partnership. The estate owner would subscribe for the entire limited partnership interest and would thereafter continue his or her investment in the partnership, which would have investment activities, etc. No gift is made by the estate owner, and the purpose of the transaction would be to obtain a discount in the estate owner's estate of at least 40 percent of the date-of-death value of his or her interest in the partnership. The larger the investment, the greater the size of the discount and the more the estate tax savings.

During the estate owner's lifetime, the partnership will need to invest and have activities (purchasing/selling, etc.).

Family Split Dollar

The Family Split Dollar planning possibilities are numerous. Family Split Dollar arrangements are particularly well suited for estate owners with taxable estates who do not wish to give up control over their life insurance policies. Many individuals with taxable estates die owning their personal life insurance policies. They fail to transfer the ownership of the policies out of concern that they may need access to the policies' cash values. Family Split Dollar may be the perfect solution.

What Is Family Split Dollar?

In general, Family Split Dollar is a shared premium arrangement between two parties in a nonemployment context. Typically, the owner of the policy will be an irrevocable trust. Rather than contributing to the trust an amount equal to the entire required premiums, the grantor can avoid estate, gift, and generation skipping taxes on the funding of a life insurance policy by obtaining the necessary cash from any available source. The only gifts required to be made to the trust are smaller amounts equal to the annual economic benefit cost of the life insurance death benefit that will be paid to the trust. In other words, rather than having to gift the entire life insurance premium to the irrevocable trust, the grantor will only have to gift the federally published annual P.S. 58 table rates (or the so-called P.S. 38 costs for a survivorship policy) or the insurer's alternative term rates into the trust each year.

In Private Letter Ruling 9636033, the Internal Revenue Service ruled favorably for the first time on the validity of a Family Split Dollar arrangement.

The arrangement in the Private Letter Ruling was an agreement between the insured's spouse and the insured's irrevocable trust. The insured's irrevocable trust applied for, owns, and is the beneficiary of a life insurance policy on the life of the insured. The trust will contribute toward the annual policy premiums an amount equal to the economic benefit cost (the P.S. 58 table rate or the insurer's alternative term rate in accordance with Rev. Ruls. 64-328 and 66-110). The amount of the economic benefit cost will be gifted to the trust each year by the insured. The insured's spouse will pay all of the policy premiums in excess of the economic benefit cost, in accordance with the split dollar agreement signed by the spouse and the irrevocable trust. The split dollar agreement provides that the insured's spouse owns all of the cash value of the policy. The policy is collaterally assigned by the trust to the spouse as security for the spouse's interest. The collateral assignment utilized gives the assignee (the spouse) the right to execute policy loans and surrenders (partial and full), and the right to change the dividend option. As long as the parties' marriage is stable and as long as the spouse does not predecease the insured, the economic unit of the insured and spouse always have complete unencumbered access to the cash value of the policy. The pure death benefit in excess of the policy cash value is owned by and is payable to the irrevocable trust and therefore escapes taxation in the estates of both the insured and the insured's spouse.

The Service ruled in PLR 9636033 that as long as the irrevocable trust contributed an amount equal to the economic benefit cost of the insurance coverage, there would be no estate or gift tax (and presumably no income tax) consequences resulting from the split dollar arrangement (assuming that gifts into the trust are covered by the annual gift tax exclusion).

Owner of Life Insurance: FLP versus Irrevocable Trust

Family Limited Partnerships are entities that may be used to further business and family planning objectives while at the same time providing gift and estate tax benefits through the application of marketability and minority interest discounts. Given the right circumstances, the Family Limited Partnership may be a viable alternative to the irrevocable life insurance trust.

The real and perceived disadvantages of irrevocable life insurance trusts have prompted many financial and tax advisers to recommend that their clients consider the use of a partnership as an alternative ownership vehicle for needed life insurance coverage. We all know the general problems with life insurance trusts. Generally, these arrangements are irrevocable in nature, which means that changes in family and financial situations may not be adequately met by the inflexibility of in most trust agreements.

Since trusts are creatures of state law, they normally require a judge's approval for modification, which translates into added legal costs. In addition, the insureds should probably not serve as their own trustees because having some personal decision-making power over how trust assets are distributed may result in potentially adverse tax consequences. These issues of "irrevocable commitment" and "surrender of control" are two of the major reasons why many life insurance trusts are never completed.

In addition, the Crummey clause provisions for irrevocable life insurance trusts are under continued intense scrutiny by the Internal Revenue Service. It is the Crummey power language that allows the premium payments to be characterized as present interest gifts eligible for the gift tax annual exclusion.

Thus, many individuals have begun to speculate on how long it will be before congressional action either eliminates, or severely restricts, this approach to life insurance planning. Although predicting what Congress might or might not do is at best a chancy proposition, there's no denying that the loss or severe limitation of the Crummey powers could bring into question the continued viability of the irrevocable life insurance trust as an estate planning technique.

For all these reasons, the use of a family limited partnership (FLP) should be considered. What we are talking about, of course, is a bona fide partnership that has legitimate business purposes and has not been established solely for tax avoidance purposes or simply to hold life insurance policies.

Typically, the life insurance need is for estate liquidity or to permit an orderly business continuation program. This need remains the same under either approach. We are simply substituting partnership ownership for trust ownership. In doing so, however, there are numerous advantages to the partnership that are not available when an irrevocable trust arrangement is used.

Partnerships do not require judicial involvement to make changes in ownership, management, or even in distribution patterns for profits and losses. Thus, all parties to the transaction—even senior family members—retain some control over being able to revoke or modify the terms of the partnership arrangement. Since the partnership is the owner of the life insurance policy(ies), these powers give the individuals indirect control over the life insurance policy(ies). Further, partnership tax provisions have many advantages over tax provisions for estates and trusts.

If the FLP Owns the Coverage

In effect, a bona fide Family Limited Partnership (FLP) becomes the vehicle for investing in the same needed life insurance coverage that would have been purchased under the irrevocable life insurance trust. Generally, the insured (or insureds) would be the senior family member(s) who will also be acting as the managing partner(s) of the FLP but who would own only a small equity interest. The FLP itself, however, is the owner and beneficiary of the policy and would pay the premiums from its funds.

The partnership form of ownership also assures that there will be no potential transfer-for-value problems if the ownership of the policies needs to be restructured within the terms of the FLP itself. Transfers of life insurance policies to and from the FLP itself or among the various partners are statutory exceptions to the transfer-for-value rules. This exception would also apply to transfers of any other life insurance policies outside the FLP among the various partners. Thus, the income tax–free nature of the insurance death proceeds is not in danger of being lost because of potential changes in policy ownership.

The Flexible Irrevocable Trust

These devices, in addition to the basic estate planning tools, such as the By-Pass or Credit Shelter Trust, Irrevocable Life Insurance Trust, Family Limited Partnership, and the Qualified Personal Residence Trust, are the basic programs being used in sophisticated estate planning today.

The gross estate of every individual includes not only property owned at death but also property the person gave away during his or her lifetime, over which particular rights or benefits were retained so as to be included under various sections of the Code.

The two common thrusts of the two important provisions of the Code (Sec. 2036 and Sec. 2038) are that (1) the estate owner gratuitously transferred property (gift) and (2) the estate owner kept some right, benefit, or power prohibited by the Code.

Section 2038 causes property to be included in the decedent's gross estate if he or she transferred property by gift and, at the date of his or her death, the enjoyment of the property was subject to change through the exercise of a power by the decedent alone or in conjunction with others to amend, revoke, or terminate.

Section 2036 requires the decedent to possess the prohibited powers and does not cause inclusion if any family member of the decedent has such powers.

The Code, the cases, and the revenue rulings are clear that estate tax inclusion under Sections 2036 and 2038 can be avoided if the decedent does not keep (1) any right to enjoy or possess the property; (2) any income from the property; (3) any right to determine who will enjoy or possess the property; (4) any right to determine who will receive the income; and (5) any right to amend, revoke, or terminate the trust.

Giving Rights to Others

Nothing in the Code prohibits a person from giving such rights to another person (i.e., your spouse) and not having these sections apply.

Accordingly, if one wishes to "have his or her cake and eat it too" and not have the property included in his or her estate and that of his or her spouse, one can establish a trust for the benefit of his or her children, and the grantor and the trustee may have the following powers:

The Grantor may have:

- The power to substitute assets of an equivalent value without the consent of the trustee
- The power to allocate receipts and disbursements as between principal and income, even though expressed in broad language
- The power to change the trustees, but cannot name himself or herself as a trustee
- The right to direct investments and vote stock held by the trust other than stock of a controlled corporation

The Trustee may:

- Be a spouse and be granted broad discretionary powers over the distribution of the trust income and principal to his or her children, but he or she cannot make any distribution that would satisfy a legal obligation of either spouse
- Be granted discretionary powers to distribute trust income and principal for his or her health, education, support, and maintenance
- Have a broadly stated limited power of appointment that would allow him or her to appoint the property (income and principal) to the grantor but not to himself or herself, his or her creditors, his or her estate, or the creditors of his or her estate

In addition, the children may have the power to appoint trust principal to the grantor.

In summary, one would not have the right to dictate or control what is to be done with the property given away. There must be no existing agreement between the spouses to exercise a power that has been given to the trustee.

The estate tax laws have historically permitted spouses to act in concert and allow a spouse or other family members to hold powers over property that the estate owner (decedent) could not hold.

CHAPTER 29

Concluding Thoughts

As far as I am concerned, everyone should have a living trust, regardless of the size of his or her estate. A simple $100,000 estate owned by a husband and wife could go through two probate proceedings that could cost no less than $3,000 to $5,000 plus be exposed to the administrative procedures and delays of the system itself. Besides all of the benefits we have discussed, the fact that your estate is completely organized and funded, thereby making orderly and quick settlements possible, is a crucial byproduct of owning and holding property in a living trust. One of the agonies of the probate process is the searching out, marshalling, and identifying a person's assets after that person is no longer alive.

Probably one of the greatest benefits you can give to your loved ones is a complete and orderly estate plan of which a living trust is a part.

Net Worth Worksheet

*D*etermining your net worth is the first step in preparing an estate plan. This worksheet will help you to organize your inventory for easy reference.

ASSETS	IN YOUR NAME	IN SPOUSE'S NAME	IN JOINT NAMES
Residence (current market value)	$ _____	$ _____	$ _____
Other real estate	$ _____	$ _____	$ _____
Bank accounts (checking and savings)	$ _____	$ _____	$ _____
Other cash accounts (money market funds, savings bonds, CDs, credit union accounts, etc.)	$ _____	$ _____	$ _____
Stocks, bonds, and mutual funds	$ _____	$ _____	$ _____
Life insurance (face value)	$ _____	$ _____	$ _____
Disability insurance (monthly benefit)	$ _____	$ _____	$ _____
Business partnership interests	$ _____	$ _____	$ _____
Retirement plan accounts:			
Pension plans	$ _____	$ _____	$ _____
Annuities	$ _____	$ _____	$ _____
IRA and Keogh accounts	$ _____	$ _____	$ _____
Stock option or savings plans	$ _____	$ _____	$ _____
Other (such as 401(k), profit-sharing, and deferred compensation plans)	$ _____	$ _____	$ _____
Personal property (replacement value of jewelry, vehicles, boats, household furnishings, etc.)	$ _____	$ _____	$ _____
Receivables, trusts, tax shelters, and other assets	$ _____	$ _____	$ _____

ASSETS	IN YOUR NAME	IN SPOUSE'S NAME	IN JOINT NAMES
Collectibles (market value of antiques, fine arts, precious metals, etc.)	$ _____	$ _____	$ _____
Other assets (specify)	$ _____	$ _____	$ _____
TOTAL ASSETS	$ _____	$ _____	$ _____
LIABILITIES			
Mortgages	$ _____	$ _____	$ _____
Life insurance loans	$ _____	$ _____	$ _____
Notes and trust deeds	$ _____	$ _____	$ _____
Other loans or debts (personal loans, credit cards, etc.)	$ _____	$ _____	$ _____
TOTAL LIABILITIES	$ _____	$ _____	$ _____
NET ESTATE (assets minus liabilities)	$ _____	$ _____	$ _____

❖

Glossary of Terms

Abatement: A priority system of reducing or eliminating bequests that an estate cannot afford to pay.

Actuary: One who calculates various insurance and property costs; particularly, one who computes the cost of life insurance risks and insurance premiums.

Ademption: Property left to a beneficiary in a will that is no longer in the decedent's estate upon death.

Adjusted Gross Estate: During administration, debt administration expenses and losses are deducted. What is left is the adjusted gross estate.

Administration of the Estate: When the court supervises the distribution of the probated estate.

Administrator: A personal representative appointed by the court to administer the estate of an intestate.

Alternate Valuation Date: A date six months after the date of the decedent's death.

Alternative Minimum Tax: A way of computing income tax disallowing certain deductions, credits, and exclusions.

Annual Exclusion: Under gift tax laws, each person may give as much as $10,000 per year to whomever he or she wishes.

Annuity: A right to receive fixed, periodic payments, either for life or for a term of years, payable at specific intervals.

Ascendant or Ancestor: A person related to an intestate or to a claimant to an intestate share in the ascending lineal line.

Attested Will: A will signed by a witness.

Augmented Estate: Property owned at the time of a person's death as well as the value of any property transferred during his or her lifetime without consideration (gifts).

Basis: What one has invested or put into property, real or personal. For tax purposes, subtract the basis from the proceeds of a property sale to determine the net gain.

Beneficiary: A person or entity selected by the testator to receive a portion of the estate upon the testator's death.

Bequest: A clause in a will directing the disposition of personal property.

By-pass Trust: Also known as a credit shelter trust. This is an estate tax–skipping trust used in conjunction with the unlimited marital deduction.

Charitable Lead Trust: Trust in which a charitable organization receives income for a certain period with the remainder passing to the donor's beneficiaries after a set period.

Charitable Remainder Trust: Trust created to pay income to beneficiary for a certain period and assets remaining in the trust pass to a charitable organization. There are three types of charitable remainder trusts.

Charitable Trust: A trust created for the benefit of a charitable organization. There are several different kinds of charitable trusts that can be created.

Closely Held Corporation: A corporation with less than twenty-five shareholders. Usually, all the issued shares are held by only those who work in the corporation.

Codicil: A testamentary instrument, which, after it has been properly executed, is added to the will.

Community Property: A property system premised on the belief that everything acquired during marriage belongs equally to each spouse.

Compromise Settlement: In a civil action, where two or more persons mutually bind themselves to refer their legal dispute to a third-party arbitrator.

Contingency Beneficiary: An alternative beneficiary selected by the testator in case the primary beneficiary dies prior to the testator.

Contingent Remainder: A remainder interest that does not become possessory until a certain specified event takes place.

Corpus: Property the settlor/transferor places in the trust. (Also known as the trust res or trust principal.)

Credit Shelter Trust: Also known as the by-pass trust. This is an estate tax–skipping trust used in conjunction with the unlimited marital deduction.

Crummey Power: The right of a beneficiary of a trust to withdraw a portion of a gift made to the trust equal to the lesser of the annual exclusion ($10,000) or the value of the gift made to the trust that year.

Custodian: General term to describe anyone who has charge or custody of property. Also, person named to care for property left to minor under Uniform Gift to Minors Act.

Death Taxes: Taxes on the estate of the decedent. Federal death taxes are called estate taxes and state death taxes can be termed inheritance taxes, among other names.

Devise: A clause directing the disposition of real property in a will. The person named to take the real property is called the devisee.

Discretionary Trust: A trust that allows the trustee to distribute as much trust income to the beneficiary as he or she deems proper.

Disinheriting: When a testator cuts someone out of his or her will. A spouse cannot legally disinherit another spouse, but a parent can disinherit a child or another by stating so specifically in his or her will or living trust.

Distributee or Next of Kin: That person or persons who are or who may be entitled to the property of an intestate.

Domicile: The permanent residence of a person or the place to which he intends to return even though he may reside elsewhere.

Dower or Curtesy: A statutory right to inherit a certain portion of the estate of the deceased spouse.

Elective Share: A portion of the estate that a surviving spouse is entitled to by statute.

Escheat: A reversion of property to the state if no relatives are living to inherit.

Estate Planning: The development of a plan to provide for effective and orderly distribution of an individual's assets at the time of death.

Estate Tax: Tax imposed on the fair market value of the net asset value of a descendent's estate.

Execution: Making a written document complete by meeting the legal requirement of the completion, usually signing, witnessing, and notarizing.

Executor or Personal Representative: The administrator named in a will.

Executory Interest: Interests that will take place in the future.

Exemption: A deduction allowed to a taxpayer because of his status (i.e. over sixty-five, being blind, particular dependents, etc.)

Fair Market Value: The average value that can be placed on an asset as determined by market forces.

Family Limited Partnership: A legal entity that can provide asset protection and allows for management and control of assets.

Fee Simple Absolute: The complete, outright right to ownership of land, present and future.

Fiduciary: A person having a duty created by his, her, or its undertaking to act primarily for the benefit of others, such as an executor, personal representative, or trustee.

Generation-Skipping Tax: Tax imposed to prevent you from passing property to two or more generations below you without paying a transfer tax.

Gift Tax: A tax imposed on transfers of property by gift during the donor's lifetime.

Grant: Formal transfer of real property.

Grant of Probate: The actual validating of a will.

Grantee: Person to whom grant is made.

Grantor: The person by whom the grant is made.

Grantor Retained Annuity Trust (Grat): Irrevocable trust into which the grantor transfers property in return for the right to receive fixed payments on at least an annual basis based upon the initial fair market value of the property.

Grantor Retained Income Trust (Grit): Trust created so that the value of a gift can be lessened by the grantor retaining an income interest, for a certain time, in the property gifted away.

Grantor Retained Unitrust (Grut): Same as a grat, except that annual payments will fluctuate each year as the value of the property increases or decreases.

Grantor Trust: A trust where income is taxable to grantor because he or she retains substantial control over the trust assets or retains certain prohibited administrative powers.

Gross Estate: The value of all property left by the deceased person required to be included in his or her estate for estate tax purposes.

Guardian: A court-appointed person who is legally responsible for the care and well-being of a minor. The only device parents can use to select a guardian for their child or children upon their deaths is a will.

Heir: A person entitled by statute to the assets of the intestate is called an heir at law.

Holographic Will: A will entirely in the handwriting of a testator.

Homestead: That part of a homeowner's real property that is exempt from attachment or sale by a creditor for the homeowner's general debts.

Honorary Trust: Not a legal trust. Some states allow people to leave part of their estate to an animal "in honorary trust."

Individual Retirement Account: A tax-deductible savings account that sets aside money for retirement.

Inheritance Tax: A tax levied on the heir of a decedent for property inherited.

Insurance Trust: A trust created to own and be the beneficiary of an insurance policy.

Inter Vivos Trust: A trust made during one's lifetime.

Intestacy: If one dies owning assets and does not have a valid distribution instrument, the property will pass to the closest blood heirs of the deceased person.

Intestate: Dying without a will or with a will found not to be legally valid.

Irrevocable Trust: A trust that cannot be revoked or amended by the creator of the trust.

Issue: Offspring, children, and their children.

Joint Ownership: Property owned by two or more persons. Upon the death of one joint owner, ownership is transferred to the surviving owners.

Joint Tenancy: Property held by two or more persons with the right of survivorship between them.

Keogh Plan: A retirement plan established by a self-employed individual.

Kiddie Tax: The federal income Tax Code provision that any unearned income of a child is taxed at the child's parent's rate.

Lapse: An inheritance "lapses" when the intended beneficiary predeceases the testator.

Legacy: A clause in a will directing the disposition of money.

Life Estate: An estate in property held by a person for his or her lifetime or measured by the life of another; the estate ends upon the death of the holder or the measuring life, whoever dies first.

Life Insurance Trust: Trust that collects and holds proceeds of life insurance for distribution to beneficiary and investment so as to exclude these monies from insured's estate for tax purposes.

Living Trust: A trust established by a person during his or her lifetime.

Living Will: A document that states that a person does not want his or her life prolonged by artificial means.

Marital Deduction: A deduction allowed by estate law for all property passed to a surviving spouse. Use of this deduction allows estate tax to be computed only after the death of the second spouse.

Material Provision: A provision that is important and necessary to a will or trust.

Multiple Probate: This occurs when decedent owns real estate or other property in more than one state that becomes subject to probate in each state at time of death.

No-Contest Clause: A clause in a will attempting to disinherit a person who attacks the will's legal validity.

Noncupative Will: An oral will.

Nonprobate Asset: Property that you have transferred during your lifetime, except that you have retained the total right, at anytime during your lifetime, to alter the distribution upon your death.

Per Stirpes: In Latin, "through or by the roots." Gives a beneficiary a share in the property to be distributed, not necessarily equal but in proportion to which, the person through whom he claims from the ancestor would have been entitled, i.e., a child claiming through his or her predeceased parent.

Personal Property: Holdings such as furniture, jewelry, stocks, cash, and other items of personal possession.

Pickup Tax (Sponge Tax): Permits the state in which one dies to receive a portion of the estate taxes that would have been paid to the federal government.

Pooled Income Fund: A fund among multiple donors, wherein each reserves a pro rata share of its assets. The amount of income paid to each donor is determined by the performance of the fund and the individual's proportionate share.

Pour-Over Trust: A trust into which assets are poured or added from another source.

Pour-Over Will: A will used in conjunction with a revocable living trust to "pour-over" or transfer to the trust any assets that were not transferred to the trust before death.

Pour-Up Trust: Assets of a living trust are poured into a testamentary trust or an estate, reversing the flow found in a pour-over trust.

Power of Attorney: A document by which one person grants to another the legal right to act on his or her behalf with regard to specific situations.

Preliminary Distribution: Assets distributed prior to the close of the estate.

Probate: The procedure by which a transaction alleged to be a will is judicially established as a testamentary disposition, and also applies to the administration process of an estate.

Qualified Disclaimer: Acceptance of bequest and subsequent disapproval. Must be executed in writing and communicated to the executor or administrator within nine months after the transfer or, in the case of a minor, by the age of twenty-one.

Qualified Domestic Trust (QDOT): Trust for a noncitizen that defers estate taxes in the estate of a citizen until the death of the noncitizen surviving spouse.

Qualified Terminable Interest Property (QTIP): Trust created for the benefit of a spouse and entitled to a marital deduction.

Remainder: Property left over after all will distribution provisions have been satisfied.

Remainder Beneficiary: A beneficiary named in the will or trust to receive the remainder property.

Res or Principal: The property the settlor/transferor places into a trust.

Residuary Beneficiary: General legacy to persons or organizations that will receive the balance of property not specifically given or legacies that have lapsed.

Residuary Clause: Provides for a distribution of the remainder of the estate after all of the other specific and cash bequests have been made.

Retained Income Trust: A trust created to give a gift of a future interest whose value is discounted for gift tax purposes.

Reversionary Interest: A right to receive property back at some future date provided that the value of such a right immediately before death is in excess of 5 percent of the value of the entire property.

Revocable Trust: A trust that can be changed or revoked by the creator.

Rule against Perpetuities: The rule that no contingent interest is good unless it must vest, if at all, no later than twenty-one years after the death of all the beneficiaries who wer in being (alive) at the time of the creation of the interest.

Self-Proving Procedure: Adopted by majority of states. Affidavit stating that all the requisites for due execution have been complied with.

Settlor: The person who creates a trust.

Spendthrift Trust: A trust established by a third party to protect the interests of another party (i.e. spouse) from claims of future creditors.

Sponge Tax: In a state such as Florida, where there is no estate tax per se, the state receives from the estate the credit calculated in a taxable estate as its state death tax.

Springing Trust: When the management of a living trust will only shift to a successor trustee when incapacity or other specified event occurs, as defined in the trust.

Sprinkle Trust: Trustee has the discretion to distribute income to a number of beneficiaries. Also known as a discretionary trust.

Sprinkling or Spray Provision: Provision in discretionary trust that allows trustee to make distributions to a number of beneficiaries without regard to equality as to amounts or times.

Standby Trust: A trust created to manage a person's assets while he or she is abroad or disabled.

Statute of Descent and Distribution: The law that sets forth the order of distribution of the property of a decedent that is not disposed of by will or trust.

Statutory Will: Form will with fill-in-the-blanks; authorized in a few states.

Stepped-up Value: The value property is increased to (fair market value) at the time of the owner's death that will reduce or eliminate capital gains taxes upon its eventual sale.

Stopgap: Additional tax designated as the generation-skipping transfer tax that prevents property from passing over a generation without estate taxes being imposed on such a transfer.

Succession: Process by which the property of a decedent is inherited by will or through descent.

Support Trust: Trust created to provide beneficiary with only as much principal or income as necessary for support and education.

Tenancy by the Entirety: Ownership of property by a husband and wife together. Neither spouse is allowed to alienate any part of the property so held without consent of the other.

Tenancy in Common: When each co-owner owns an undivided fractional interest in the property.

Terrorem Clause: Provides for forfeiture of legacy in the event of a challenge by a beneficiary.

Testamentary Capacity: Criteria established by the laws of our states required to be met by you in order for you to create a legally valid will.

Testamentary Substitute: Transfers usually made during a spouse's lifetime but which usually do not pass to the beneficiary of such an account until the death of the person that created it.

Testamentary Trust: A trust created in accordance with instructions contained in your will. Takes effect only after death.

Testate: One passes "testate" when he or she leaves behind a valid will.

Testator or Testatrix (female): Name for person who has created a legally valid will.

Throwback Rule: Rule that applies only to trusts, not estates. If property is distributed to a beneficiary and the distribution results in a loss, the loss could be disallowed.

Totten Trust: A bank account created that prevents a joint owner from withdrawing any funds before your death. If the beneficiary of such an account predeceases you, the account will pass under the residuary clause of your will.

Trust: A legal entity created to control the distribution of property.

Trustee: The person holding legal title to a trust for the benefit of a beneficiary.

Unified Credit against Estate and Gift Tax: Credit up to $192,800 (equivalent to $600,000 in property) that can be credited against the federal estate and gift tax.

Uniform Gifts to Minors Act: Law that permits you to give a gift to a minor by giving the gift to a custodian who holds title to the property for the benefit of the minor.

Uniform Marital Deduction: Unlimited amounts of property that can pass or be gifted to a surviving spouse without estate or gift tax consequences.

Uniform Probate Code: A model statute governing distribution of estate assets. This may be adopted, used as a guide, or wholly ignored by the various states.

Unitrust: A qualified trust in which the grantor retains certain income rights.

Will: An expression, either written or oral, of a person's intentions concerning disposition of property at death.

❖

Index

personal property and, 38
safe deposit boxes and, 32
simultaneous death and, 34–35
tax liabilities and, 36
tax rules and, 35
tenancy by the entirety, 30
tenancy in common, 29, 30–31
third parties and, 34
types of, 29
Uniform Marital Property Act
(UMPA) and, 34
See also community property; joint
tenancy
Prudent Investor Act (of New York),
41
prudent man rule, 41
publicity, avoiding, 65–66

qualified disclaimer, 90–91
qualified domestic trust (QDOT),
56–57, 98, 230
Qualified Subchapter S Trust (QSST),
281
qualified terminable interest property
(QTIP) trust
generation-skipping transfer tax
(GST) and, 142
gifts and, 123–124, 125
multiple marriages and, 178, 180
retirement benefits and, 230–231,
236
surviving spouses and, 173–174,
285, 286–287, 288
taxes and, 83, 84–85, 88, 98
wills and, 17, 20

residences
disabilities and, 201–202
establishing legal, 165–168
grits and, 150–151
Medicaid and, 244–245
residuary beneficiary, 9
residuary clauses, 15, 34
retirement benefits, 227–238
charities and, 232, 236–237
distributions from, 228–229,
233–237
estate plans and, 228
gifts and, 236–237
life insurance and, 237
living trusts and, 232
QDOTs and, 230
QTIPs and, 230–231, 236

Roth IRAs, 232
spouses and, 229–230, 285
taxes and, 227–228, 229
unified credit shelter trusts and,
231–232
See also individual retirement
accounts (IRAs)
Revenue Reconciliation Act of 1993,
46
reversionary interests, 85
revocable bank accounts, 31
Roth IRAs, 232

safe deposit boxes, 32
San Francisco, 214
S corporations, 280, 281–282, 293
See also businesses
self-proving wills, 13
senior citizens, 53, 219–225
skip person, defined, 143–144
Small Business Job Production Act of
1996, 228
South Carolina, 32
spendthrift provisions, 43–44, 68, 69,
201
sponge tax, 91, 113
spouses
living trusts and, 68–69
Medicaid and, 241–242, 252–253
retirement benefits and, 229–230,
235
surviving, 8, 169–175, 179, 283–289
See also marriage
spray provision, 55
springing trusts, 66
sprinkling provision, 55, 201
standby trusts, 52
state taxes, 2, 91–92, 95, 105–107,
109, 113
statutory wills, 14
stepped-up value, of property, 29–30
successor trustees, 71
sunset provision, 112, 114
Supplemental Medical Insurance (SMI),
under Medicare, 240
Supplemental Needs Trust (SNT),
202–203, 248–249
Supplemental Security Income (SSI),
193–195, 240, 242–243
support trusts, 55

taxes, 2, 81–115
annuities and, 84

Books from Allworth Press

Estate Planning and Administration: How to Maximize Assets and Protect Loved Ones by Edmund T. Fleming (paperback, 6 × 9, 224 pages, $14.95)

Legal Forms for Everyone by Tad Crawford (paperback with CD-ROM, 8½ × 11, 224 pages, $24.95)

The Retirement Handbook: How to Maximize Your Assets and Protect Your Quality of Life by Carl W. Battle (paperback, 6 × 9, 256 pages, $18.95)

Retire Smart by David and Virginia Cleary (paperback, 6 × 9, 224 pages, $12.95)

Turn Your Idea or Invention into Millions by Don Kracke (paperback, 6 × 9, 224 pages, $14.95)

The Money Mentor: A Tale of Finding Financial Freedom by Tad Crawford (paperback, 6 × 9, 272 pages, $14.95)

The Secret Life of Money: How Money Can Be Food for the Soul by Tad Crawford (paperback, 5½ × 8½, 304 pages, $14.95)

Winning the Divorce War: How to Protect Your Best Interests by Ronald Sharp (paperback, 5½ × 8½, 192 pages, $14.95)

Money Secrets of the Rich and Famous by Michael Reynard (hardcover, 6 × 9, 288 pages, $24.95)

Old Money: The Mythology of Wealth in America by Nelson W. Aldrich, Jr. (paperback, 6 × 9, 340 pages, $16.95)

The Money Mirror: How Money Reflects Women's Dreams, Fears, and Desires by Annette Lieberman and Vicki Lindner (paperback, 6 × 9, 232 pages, $14.95)

To request our free catalog or to order by credit card, call 1-800-491-2808.

To see our complete catalog on the World Wide Web, or to order online, you can find us at *www.allworth.com*.